The Frog Principle

The Loss of Freedom in America

by

Walter A. Ascher

authorHOUSE™
1663 Liberty Drive, Suite 200
Bloomington, Indiana 47403
(800) 839-8640
www.AuthorHouse.com

First published by AuthorHouse 03/10/05

ISBN: 1-4208-2024-9 (sc)

Printed in the United States of America
Bloomington, Indiana

This book is printed on acid-free paper.

Table of Contents

Chapter I

"I have sworn upon the altar of God, eternal hostility against every form of tyranny over the mind of man."

-Thomas Jefferson, 3rd President of the USA, 1800

Immerse a frog into a pot of hot water and it will instantly jump out. Immerse a frog into a pot of cold water and slowly heat it up, it will tolerate the heat until it is cooked.

In my travels around the world, I constantly am amazed as to what has happened to our personal freedom. The nation that prides itself on being built on freedom would be the envy of George Orwell's Novel "1984".

We have succeeded beyond the wildest dreams of big Brother in our slowly heated pot. In the name of letting the government care for us from the cradle to the grave, we have handed over almost all of the freedom this country was founded upon a little over 200 years ago.

We gave the government after 9/11 Carte Blanche to take away our rights and the government has taken it with a vengeance.

Citizens of other nations are stunned by our court decisions they read or hear. They are stunned upon their arrival as a visitor into the United States having to prepare a form for Immigration as if everyone who visits Disney World wants to stay here forever. They are stunned by Passport Control asking where they are staying, how long and how much money they have with them. Even the possession of a credit card alone prevents the ease of entry into the United States of America. They are stunned at the agricultural inspections upon arrival causing flowers, fruit or meat products to be confiscated. Yet, tons of drugs reach our citizens on a daily basis.

The United States has forced the world to provide fingerprints or iris imaging contained passports for anyone entering the United States. Most visitors must submit to a fingerprint identification upon entering and upon leaving the U.S.A.

Equate our visiting procedures with other nations. A trip to England, Germany or France requires nothing more than you holding up your passport as you walk past the Passport control. That is it, nothing more.

Just the arrival into the U.S. requires declaration of all goods, gifts, or articles you are bringing into the U.S. Moreover. You are required to submit to a strip search so that someone can stick their fingers up your behind and in other places before they let you enter our free country if the Government Officials feel like it.

We have lost your freedom in the past 30 years at a mind boggling pace.

If there is a shooting, lets confiscate all guns. We have installed metal detectors in airports, public buildings, and high schools and in our courts. Imagine having to go to court for a traffic ticket in the winter being told to remove your belt and jacket before you are allowed to enter the court building to enforce your right as a citizen for a fair trial.

The government has taken away most of our personal freedom. It has taken away our rights to raise our children. We have lost many of our property rights. Our phone may be tapped without a court order and computers listen for certain words. If they occur the police will show up at your door. Laws have been enacted that can confiscate all of your property just on a hunch without any court proceeding or chance of defending yourself.

The daily headlines in our newspapers are accepted without any public outcry.

"Child divorces parent".

"Cops plant knife".

"17 1/2 years jail for pawning a gun".

"Car confiscated for playing music to loud".

"State takes children while parents are on vacation".

"Victim jailed for not testifying".

"Social Security card becomes national ID".

"Wife loses car for husband's tryst with prostitute".

"Twice on death row police and prosecutors lied".

"House and bank account confiscated from suspected terrorist".

"Joint in ashtray, boat seized".

"IRS tracks your money".

These headlines are real. This is the Nation we have become.

...And the cold frog likes the tepid warm water...

Chapter II
A New Day

"Government is not the solution to our problem, government is the problem."

-Ronald Reagan

A new child arrives into this world being delivered in a Hospital since in most states, mid-wivery (the act of having a mid-wife assist in the birth usually in an at home setting) is illegal.

Before the father can wipe off his brow and take his child in hand, a footprint is made and a DNA blood sample is taken. With this DNA sample the government can positively identify the child for the rest of its life and further can tell any potential health problems the child may incur in its lifetime, allowing the insurance company to decide what insurance risk the child will face and if they will insure at all. The DNA sample will further allow the government to determine the learning potential of the child thereby predetermining the child's status in its academic life and how much effort the state should spend on the child's development.

Before the child is handed to its mother, a social security form is prepared by the hospital and along with the child's DNA sample the government will be in control of the child's growth, social status and eventual death.

The identity will also be transmitted to the Internal Revenue Service and when the child opens its first bank account, its income will be taxed for the rest of the child's life. The government computer will track all of the income, expenses, bank records, credit card purchases, cash transactions and the eventual lifestyle to match the reported income. The DNA sample will be used by the heath insurance company to provide a basis for determining the insurance rates for the child.

A microchip will be implanted in the child's shoulder to allow the police to locate the child via GPS (Geophysical Positioning System) developed by the U.S. Government for military use. GPS can locate via satellite, the child in case it were to be kidnapped. Obviously this would also allow the government to track each person's whereabouts to within a few feet. If a criminal wanted to really kidnap a child with an implanted microchip it would be easily located and cut out. The implanted chip would allow the police or government to immobilize any person they deem a danger to society.

In school the chip can administer the proper medicated such as Ritalin or Prozac to have the child to the schools desired behavior.

Any and all activities of the child may be recorded for future use. Any potential employer would have equal access to all of the historical records of the child and based on the developed database, whether it covers the religious practices the child has or for the matter the spending habits may determine the company's decision on employment or promotions.

A similar chip will be integrated into each motor vehicle allowing the government to charge taxes based on road use or miles traveled. The policemen no longer have to hide for new satellites can track a vehicle and print out a ticket if you are speeding. Obviously, a chip in each vehicle will allow the government to locate any vehicle if stolen but it will also allow the vehicle to be incapacitated via satellite if the government wants to.

No passports will be required in that each entry and exit into the country will be recorded by precise recognition finger print technology or IRIS imaging, as will each bank transaction for our newly designed bills have already imprinted in them the capacity to track each use under the guise of preventing counterfeiting.

Each doctor visit and medication will be recorded as well as any participation in any political party or other clubs. Sport activities as well as social activities will be tracked.

Since the local government already has for property tax purposes, the layout of each home it may know how much time you spend in the bathroom, bedroom or watching TV. The government may deny you medicine it has not approved or a medical procedure it deems unnecessary.

Under the patriot act the government can access citizens records whether telephone, financial, rental, internal, medical, educational and even kill a U.S. citizen without a trial for national security.

Even in death the government has decided via courts you do not have any rights to die when you choose.

This is the world we have created for our children.

...It is so cozy in the warm water that the frog closes his eyes and dreams...

Chapter III
The War on Terrorism.

"A patriot must always be ready to defend his country against his government."

-Edward Abbey (1927-1989) US author

In 1759, Benjamin Franklin wrote: "They that can give up essential liberty to obtain a little temporary safety deserve neither." In the months ahead, I believe, we can both obtain our security and preserve our essential liberty, but only so long as we have courage from our courts, commitment from our citizens, and pressure from our foreign allies.

Who could have foreseen that a few tiny chad's that were not totally removed changed the whole future of the world? Who could have known that a president who in his pre- election rhetoric stressed family values and world peace would implement the right to a pre-emptive war on a sovereign nation, who would implement a law that takes away the rights of its citizens and have an arrogant attitude that has caused other countries to loathe the United States and instead of stopping terrorism, we have become the target for all that hate us.

Just six weeks after the September 11th terrorist attacks on the World Trade Center, the Pentagon and a jittery Congress-exiled from its anthrax-contaminated offices and continuous warnings that more terrorist assaults were soon to come capitulated to the Bush Administration's demands for a new arsenal of anti-terrorism weapons. Over vigor objections from civil liberties organizations on both ends of the political spectrum, The Patriot Act was approved.

The House vote was 356 to 66, and the Senate vote was 98 to 1. The hastily-drafted complex and legislation spans 342 pages. Yet it was passed with virtually no public hearing and was signed into law by a triumphant President George W. Bush.

THE USA PATRIOT ACT CONFERS VAST AND UNCHECKED POWERS TO THE EXECUTIVE BRANCH

The USA PATRIOT ACT stands out as radical in its design. To an unprecedented degree, the Act Sacrifices freedoms in the name of national security and upsets the democratic values and freedom of our nation by consolidating vast new powers in the executive branch of government. Enhancing the executive's ability to conduct surveillance and greater intelligence, placing array of new tools at the disposal of the prosecution, including new crimes, enhancing penalties, and longer statutes of limitations, and grants the Immigration and Naturalization Service (INS) the authority to detain immigrants suspected of terrorism for lengths, some cases indefinite, periods of time. At the same time it gives the executive, rights without any meaningful judicial Congressional oversight.

Since September 11, there has been a flagrant disregard of the rule of law by those charged with its enforcement. Already Department of Justice (DOJ) has admitted to detaining more than 1,000 immigrants none whom has been charged with committing a terrorist act. Many in this group are being held without bond under unrelated criminal charges or minor immigration violations, in a modern-day form preventive detention. Chillingly, the Attorney General's response to the passage of Patriot Act was not a pledge to use his new powers responsibly and guard against abuse, but instead was a vow to step up his detention efforts. Labeling immigrants with terrorist status, he declared: "Let the terrorists among us be warned, if you overstay your visa, even by one day, we will arrest you."

Furthermore, the Administration has made no secret of its hope that the judiciary in its broad reading of the USA PATRIOT ACT will read its content liberally.

USA Patriot Act Boosts Government Powers While Cutting Back on Traditional Checks and Balances

When President Bush signed the USA Patriot Act, he significantly boosted the government's law enforcement powers while continuing a trend to cut back on the checks and balances that Americans have traditionally relied on to protect individual liberty.

"This law is based on the faulty assumption that safety must come at the expense of civil liberties."

Among the USA Patriot Act's most troubling provisions are measures that:

- Allow for indefinite detention of non-citizens who are not terrorists on minor visa violations if they cannot be deported because they are stateless, their country of origin refuses to accept them or because they would face torture in their country of origin.
- Minimize judicial supervision of federal telephone and Internet surveillance by law enforcement authorities.
- Expand the ability of the government to conduct secret searches.
- Give the Attorney General and the Secretary of State the power to designate domestic groups as terrorist organizations and deport any non-citizen who belongs to them.
- Grant the FBI broad access to sensitive business records about individuals without having to show evidence of a crime.
- Lead to large-scale investigations of American citizens for "intelligence" purposes.

The bill's expanded definition of terrorism will inevitably ensnare many non-citizens who have done nothing wrong on the basis of their political beliefs and associations. For the first time, domestic groups can be labeled terrorist organizations, making membership or material support a deportable offense. Non-citizens could also be detained or deported for providing assistance to groups that are not designated as terrorist organizations at all, as long as activity of the group satisfies an extraordinarily broad definition of terrorism that covers virtually any violent activity. It would then fall on the non-citizen to prove that his or her assistance was not intended to further terrorism.

Such groups as the World Trade Organization protesters and even People for the Ethical Treatment of Animals (PETA) would, on the basis of minor acts of violence or vandalism, meet this overbroad definition. Non-citizens who provide assistance to such groups—such as paying membership dues—will run the risk of detention and deportation.

Wiretapping and Intelligence Surveillance

The USA Patriot Act allows the government to use its intelligence gathering power to circumvent the standard that must be met for criminal wiretaps. The new law allows use of surveillance authority as if the primary purpose were a criminal investigation. Intelligence surveillance merely needs to be only a "significant" purpose. This provision authorizes unconstitutional physical searches and wiretaps.

The USA Patriot Act extends a very low threshold of proof for access to internet communications that are far more revealing than numbers dialed on a phone. The new provisions allow law enforcement efforts to determine what websites a person has visited, this is likely giving law enforcement the power-based only on its own certification—to require the librarian to report on the books you had perused while visiting the public library. This provision extends a low standard of proof, far less than probable cause—to actual "content" information.

The law further marginalizes the role of the judiciary. It authorizes what would be the equivalent of a blank warrant in the physical world. The court issues the order, and the law enforcement agent fills in the places to be searched. This is not consistent with the important Fourth Amendment privacy protection of requiring that warrants specify the place to be searched. Under this legislation, a judge is unable to meaningfully monitor the extent to which their order was being used to access information about Internet communications.

The act also grants the FBI broad access in "intelligence" investigations to records about a person maintained by a business. The FBI need only certify to a court that it is conducting an intelligence investigation and the records it seeks may be relevant. With this new power, the FBI can force a business to turn over a person's educational, medical, financial, mental health and travel records based on a very low standard of proof and without meaningful judicial oversight.

Criminal Justice

The law dramatically expands the use of secret searches. Normally, a person is notified when law enforcement conducts a search. In some cases regarding searches for electronic information, law enforcement authorities can get court permission to delay notification of a search. The USA Patriot

Act extends the authority of the government to request "secret searches" to every criminal case. This vast expansion of power goes far beyond anything necessary to conduct terrorism investigations.

The Act also allows for the broad sharing of sensitive information in criminal cases with intelligence agencies, including the CIA, the NSA, the INS and the Secret Service. It permits sharing of sensitive grand jury and wiretap information without judicial review or any safeguarding the future use of dissemination of such information.

These information sharing authorizations and mandates effectively put the CIA back in the business of spying on Americans: Once the CIA makes clear the kind of information it seeks, law enforcement agencies can use tools like wiretaps and intelligence searches to provide data to the CIA. In fact, the law specifically gives the Director of Central Intelligence who heads the CIA—the power to identify domestic intelligence requirements.

The law also creates a new crime of "domestic terrorism." The new offense threatens to transform protestors into terrorists if they engage in conduct that "involves any act dangerous to human life." Member of Operation Rescue, the Environmental Liberation Front and Greenpeace, for example, have all engaged in activities that could subject them to prosecution as terrorists. Then, under this law, the dominoes begin to fall. Those who provide lodging or other assistance to these "domestic terrorists" could have heir homes wiretapped and could be prosecuted.

Financial Privacy

The USA Patriot Act continues the unfortunate trend of expanding government access to personal financial information rather than safeguarding it against intrusion. While there is certainly a need to shut down the financial resources used to further acts of terrorism, the USA Patriot Act goes beyond its stated goal of combating international terrorism and instead reaches into innocent customers' personal financial transactions.

Under the new law, financial institutions are required to monitor daily financial transactions even more closely and to share information with other federal agencies, including foreign intelligence services such as the CIA. The law also allows law enforcement and intelligence agencies to get easy access to individual credit reports in secret. The law provides for no judicial review and does not mandate that law enforcement give the person whose records are being reviewed any notice.

Student Privacy

The USA Patriot Act allows law enforcement officials to cast an even broader net for student information without any particularized suspicion of wrongdoing. When the changes in federal law dealing with student records privacy are combined with other information-sharing provisions contained in the new law, it becomes clear that highly personal student information will be transmitted to many federal agencies in ways likely to harm innocent students' privacy.

The USA Patriot Act allows law enforcement agencies to get access to private student information based on a mere certification that the records are relevant to an investigation. This certification, which a judge cannot challenge, is insufficient to protect the privacy of sensitive information contained in students' records.

Security Versus Liberty

The war on terrorism has finally arrived at the doorstep of the U.S. Supreme Court.

The court has accepted the appeals of two groups of prisoners from the Afghanistan conflict and has other cases before it that stem from the Bush administration's treatment of terrorist suspect. Up to this point, the federal appellate courts have largely allowed the administration to bend the rules of due process in the name of national security. Now the high court has the opportunity to set some limits.

Twelve Kuwaitis, two Britains, and two Australians held at Guantanamo Bay, Cuba, are challenging their open-ended detention and the administration's refusal to provide them hearings before a tribunal. To date, they have had no way to challenge the legitimacy of their captivity. All have been detained for at least 18 months without charge.

The high courts have a duty to bring some balances to the civil liberties side of the freedom-versus-security equation. In a recent speech, President Bush, speaking on another issue, said: "In the long run, stability cannot be purchased at the expense of liberty." How true, and we hope the court is listening.

The Republic of Fear

Since 9/11 the administration has led us to believe that there is a terrorist behind every bush. The news media reports the terror alert go from yellow to orange and we have roadside searches of our vehicles and our persons under the suspicion that we are carrying chemical or nuclear weapons in the trunk of our cars.

Since then the administration's answer has been "homeland security." To preserve American power and prevent future attack, the government has asserted a novel right under international law to disarm through "pre-emptive self-defense" any country that poses a threat. At home it has instituted sweeping strategies of immigration control, security detention, governmental secrecy and information awareness.

The administration has also radically shifted its emphasis on human rights. In 1941, Franklin Delano Roosevelt called the Allies to arms by painting a vision of the world we were trying to make: a postwar world of four fundamental freedoms: freedom of speech, freedom of religion, freedom from want, freedom from fear.

This framework foreshadowed the postwar human rights construct- embedded in the Universal Declaration of Human Rights and subsequent international covenants- that emphasized comprehensive protection of civil and political rights (freedom of speech and religion), economic, social and cultural rights (freedom from want), and freedom from gross violations and persecution (the Refugee Convention, the Genocide Convention, and the Torture Convention). But Bush Administration officials have now reprioritized "freedom from fear" as the No.1 freedom we need to preserve. Freedom from fear has become the obsessive watchword of America's human rights policy.

The following changes illustrate this transformation of human rights.

1. **Closed government and invasions of privacy.** Two core tenets of post-Watergate world had been that our government does not spy on its citizens, and that American citizens should see what our government

is doing. But since Sept.11, classification of government documents has risen to new heights.

The Patriot Act, passed almost without dissent after Sept. 11, authorizes the Defense Department to develop a project to promote something called "total information awareness." Under this program, the government may gather huge amounts of information about citizens without proving they have done anything wrong. They can access a citizen's records-whether telephone, financial, rental, Internet, medical, educational or library-without showing any involvement with terrorism. Internet service providers may be forced to produce records based solely on FBI declarations that the information is for an antiterrorism investigation.

Many absurdities follow: The Lawyers Committee for Human Rights, reports that 20 American peace activists, including nuns and high school students, were recently flagged as security threats and detained for saying that they were traveling to a rally to protest military aid to Columbia. The entire high school wrestling team of Juneau, Alaska was held up at airports seven times just because one member was the son of a retired Coast Guard officer on the FBI watch list.

2. Scapegoating immigrants. 1200 immigrants were detained, more than 750 on charges bases solely on civil immigration violations. The Justice Department's own inspector general called the attorney general's enforcement of immigration laws "indiscriminate and haphazard." The Immigration and Naturalization Service, which formerly had a mandate for humanitarian relief as well as for border protection, has been converted into an arm of the Department of Homeland Security.

The impact on particular groups has been devastating. The number of refugees resettled in America declined from 90,000 a year before Sept.11 to less than a third that number, 27,000, this year. The Pakistani population of Atlantic County, NJ, has fallen by half.

3. The creation of extralegal zones. Some 660 prisoners from 42 countries are being held in Guantanamo Bay, some for nearly two years. Three children are apparently being detained, including a 13-year-old, several of the detainees are over 70, and one claims to be over 100. Courtrooms are being built to try six detainees, including two

British subjects who have been declared eligible for trial by military commission. There have been 32 reported suicide attempts. Yet the administration is literally pouring concrete around its detention policy, spending another $25-million on buildings in Guantanamo that will increase the detention capacity to 1,100.

4. **The creation of extralegal persons.** In two cases that are quickly working their way to the Supreme Court, Yasser Hamdi and Jose Padilla are two American citizens on American soil who have been designated as "enemy combatants" and who have been accorded no legal channels to assert their rights. The racial disparities in the use of the "enemy combatant" label are glaring. Contrast, for example, the treatment of Hamdi, from Louisiana but of Saudi Arabian ancestry, with that of John Walker Lindh, the famous "American Taliban," who is white American from a comfortable family in the San Francisco Bay area. Both are American citizens; both were captured in Afghanistan in late 2001 by the Northern Alliance; both were handed over to American forces, who eventually brought them to the United States. But federal prosecutors brought criminal charges against Lindh, who got an expensive lawyer and eventually plea-bargained to a prison term. Meanwhile, Hamdi has remained in incommunicado detention, without a lawyer, in a South Carolina military brig.

5. **The effect of the rest of the world.** America's antiterrorist activities have given cover to many foreign governments who want to use "antiterrorism" to justify their own crackdowns on human rights. Examples abound. In Indonesia, that army has cited America's use of Guantanamo to propose building an offshore prison camp on Nasi Island to hold suspected terrorists from Aceh. In Australia, Parliament passed laws mandating the forcible transfer of refugees seeking entry to detention facilities in Nauru, where children as young as three years old are being held, so that Australia does not (in the words of its defense minister) become a "pipeline for terrorists."

Who are the terrorists

Our current national leadership appears to have been taken over by a recruitive group of enlists who profess democracy while dragging the country into a totalitarian nightmare. Confusion and fear take hold, civil rights are eroded in the name of fighting a terror war, and impersonal governmental bodies with names like "Committee of General Security" start labeling dissenters as enemies of the state. Secretive courts with limited accountability punish civilians who object. Tightening its grip on power, the government creates public crises it can later be seen as solving, and military service is made mandatory for young men. The ongoing terror war drains the country's resources, foreign relations hit rock bottom, and the economy slides even further. But since fear is the government's most effective weapon against its own population, the terror war is expanded.

America is a nation on edge; 9-11, anthrax attacks and color-coded danger alerts have seen to that. Few have questioned the Bush administration's unprecedented increase in military spending or why social programs were cut to fund it. Even fewer realize our government has considered -in the name of fighting a war on terror- provoking attacks against Americans. No surprise that mandatory military service is once again a hot topic. Meanwhile, the Land of the Free has been usurped by Big Brother nightmares like the Pentagon's "total information awareness" program, and citizens have become enemy combatants, shorn of legal rights.

Just in Napolean time our country will grow used to the iron hand of the governments' force and secretive military government that Napolean could easily pick up the pieces and impose another dictatorship. People have forgotten what freedom was. Patriotism had become a tool for social control, rather than social justice, and civil liberties were a thing of the past.

So how different are we today? The issue isn't Iraq, the Patriot Act, or Bush. The issue is freedom: if we want it, we'd better let go of fear, the ultimate Weapon of Mass Distraction. We'd better confront the hysteria-inducing tactics asking us to equate freedom with corporate pork for defense contractors. We'd better think twice about tossing aside fundamental constitutional rights in the so-called pursuit of liberty. Because if we don't, what's coming next could be even worse.

The United Nations Covenant on Civil and Political Rights

Preamble

The States Parties to the present Covenant,

Considering that, in accordance with the principles proclaimed in the Charter of the United Nations, recognition of all members of the human family is the foundation of freedom, justice and the peace in the world,

Recognizing that these rights derive from the inherent dignity of the human person,

Recognizing that, in accordance with the Universal Declaration of Human Rights, the ideal of free human beings enjoying civil and political freedom and freedom from fear and want can only be achieved if conditions are created whereby everyone may enjoy his civil and political rights, as well as his economic, social and cultural rights,

Considering this obligation of States under the Charter of the United Nations to promote universal respect for, and observance of, human rights and freedoms,

Realizing that the individual, having duties to other individuals and to the community to which he belongs, is under a responsibility to strive for the promotion and observance of the rights recognized in the present Covenant, Agree upon the following articles:

PART I

Article 1

1. All peoples have the right of self-determination. By virtue of that right they freely determine their political status and freely pursue their economic, social and cultural development.

2. All peoples may, for their own ends, freely dispose of their natural wealth and resources without prejudice to any obligations arising out of international economic co-operation, based upon the principle of mutual benefit, and international law. In no case may a people be deprived of its own means of subsistence.

3. The States Parties to the present Covenant, including those having responsibility for the administration of Non-Self-Governing and Trust Territories, shall promote the realization of the right of self-determination, and shall respect that right,

in conformity with the provisions of the Charter of the United Nations.

PART II

Article 2

1. Each State Party to the present Covenant undertakes to respect and to ensure to all individuals within its territory and subject to its jurisdiction the rights recognized in the present Covenant, without distinction of any kind, such as race, colour, sex, language, religion, political or other opinion, national or social origin, property, birth or other status.

2. Where not already provided for by existing legislative or other measures, each State Party to the present Covenant undertakes to take the necessary steps, in accordance with its constitutional processes and with the provisions of the present Covenant, to adopt such laws or other measures as may be necessary to give effect to the rights recognized in the present Covenant.

3. Each State Party to the present Covenant undertakes:

(a) to ensure that any person whose rights or freedoms as herein recognized are violated shall have as effective remedy, notwithstanding that the violation has been committed by persons acting in an official capacity;
(b) to ensure that any person claiming such a remedy shall have his right thereto determined by competent judicial, administrative or legislative authorities, or by any other competent authority provided for by the legal system of the State, and to develop the possibilities of judicial remedy;
(c) To ensure that the competent authorities shall enforce such remedies when granted.

Article 3

The States Parties to the present Covenant undertake to ensure the equal right of men and women to the enjoyment of all civil and political rights set forth in the present Covenant.

Article 4

1. In time of public emergency which threatens the life of the nation and the existence of which is officially proclaimed, the States Parties to the present Covenant may take measures derogating from their obligations under the present Covenant to the extent strictly required by the exigencies of the situation, provided that such measures are not inconsistent with their other obligations under international law and do not involve discrimination solely on the ground of race, color, sex, language, religion or social origin.

Article 5

2. Nothing in the present Covenant may be interpreted as implying for any State, group or person any right to engage in any activity or perform any act aimed at the destruction of any of the rights and freedoms recognized herein or at their limitation to a greater extent than is provided for in the present Covenant.

3. There shall be no restriction upon or derogation from any of the fundamental human right recognized or existing in any State Party to the present Covenant pursuant to law, conventions, regulations or custom on the pretext that the Present Covenant does not recognize such rights or that it recognizes them to a lesser extent.

PART III

Article 6

1. Every human being has the inherent right to life. This right shall be protected by law. No one shall be arbitrarily deprived of his life.

2. In countries which have not abolished the death penalty, sentence of death may be imposed only for the most serious crimes in accordance with the law in force at the time of the commission of the crime and not contrary to the provisions of the present covenant and to the Convention on the Prevention and Punishment of the Crime of Genocide. This penalty can only be carried out pursuant to a final judgement rendered by a competent court.

3. When deprivation of life constitutes the crime of genocide, it is understood that nothing in this article shall authorize any State Party to the present Covenant to derogate in any way from any obligation assumed under the provisions of the Convention on the Prevention and Punishment of the Crime of Genocide.

4. Anyone sentenced to death shall have the right to seek pardon or commutation of the sentence. Amnesty, pardon or commutation of the sentence of death may be granted in all cases.

5. Sentence of death shall not be imposed for crimes committed by persons below eighteen years of age and shall not be carried out on pregnant women.

6. Nothing in this article shall be invoked to delay or to prevent the abolition of capital punishment by any State Party to the present Covenant.

Article 7

No one shall be subjected to torture or to cruel, inhuman or degrading treatment or punishment. In particular, no one shall be subjected without his free consent to medical or scientific experimentation.

Article 8

1. No one shall be held in slavery; slavery and the slave trade in all their forms shall be prohibited.

2. No one shall be held in servitude.

3. No one shall be required to perform forced or compulsory labor;

(a) Paragraph 3 (a) shall not be held to preclude, in countries where imprisonment with hard labor may be imposed as a punishment for a crime, the performance of hard labor in pursuance of a sentence to such punishment by a competent court;

(b) For the purpose of this paragraph, the term "forced or compulsory labor" shall not include:

(i) Any work or service, not referred to in subparagraph (b), normally required of a person who is under detention in consequence of a lawful order of a court, or of a person during conditional release from such detention;

(ii) Any service of a military character and, in countries where conscientious objection is recognized, any national service required by law of conscientious objectors;

(iii) Any service exacted in cases of emergency or calamity threatening the life or well-being of the community;

(iv) Any work or service which forms part of normal civil obligations.

Article 9

1. Everyone has the right to liberty and security of person. No one shall be subjected to arbitrary arrest or detention. No one shall be deprived of his liberty except on such grounds

and in accordance with such procedure as are established by law.

2. Anyone who is arrested shall be informed, at the time of arrest, of the reasons for his arrest and shall be promptly informed of any charges against him.

3. Anyone arrested or detained on a criminal charge shall be brought promptly before a judge or other officer authorized by law to exercise judicial power and shall be entitled to trial within a reasonable time or to release. It shall not be the general rule that persons awaiting trial shall be detained in custody, but release may be subject to guarantees to appear for trial, at any other stage of the judicial proceedings, and, should occasion arise, for execution of the judgement.

4. Anyone who is deprived of his liberty by arrest or detention shall be entitled to take proceedings before a court, in order that court may decide without delay on the lawfulness of his detention and order his release if the detention is not lawful.

5. Anyone who has been the victim of unlawful arrest or detention shall have an enforceable right to compensation.

Article 11

No one shall be imprisoned merely on the ground of inability to fulfill a contractual obligation.

Article 12

1. Everyone lawfully within the territory of a State shall, within that territory, have the right to liberty of movement and freedom to choose his residence.

2. Everyone shall be free to leave any country, including his own.

3. The above-mentioned rights shall not be subject to any restrictions except those which are provided by law, are necessary to protect national security, public order (order public), public health or morals or the rights and freedoms of

others, and are consistent with other rights recognized in the present Covenant.

4. No one shall be arbitrarily deprived of the right to enter his own country.

Article 13

An alien lawfully in the territory of a State Party to the present Covenant may be expelled therefrom only in pursuance of a decision reached in accordance with law and shall, except where compelling reasons of national security otherwise require, be allowed to submit the reasons against his expulsion and to have his case reviewed by, and be represented for the purpose before, the competent authority or a person or persons especially designated by the competent authority.

Article 14

1. All persons shall be equal before the courts and tribunals. In the determination of any criminal charge against him, or of his rights and obligations in a suit at law, everyone shall be entitled to a fair and public hearing by a competent, independent and impartial tribunal established by law. The press and the public may be excluded from all or part of a trial for reasons of morals, public order (order public) or national security in a democratic society, or when the interest of the private lives of the parties so requires, or to the extent strictly necessary in the opinion of the court in special circumstances where publicity would prejudice the interests of justice; but any judgement rendered in a criminal case or in a suit at law shall be made public except where the interest of juvenile persons otherwise requires or the proceedings concern matrimonial disputes or the guardianship of children.

2. Every one charged with a criminal offense shall have the right to be resumed innocent until proven guilty according to law.

3. In the determination of any criminal charge against him, everyone shall be entitled to the following minimum guarantees, in full equality:

> (a) to be informed promptly and in detail in a language which he understands of the nature and cause of the charge against him;
> (b) to have adequate time and facilities for the preparation of his defense and to communicate with counsel of his own choosing;
> (c) to be tried without undue delay;
> (d) to be tried in his presence, and to defend himself in person or through legal assistance of his own choosing; to be informed, if he does not have legal assistance, of this right; and to have legal assistance assigned to him, in any case where the interests of justice so require, and without payment by him in any such case if he does not have sufficient means to pay for it;
> (e) to examine, or have examined, the witnesses against him and to obtain the attendance and examination of witnesses on his behalf under the same conditions as witnesses against him;
> (f) to have the free assistance of an interpreter if he cannot understand or speak the language used in court;
> (g) not to be compelled to testify against himself or to confess guilt.

4. In the case of juvenile persons, the procedure shall be such as will take account of their age and the desirability of promoting their rehabilitation.

5. Everyone convicted of a crime shall have the right to his conviction and sentence being reviewed by a higher tribunal according to law.

6. When a person has by a final decision been convicted of a criminal offence and when subsequently his conviction has been reversed or he has been pardoned on the ground that a

new or newly discovered fact shows conclusively that there has been a miscarriage of justice, the person who has suffered punishment as a result of such conviction shall be compensated according to law, unless it is proved that the nondisclosure of the unknown fact in time is wholly or partly attributable to him.

7. No one shall be liable to be tried or punished again for an offence for which he has already been finally convicted or acquitted in accordance with the law and penal procedure of each country.

Article 15

1. No one shall be held guilty of any criminal offence on account of any act or omission which did not constitute a criminal offence, under national or international law, at the time when it was committed. Nor shall a heavier penalty be imposed than the one that was applicable at the time when the criminal offence was committed. If, subsequent to the commission of the offence, provision is made by law for the imposition of the lighter penalty, the offender shall benefit thereby.

2. Nothing in this article shall prejudice the trial and punishment of any person for any act or omission which, at the time when it was committed, was criminal according to the general principles of law recognized by the community of nations.

Article 16

Everyone shall have the right to recognition everywhere as a person before the law.

Article 17

1. No one shall be subjected to arbitrary or unlawful interference with his privacy, family, home or correspondence, nor to unlawful attacks on his honor and reputation.

2. Everyone has the right to the protection of the law against such interference or attacks.

Article 18

1. Everyone shall have the right to freedom of thought, conscience and religion. This right shall include freedom to have or to adopt a religion or belief of his choice, and freedom, either individually or in community with others and in public or private, to manifest his religion or belief in worship, observance, practice and teaching.

2. No one shall be subject to coercion which would impair his freedom to have or to adopt a religion or belief of his choice.

3. Freedom to manifest one's religion of beliefs may be subject only to such limitations as are prescribed by law and are necessary to protect public safety, order, health, or morals or the fundamental rights and freedoms of others. The States Parties to the present Covenant undertake to have respect for the liberty of parents and, when applicable, legal guardians to ensure the religious and moral education of their children in conformity with their own convictions.

Article 19

1. Everyone shall have the right to hold opinions without interference.

2. Everyone shall have the right to freedom of expression; this right shall include freedom to seek, receive and impart information and ideas of all kinds, regardless of frontiers, either orally, in writing or in print, in the form of art, or through any other media of his choice.

3. The exercise of the rights provided for in paragraph 2 of this article carries with it special duties and responsibilities. It may therefore be subject to certain restrictions, but these shall only be such as are provided by the law and are necessary:

(a) For respect of the rights or reputations of others;
(b) For the protection of national security or of public order (order public), or of public health or morals.

Article 20

1. Any propaganda for war shall be prohibited by law.

2. Any advocacy of national, racial or religious hatred that constitutes incitement to discrimination, hostility or violence shall be prohibited by law.

Article 21

The right of peaceful assemble shall be recognized. No restriction may be placed on the exercise of this right other than those imposed in conformity with the law and which are necessary in a democratic society in the interests of national security or public safety, public order (order public), the protection of public health or morals or the protection of the rights and freedoms of others.

Article 22

1. Everyone shall have the right to freedom of association with others, including the right to form and join trade unions for the protection of his interests.

2. No restrictions may be placed on the exercise of this right other than those which are prescribed by law and which are necessary in a democratic society in the interests of national security or public safety, public order the protection of public health or morals or the protection of the rights and freedoms of others. This article shall not prevent the imposition of lawful restrictions on members of the armed forces and of the police in their exercise of this right.

3. Nothing in this article shall authorize States Parties to the International Labour Organization Convention of 1948 concerning Freedom of Association and Protection of the

Right to Organize to take legislative measures which would prejudice, or to apply the law in such a manner as to prejudice, the guarantees provided for in that Convention.

Article 23

1. The family is the natural and fundamental group unit of society and is entitled to protection by society and the State.

2. The right of men and women of marriageable age to marry and to found a family shall be recognized.

3. No marriage shall be entered into without the free and full consent of the intending spouses.

4. States Parties to the present Covenant shall take appropriate steps to ensure equality of rights and responsibilities of spouses as to marriage, during marriage and at its dissolution. In the case of dissolution, provision shall be made for the necessary protection of any children.

Article 24

1. Every child shall have, without any discrimination as to race, color, sex, language, religion, national or social origin, property or birth, the right to such measures of protection as are required by his status as a minor, on the part of his family, society and the State.

2. Every child shall be registered immediately after birth and shall have a name.

3. Every child has the right to acquire a nationality.

Article 25

Every citizen shall have the right and the opportunity, without any of the distinctions mentioned in article 2 and without unreasonable restrictions:

(a) To take part in the conduct of public affairs, directly or through freely chosen representatives;

(b) To vote and to be elected at genuine periodic elections which shall be by universal and equal suffrage and shall be held by secret ballot, guaranteeing the free expression of the will of the electors;
(c) To have access, on general terms of equality, to public service in his country.

Article 26

All persons are equal before the law and are entitled without any discrimination to the equal protection of the law. In this respect, the law shall prohibit any discrimination and guarantee to all persons equal and effective protection against discrimination on any ground such as race, colour, sex, language, religion, political or other opinion, national or social origin, property, birth or other status.

Article 27

In those States in which ethnic, religious or linguistic minorities exist, persons belonging to such minorities shall not be denied the right, in community with the other members of their group, to enjoy their own culture, to profess and practice their own religion, or to use their own language.

Part IV

Article 28 through article 47 deals with the establishment of a Human Rights Committee (hereafter referred to in the present Covenant as the Committee). And the rules concerning the operation of the committee.

Part V

Article 48 through article 53 deals with the notification of these articles.

1. The present Covenant is open for signature by any State Member of the United Nations or member of any of its specialized agencies, by any State Party to the Statute of the International Court of Justice, and by any other State which

has been invited by the General Assembly of the United Nations to become a Party to the present Covenant.

2. The present Covenant is subject to ratification. Instruments of ratification shall be deposited with the Secretary-General of the United Nations.

3. The present Covenant shall be open to accession by any State referred to in paragraph 1 of this article.

4. Accession shall be effected by the deposit of an instrument of accession with the Secretary-General of the United Nations.

5. The Secretary-General of the United Nations shall inform all States which have signed this Covenant or acceded to it of the deposit of each instrument of ratification or accession.

The United States is a signer with these United Nations resolutions but in the year 2002 we were ousted as a member from the U.N. board dealing with human rights.

The United States refused to sign a resolution to eliminate the use of cluster bombs and personal mines which are armed mainly on killing civilians. The United States has also refused to acknowledge the World court in Europe. It clearly appears that the United States leadership chooses to enforce its world participation on the basis of what we want contrary to what the U.N. wants or what all the other World Nations agreed to.

Out of the mouth of Government Comes Lies Lessons on Misplaced Trust

In the current "war on terrorism" the government has said that the people are going to have to give up some freedom so that government can combat terrorists. Of course, the government has yet to tell the public what will happen if the government is unable to keep its end of the bargain and the public is no more safe after all is said and done. In fact, it is pretty evident that the successful terrorist attacks of September 11 are evidence of a massive failure by the very government that now seek even more power over ordinary citizens. Furthermore, what type of recourse would be left to the public demand back its lost freedoms? History has shown the answer to be rebellion, pure and simple.

According to several polls of the American public conducted since the September 11 terrorist attacks, a majority of the public agrees with the idea of trading liberty for security. Now, it behooves us to ask if less freedom has ever resulted in greater security. A cursory review of the 20th century shows that to just not be the case. Civil populations tend to be a greatest risk from their own governing authorities.

According to author RJ Rummel, who wrote Death by Government, government is the great killer of ordinary human beings due to a combination of both a monopoly of force within a country's borders and a natural instinct for social engineering that seems inherent to all governing authorities. According to Rummel governments killed between 100 to 120 million of their own citizens during the 20th century. Terrorists do not even come close to that figure.

Now why has such genocide been avoided in the United States so far? Is there something inherent in US society or culture that makes genocide unlikely? No. The difference is due to the US Constitution and a Bill of Rights that has restricted the government for wielding the power that would make genocide easy and therefore probable. The 2nd Amendment is especially prominent in this issue as the ability to protect oneself from government aggression dissuades the government from acting. A heavily armed and unmonitored population is a difficult and dangerous target. However, the US now has a civil population that does not understand the basis of freedom now how to maintain that freedom. We can thank compulsory public education and privacy and believe in some vague government promises of greater security, totally forgetting the lessons of history.

The founding fathers of the Republic knew only too well how dangerous government could be as they had experienced abusive government in person. Because of their experiences, they created a national government of very limited power, knowing only too well all government will abuse any power at their disposal and so the less power available to government, the better.

George Washington said in his farewell address in 1796, "Government is not reason, it is not eloquence-it is force! Like fire it is a dangerous servant and a fearful master; Never for a moment should it be left to irresponsible action." Finally Benjamin Franklin summed it up best when he said, "They that can give up essential liberty to purchase a little temporary safety deserve neither liberty nor safety."

We can only hope that what both President Washington and Mr. Franklin said will be warning enough for today's innocent, misguided generation. To not heed their learned advice only invites tragedy.

You're either with us or against us.

Since the attacks of September 11th, we have witnessed a sweeping revision of our country's immigration laws, foreign intelligence gathering operations, and domestic law enforcement procedures. These changes, like those adopted during some of the most notorious episodes in our nation's history, involve a profound curtailment of our civil liberties. In the no-too-distant past, the government of this country reacted to threats to our national security with policies that we now look upon with horror. The Red scare and the Palmer raids after the First World War, the internment of Japanese Americans during the Second World War, the repressive and chilling measures of the McCarthy era, and the harassment and prosecution of political dissidents during and after the Vietnam War all represent policies that we all recall with regret and shame. Given this unfortunate history, perhaps before we accept arguments regarding the need for more restrictions on our civil liberties and fully acquiesce in their adoption, we need to examine more closely some of the current Administration's recent policy pronouncements and actions and assess what they mean in terms of our commitment to democratic principles both in this country and abroad. We must take a thoughtful look at what this country is doing in the name of defense of our democracy; indeed, this very exercise is demanded of us by it. Yet, the President took action without Congress to make himself king.

Who Does The Military Order Cover And What Types of Trials Does It Permit?

The Military Order gives the President the power to identify the particular persons who will be tried by military commission, to create the rules that the commission will operate under, to appoint those who will be the judges, prosecutors and defense lawyers, to decide the sentence upon conviction, and to decide all appeals. The entire process can be held in secret including execution; there is no mechanism to provide for any accountability to Congress, the courts or the American public. In this way, the Order provides the President, and in some instances the Secretary of Defense, with the greatest array of legal powers to be exercised in the justice system that has ever been vested in a single person, office or branch of government since the birth of this nation. In fact, the Order is breathtaking in its abandonment of the doctrine of separation of powers and in its forsaking of cherished constitutional principles.

What Are the Rules for the Military Commissions?

The Military Order leaves to the President alone the decision of who will be brought before the military commissions. Under the Order, the "non-citizens" prosecuted by military commissions will be those people that the President has "reason to believe": (1) are a member of Al Qaeda; (2) are in any way involved in "acts of international terrorism;" or (3) have "knowingly harbored" persons falling within either of the first two categories.

Who is covered by the Military Order?

The Military Order covers non-United States citizens, a term that, literally read, includes legal permanent residents of this country as well as people who may be entitled to citizenship status but have not yet been officially granted that status. In addition, while the Order states that it applies only to individuals who are non-citizens, nowhere does it specify what will happen in those cases in which the question of citizenship status is in doube, as it may be for people who have applied for political asylum. The discretion to decide this issue is also vested solely in the President.

The Administration's effort to defend the Military Order's elimination of constitutional rights on the ground that the Order does not apply to U.S. citizens is deeply troubling. This country has never accepted the principle that only citizens are entitled to the benefits of our constitutional guarantees when they are subject to criminal prosecution. In fact, the United States Supreme Court has held steadfast to this deeply rooted principle of equal protection under the Bill of Rights even in those periods in which the country sought to impose harsh measures to address threats to national security.

The Supreme Court emphasized our Constitution's commitment to this key democratic principle in 2001, when it held "the Due Process Clause applies to all 'persons' within the United States, including aliens, whether their presence here is lawful, unlawful, temporary, or permanent."

The Military Order's disavowal of our core constitutional rules is even more disturbing when we look at the breadth of the net that it creates. A quick look at the three categories of "non-citizens" covered by the Order shows that, even though the Administration painted the Order as an effort to address the limited situation in which Al Qaeda leaders might be captured and held for trial, two of the three categories set forth do not mention Al Qaeda at all, and instead reach a much broader group of immigrants.

The second category of those covered by the Order is vague and ambiguous and therefore extremely broad as well. Because the Order contains no definition of the term "international terrorism," it leaves the determination of the type of conduct that will be held to violate the law and subject an individual to prosecution by military commission entirely up to the President. Unlike our criminal justice system, in which the prosecution tries people for violating specific criminal laws that have been written and adopted either by our state legislatures or by Congress, under the Military Order, the President alone decides what types of acts having "an adverse effect on the United States, its citizens, national security, foreign policy, or economy: will be punishable as "international terrorism."

The range of lawful activities that could be reached by this undefined and extremely broad category of offenses is staggering. In the absence of any definition of the offense of "international terrorism," the potential for conveniently changing the rules to include different conduct as new circumstances arise is great, as is the potential for the use of military commissions to serve ends other than the furtherance of justice. Even if the phrase "international terrorism" were to be defined in terms of its use in existing laws, the concerns raised above would not diminish. Under the Anti-Terrorism and Effective Death Penalty Act of 1996, "terrorism" is defined as the use of any force or violence to achieve a political aim. The use of such a definition here would mean that persons engaging in lawful, non-violent political activities—such as civil disobedience protests—which result in minor property damage or any measure of physical interaction with police officers, could be subjected to trial by a military commission.

Similarly, because the federal criminal code now prohibits the provision of material support to a terrorist organization, regardless of whether that support actually furthers any terrorist activity, people who, for example, provide money for humanitarian medical assistance to an organization allegedly linked to a terrorist group may be prosecuted by military commission even if they are unaware of the link. Given these circumstances, the risk that the Military Order will catch in its net those innocent persons seeking to help relief efforts in other nations seems very hign indeed.

In addition to the vague, ambiguous, and broad definitions of who may be covered, the tentacles of the Order also reach out broadly by means of another mechanism. The Military Order simply states that the people who will be subject to the Order are those whom the President "determine[s] from time to time in writing that... there is reason to believe that such individual, at the relevant times, is or was a member of the organization known as Al Qaeda..." Although aimed at reaching members of Al Qaeda, this provision raises serious concerns as well. First, the language tells us that the decision of who to prosecute by military commission will be based entirely on the President's subjective assessment, and not upon the more stringent and objective standard of "probable cause to believe that a crime has been committed" as required by the Supreme Court's decisions interpreting the constitutional boundaries of our criminal laws. Second, this part of the Order vests the discretion of who to charge solely in the President, and does not require any further corroboration or additional evidence before the military commission process is invoked. The lack of any judicial review at this stage of the process—the charging stage—means that the President will not be called upon to explain why he has "reason to believe" someone falls within one of the three categories nor to specify what proof he has gathered in support of his determination. This circumvention of judicial review plainly contradicts settled constitutional law.

Finally, because there is no time frame governing the President's determination of who is to be charged and tried by military commission, a person who provided housing many years ago to an individual that we now suspect may be a terrorist may be caught in web of the military commission.

The Military Order permits unlimited and unappealable pretrial detention.

Even without knowledge as to what the trial procedures will be, we can already see that the President has cast aside many basic rights and guarantees in the name of expediency. The few guidelines that have been set forth in the Military Order indicate that none of the due process safeguards for which our justice system is renowned will be provided. For example, the Order makes clear in two separate provisions that the Secretary of Defense has complete authority to determine the conditions of detention of the individuals who are charged under the Order. These provisions give the Secretary license to detain individuals indefinitely in direct violation of even the most recent Congressional enactment addressing this issue, the USA Patriot Act. They also give the Secretary the authority to specify the place of detention anywhere in the world. The USA Patriot Act requires that non-citizens who are detained by the government be charged with a crime or immigration violation within seven days of their detention. It then permits judicial review of the bases for the detention through the mechanism of a petition for habeas corpus seeking release from custody. In contrast, no time limitations apply for informing those detained of the charges against them nor do any avenuses of judicial review exist for those being held. By means of the Military Order then, the President has accomplished precisely those objectives which Congress would not accept when it considered the Administration's proposal on the Patriot Act. Apparently, the Administration has used the Military Order to circumvent the considered determination of Congress on this precise issue.

The Military Order casts aside Fourth, Fifth, and Sixth Amendment rights.

In addition to the unlimited restraint on one's liberty, the Military Order makes clear that no persons brought before a military commission will be entitled to the presumption of innocence; nor will they be entitled to the protection of the requirement that there be proof of guilt beyond a reasonable doubt. The Military Order also makes clear that other fundamental principles of our justice system—principles aimed at ensuring the veracity of the evidence presented and relied upon in convictions-are not applicable in military tribunals. Under the Order, all evidence deemed to have : probative value to a reasonable person: may be used in the proceeding. This means that hearsay and other evidence that our federal courts have determined is unreliable or illegally obtained-such as testimony resulting from coerced confessions- may be used. No longer will the Fourth Amendment's guarantee against unreasonable searches and seizures or its prohibition against the use of evidence gathered in violation of this guarantee stand as guardians at the courthouse door to ensure that those who seek to gather evidence do so in accordance with our cherished rights to privacy and to be secure in our homes.

Under the Military Order, the Fifth Amendment's guarantee against compelled self-incrimination will no longer protect individuals who are suspected of wrongdoing from the psychological and physical tactics, used by governments and groups that we have historically condemned, to extract "confessions" regardless of their truth. The heart of our justice system is that it affords protection not just to the accused, but to the search for truth itself. Are we ready to forego this principle that pumps the blood to the heart of our democracy?

The Fifth Amendment's due process guarantees suffer additional blows under the Order by means of the structure and staffing of the military commissions. While in a traditional criminal trial the judge is entirely independent of the prosecutor and sits by virtue of an appointment from the judicial branch as opposed to the Executive branch, all roles in the military commission are to be filled by military officers acting upon designation by the President. The evidence will be presented by military officers acting as prosecutors, and will be weighed by military officers acting as judges, all of who report through the chain of command to the President in his role as Commander-in-chief. Even defense counsel will be selected by the U.S. military; the individual accused will have no say whatsoever in the matter. In this manner, the military commission—staffed entirely by military officers who work directly at the behest of the President—do away with the Constitution's bedrock due process principles.

Another extremely disturbing aspect of the Military Order is that double jeopardy, the constitutional principle anchored in the Fifth Amendment that the same sovereign cannot try a person twice for the same offense, is never mentioned. This omission makes possible a scenario in which an individual is charged and tried in the civilian federal court, acquitted, and then detained and brought to trial before a military commission for the same offense. Indeed, the Order seems designed to permit the Executive branch to try its hand first in the federal courts, and if unsuccessful, bring the same case before a military commission where it will be permitted to use evidence that was not admitted in the federal court case (perhaps because it was tainted by an unlawful search or coercion), thereby providing a better chance of conviction. Plainly, the Order places no constraint whatsoever on the President or the Secretary of Defense should they decide to seek a second bite at the apple.

Our Sixth Amendment guarantees have been tossed aside by the Military Order as well. The Sixth Amendment provides for the defendant in a criminal case to be afforded a speedy and public trial, to have the benefit of an impartial jury venued where the crime was committed, to informed of the accusations against him, to confront the witnesses against him, to be able to use compulsory process to obtain favorable witnesses, and to have the assistance of counsel in presenting his case. The Military Order, however, makes clear that there is no right to a jury trial, nor is there a right to a public trial. Furthermore, those who are detained pursuant to the Order apparently are not entitled to a reading of the charges brought against them, and may not even be able to see the evidence against them because of the charges brought against them, and may not even be able to see the evidence against them because of the provisions of the Order prohibiting the disclosure of classified information.

The Military Order erases the Constitutional guarantee of habeas corpus.

The Military Order's evisceration of an accuse person's right to judicial review of the decision of a military commission is also greatly troubling. The Order grants military commissions "exclusive jurisdiction" over the covered offenses such that individuals subject to the Order "shall not be privileged to seek any remedy or maintain any proceeding" in "any court of the United States," "any foreign nation," or "any international tribunal." The Order is clearly intended to eliminate all judicial review of the process, including the "privilege of habeas corpus," a fundamental constitutional right.

The bedrock principle of our justice system is that government may not deprive a person of their liberty without due process of law. The Supreme Court has long held, beginning in the nineteenth century and continuing without exception to the present day, that all "persons" within the jurisdiction of the United States are entitled to the protections of the due process clause. In fact, even during World War II, the writ of habeas corpus was available to members of the German and Japanese militaries so that they could test the authority of a military commission to detain and try them.

The writ of habeas corpus is one of the primary constitutional mechanisms intended to provide those incarcerated with due process protections against arbitrary, biased, and unlawful detention. Chief Justice Rehnquist has said that this privilege "has been rightly regarded as a safeguard against executive tyranny, and an essential safeguard to individual liberty." The language of the Constitution makes clear that only Congress, not the President, may suspend the writ of habeas corpus, and even then, this power is restricted to cases of actual rebellion or invasion. In fact, such an extreme measure has not been used since the Civil War. Nevertheless, the Military Order suspends the writ. Under the order, persons may be detained indefinitely without being charged or brought to trial, and convictions and sentences by a military commission, including "life imprisonment or death," can be reviewed only by the same officials who made the initial determination to charge the person accused: the President or the Secretary of Defense.

The sources cited by the Administration as authority for issuing the Military Order do not support the suspension of the writ of habeas corpus. The Congressional Resolution Authorizing the Use of Military Force makes no reference whatsoever to arrest, detention, trial, appeal, judicial review or habeas corpus relief. Similarly, nothing in either Section 821 or Section 836 of the Uniform Code of Military Justice provides the bases for Congressional suspension of the writ.

Not only is there no legal authority supporting the Administration's position, there is ample evidence that Congress did not intend for the writ of habeas corpus to be suspended under the present circumstances. When Congress enacted the USA Patriot Act of 2001 on October 26, it plainly intended, as the full name of the Act implies, to create a comprehensive set of tools for the federal government to use in its intelligence gathering and law enforcement efforts to combat terrorism. Accordingly, Congress specifically contemplated and addressed the issue of the availability of the writ of habeas corpus in Section 412 of the USA Patriot Act, entitled "Mandatory Detention of Suspected Terrorists; Habeas Corpus; Judicial Review." Section 412 amends a provision of the Immigration and

Nationality Act ("INA") to require that the government, when it detains immigrants subject to the INA, either criminally charged them or place them in removal proceedings within seven days of the start of their detention, unless their release would threaten the national security of the United States. If the Attorney General believes that there would be such a danger, he must issue a certification to that effect, and must re-certify his findings every six months that the individual remains in detention. This Section of the USA Patriot Act also provides for habeas corpus proceedings to review the government's decisions regarding detention: the individual may apply for such relief from the Supreme Court, any Justice of the Supreme Court, any circuit judge of the D.C. Circuit Court of Appeals, or any district court with jurisdiction.

While Section 412 of the USA Patriot Act codifies Congressional intent to ensure the availability of the writ of habeas corpus, the Military Order provides for no release process, no right to a petition for a writ of habeas corpus, and no right to appeal any decision made by the Executive branch from detention through conviction and sentencing. Congress' action on the subject of habeas corpus is clear; the USA Patriot Act preserves the writ. The President's Military Order not only seeks to exercise a power that is constitutionally reserved to Congress, but also seeks to undermine Congress' specific exercise of its power. There can be no more blatant and profound example of unlawful Presidential overreaching- of Presidential conduct taken in contravention to the expressed will of Congress- than in this instance.

The Military Order creates a system in which both secret trials and executions are authorizes.

The Military Order expressly authorizes "closure" of a military commission's proceedings, permitting the President and the Secretary of Defense to decide whether or not to conduct secret proceedings. In this was, the Military Order creates a system that answers only to the President. Under this system, individuals can be arrested, detained indefinitely without being charged, tried in secret before a military panel on evidence that may not be examined or tested, convicted by two-thirds vote, sentenced to death, and executed, without Congress, the judiciary, or the American public ever knowing anything about any aspect of the proceeding. Never before has the American public been asked to shut its eyes, stop its ears, and close its mouth when the pursuit of justice has been at stake.

Yet, even more disturbing is the fact that the Military Order gives the President completes authority to reach whatever "final decision" he deems proper. The Order provides for no constraint on the President's decision-making in this regard; it may therefore be construed as permitting the President to issue a final decision that completely contravenes the findings of the military commission, even convicting and sentencing someone to death that the military commission has determined is not guilty. The vesting of such authority in the President is so utterly inconsistent with the bedrock principles of American democracy that no argument can be made in support of such a grant of power.

With the overt goal of expediency, and the covert objective of vengeance, the Military Order deliberately sacrifices those constitutional protections that are intended to prevent the conviction and punishment of the innocent. The guarantees of trial by jury or an independent and impartial judge; a public trial attended by the presumption of innocence, evidentiary rules, requirements of proof beyond reasonable doubt, the privilege against self-incrimination, defense counsel of one's choice, and the right to appeal, are all intended to ensure that the process is fair, just, and truth-seeking. Why abandon these principles now when we have successfully prosecuted terrorists while complying with them in the past? Will we permit the subversion of these basic democratic values when their loss may affect immigrants accused of crimes unrelated to terrorism? How can the sacrifice of rules intended to safeguard the innocent be deemed morally acceptable when the potential penalties include life imprisonment or death?

What are the legal and historical grounds for the military commissions created by the President's order?

According to the Bush Administration, the Military Order is constitutional, politically necessary, and morally appropriate. The Administration points to three founts of federal authority: (I) the President's constitutional authority as Commander-in-chief of the Armed Forces of the United States; (ii) the Congressional Joint Resolution Authorizing the Use of Military Force, and (iii) two provisions of the Uniform Code of Military Justice. Not one of these sources, however, gives the President the authority that he has claimed.

Does the President have the legal authority to Create Military Commissions to try terrorists?

Neither the Constitution nor any federal statute permits the President to create a military court with the jurisdiction to try all cases of alleged international terrorism against the United States. The Constitution contains no article, section or clause that provides the President with the power to create military commissions, and the Supreme Court has never held that the President has any implied authority to do so absent Congressional action. In fact, the Constitution is quite clear that when Congress acts, it alone has the authority to create and permit the use of military commissions. This authority is created by the powers vested in Congress to "constitute tribunals inferior to the supreme Court," "to define and punish...Offenses against the Law of Nations," and "to make rules for the government and regulation of the land and naval forces." The Military Order, in direct contravention on the Separation of Powers principle of our government, lodges these powers in the Secretary of Defense, acting at the direction of the President, without congressional approval.

The Joint Resolution authorizing the use of Military Force cannot provide the President with the power he seeks to exercise here. The Joint Resolution permits the President to use "all necessary and appropriate force against those nations, organizations, or persons" that were involved in the attacks on September 11th "in order to prevent future actions of international terrorism against the United States" by them. It authorizes the President to activate the reserves and send troops to Afghanistan, but says nothing about the methods to be sued to try those who are captured and accused of participating in the attacks.

The third source of authority cited by the Administration also provides no support for the Military Order. Neither Section821 nor Section 836 of the Uniform Code of Military Justice authorizes the use of secret military tribunals by any agency or branch of government. Section 821 merely states that, if and when military commissions are properly authorized "by statute or by the law of war," the existence of courts-martial will not deprive such commissions of their ability to hear a case. This Section therefore addresses only those specific situations involving offenders and offenses that are traditionally tried under the law of war by military commissions; it cannot authorize the creation of military commissions.

What is the Historical Precedent for the Military Order? Have We Done This Before?

America's use of military commissions in the past provides no support whatsoever for the use of the military commissions contemplated by the Military Order.

As historical support for its position, the Administration has pointed to a World War II decision by the Supreme Court, in which the Court upheld the propriety of a trial of eight German saboteurs by military commission. However, that decision does not support the Administration's position. At the time, Congress had issued a formal declaration of war and had expressly authorized the trial by military commission of "enemy aliens" who violate the law of war – i.e., citizens of a state with which the United States is at war.

The circumstances under which the Court decided that case, however, are not present today. None of the proposed defendants in the current circumstances are likely to be charged with violations of the law of war committed in the context of a declared armed conflict. Congress has not made a formal declaration of war, nor or the members of Al Qaeda "enemy aliens" within the meaning of international law; they are not combatants or soldiers from an enemy state's army.

International treaty law defines the specific circumstances in which the "laws of war" apply. These rules have been accepted and adopted by the United States. Under the Geneva Conventions, a state of war exists only when a conflict arises between nation states. While the Geneva Conventions also delineate rules of war that apply for "non-international armed conflicts" or non-country conflicts, they clearly provide that such rules apply only to conflicts between a state's armed forces and dissident groups within that state that are under responsible command and exercise authority over a part of the state's territory. Plainly, neither of these definitions apply to the current situation. On September 18,2001, Congress authorized military action, but it did not declare war on any foreign nation. Moreover, even if the United States' actions with regard to Afghanistan and the Taliban government amounted to a declaration of war against those entities, the same analysis cannot applied to Al Qaeda. Al Qaeda is neither a nation nor a government. In fact, those persons being held by the Administration on suspicion of terrorism may be citizens of as many as forty-seven different nations. A number of these nations are those with which the United States maintains a close alliance (such as France, Spain, and Egypt).

Although Congress enacted legislation authorizing the use of courts-martial after the Second World War, such tribunals have limited jurisdiction and have never been used to try offenses committed by civilians. The Supreme Court addressed this issue many years ago, in a case in which the Court overturned a conviction of a civilian by a military tribunal because the tribunal had not been authorized either by the Constitution or Congress. Speaking to the issue of Presidential authority, the Court stressed that the use of military tribunals for civilians "cannot [be] justified on the mandate of the President; because he is controlled by law, and has his appropriate sphere of duty, which is to execute, not to make, the laws; and there is 'no unwritten criminal code to which resort can be had as a source of jurisdiction." The Supreme Court also expressly rejected the government's contention that the use of a military tribunal was necessary given the exigencies of the Civil War, the Court stressed that: "The Constitution of the United States is a law for rulers and people, equally in war and in peace, and covers with the shield of its protection all classes of men, at all times, and under all circumstances."

Does The Military Order Comport With International Law?

To the extent that military commissions can legally hear any cases at all, they are limited to those alleging violations of the laws of war by combatants. Violations of the laws of war, by definition, can only be committed during an armed conflict by persons who are acting on behalf of a state or as part of an insurgency that rises to the level of a civil war. Therefore, in order to assess the current situation in terms of international law,, we must determine first whether the acts of September 11th constituted violations of the laws of war-i.e., were these actions committed during a war by state actors? Although it appears that the United States cannot be at war with bands of terrorists under the principles of international law, with regard to those fighting on behalf of the Taliban regime, the answer is different. The Taliban regime was the operating government of Afghanistan, whether formally recognized by the United States or not, and once the United States attacked that country, a war was started. Under these circumstances. Taliban fighters captured on the battlefield must be treated in accordance with the requirements of the Geneva Conventions, and therefore if they are accused of committing any war crimes must be tried before courts martial and not military commissions.

What Does International Humanitarian Law say about who may be brought before the military commissions contemplated by the order?

Whether the current situation constitutes a "war" or "armed conflict" within the meaning of international law is of great importance in determining the legal status of those persons involved in the hostilities, the forum in which they can be tried for their actions, and the nature of the charges that can be brought against them. If a state of war exists, then the status of those involved in the September 11th attacks could change from that of civilian to that of combatant, and, upon capture, from that of unprivileged combatants may be tried by military commissions, POWs and civilians may not. For this reason, the question of whether the present state of affairs amounts to an armed conflict must be addressed first.

We have recently used the word "war" to refer to a wide range of governmental program designed to address major social and political problems-e.g.., the "war on poverty" or the "war on drugs"-but historically, the word's accepted meaning has been that of a conflict between traditional nations that have defined borders and organizes military forces, and in which success is measured in terms of the achievement of geographical objectives. It is from this historical understanding that the definition used in international law is derived.

International humanitarian law imposes rights and obligations on all parties to international and internal armed conflicts. The primary sources of this body of law are the four Geneva Conventions and their two additional protocols. Under international humanitarian law, war or armed conflict can, by definition, only arise between two or more nation-states or a nation state and an insurgent group within that state. A "State," for purposes of international law, is "an entity that has a defined territory and a permanent population, under the control of its own government, and that engages in, or has capacity to engage in, formal relations with other such entities." States are the principal entities that have a legal personality in the international legal order; they have the capacity to make agreements and treaties, and they have rights and corresponding obligations under them.

The answer to the question of whether the Unites States can in fact be "at war" with Al Qaeda or any other group of terrorists is clear in light of these international law principles. Although the Unites States fits squarely within the definition of a State, terrorist organizations like Al Qaeda plainly do not. Members of the network are dispersed throughout countries all over the world and are not associated with any distinct territory. Al Qaeda has never been accorded recognition as a State by any other State, and does not have the capacity to engage in relations with other entities.

The absence of a legal state of armed conflict between the United States and Al Qaeda means that those who were involve, either directly or indirectly, in the attacks of September 11th must be considered civilians, and as such, are subject only to this country's criminal jurisdiction, not its military jurisdiction. They cannot legally be brought before and tried by military commissions. However, because their acts were of such an egregious nature, in addition to prosecuting these individuals for their violations of federal and state criminal laws, the government may also prosecute them for engaging in "crimes against humanity," a crime defined by international law. (c) Enslavement; (d) Deportation or forcible transfer of population; (e) Imprisonment or other severe deprivation of physical liberty in violation of fundamental rules of international law; (f) torture; (g) Rape, sexual slavery, enforced prostitution, forced pregnancy, enforced sterilization, or any other form of sexual violence of comparable gravity; (h) Persecution against any identifiable group or collectivity on political, racial, national, ethnic, cultural, religious, gender…, or other grounds that are universally recognized as impermissible under international law, in connection with any act referred to in this paragraph or any crime within the jurisdiction of this Court; (I) Enforced disappearance of persons; (j) The crime of apartheid; (k) Other inhumane acts of a similar character intentionally causing great suffering, or serious injury to body or to mental or physical health."

The international humanitarian law analysis differs for those captured on the battlefield in Afghanistan. Individuals who meet the criteria for combatant status and who are captured in the course of an armed conflict are afforded "prisoner of war" ("POW") status, which carries with it a number of rights and protections, commensurate with the respect accorded their military status as soldiers. The protections of the Geneva Conventions provide that POWS must be quartered in conditions that meet the same general standards as the quarters available to the captor's force, i.e., the U.S. armed forces. The legal rights of POWs include: (I) the right to attack military objectives (e.g., armed forces personnel, bases, equipment); and (ii) the right not to be prosecuted for legitimate military actions (e.g., taking up arms against other combatants). Those POWs whom the government wishes to prosecute for war crimes (such as the murder of civilians), are entitled to certain minimum standards of due process in judicial proceedings, and must be tried by the same court under the same rules as those used for the detaining country's armed forces. In the current conflict, a captured Taliban soldier who fought for the regular armed forces of Afghanistan would likely be deemed a POW, and thus could not be tried by the proposed military commissions. The soldier could, however, be tried by an American court-martial for violations of the laws of war.

Some of the people captured in Afghanistan and detained by the U.S. government may not be POWs. Under the Geneva Conventions, only those who were members of the armed forces or were part of an identifiable militia group that complied with the formal requirements of combatant status may be considered POWs. For example, members of Al Qaeda, who neither wore an insignia or uniform nor complied with the laws of war, may not qualify for POW status. However in circumstances where there is doubt about a prisoner's status, the Conventions and U.S. military regulations require that the prisoner be considered a POW until a "competent tribunal" can make a determination. The presumption that a person captured on a battlefield has POW status provides protections that all nations thought necessary to codify after the Second World War. This country should embrace this set of rules that is intended to protect all people, including American servicemen and women, taken captive in war.

We must also recognize that the rules set forth in the Geneva Conventions require the humane treatment of all persons captured during armed conflict. Every captured fighter is entitled to humane treatment including basic shelter, food, clothing, and medical attention. No detainee may be subjected to torture, corporal punishment, or humiliating or degrading treatment. These rules apply regardless of whether one is found to have POW status. If we do not comply with these requirements now and show our respect for the Geneva Conventions, we will not be in a position to insist on such treatment for out soldiers captured in war.

What does international human rights law say about structure and operation of the military commissions contemplated by the order?

The Military Order allows the President to violate the United States' binding international treaty obligations. The International Covenant on Civil and Political Rights (the "ICCPR") which the United States ratified in 1992, obligates State Parties to the Covenant to protect the due process rights of all persons subject to any criminal proceeding. Once these treaty obligations were ratified by the United States, they became the "Supreme Law of the Land" under the U.S. Constitution, and must be applied by all courts in proceedings that are brought under them. These treaty obligations simply cannot be overturned by Executive fiat.

The Order is seriously flawed when examined from the perspective of the guarantees and protections afforded by international human rights law. Specifically, the Military Order raises significant concerns regarding whether the United States will comply with its obligations under the ICCPR.

Like other agreements ensuring the protection of human rights, the ICCPR permits a country to derogate form some of these obligations in times of public emergencies. However, the Covenant also provides that certain rights and freedoms are so fundamental that they may not be suspended even in a time of public emergency. These rights include: the right to live your life (Article 6); the prohibition against torture and cruel, inhuman, and degrading treatment or punishment (Article 7); the prohibition against slavery (Article 8); the prohibition against convictions based on retroactive laws (Article 15); and the right of religious freedom (Article 18).

The Covenant sets forth a specific procedure that must be followed when a State wishes to derogate from any of those rights. Under this procedure, a State must immediately inform other parties to the Covenant of the specific provisions from which it has derogated, and must use as intermediary the Secretary General of the United Nations. A State must explain its reasons for the derogation and must state the date upon which the derogation will terminate. Finally, a State may derogate from its obligations under the ICCPR only "to the extent strictly required by the exigencies of the situation" and provided that such measures are not inconsistent with its other obligations under international law.

The terms of the Military Order fall far short of meeting the high standard for derogation from the human rights guaranteed under the ICCPR. The Order sharply curtails the right to liberty and security of the person as guaranteed by Article 9 of the Covenant, and the right to a fair trial as guaranteed by Article 14 of the Covenant. The Administration has undertaken this derogation even though it has not, and indeed cannot, show that such a suspension of rights is necessary within the current situation, and it has created a military justice system that, as discussed above, will violate other international obligations as well.

The Military Order violates the ICCPR's Article 9 Guarantee of the Right to Liberty and Security of the person

Section 2 of the Military Order permits the President to authorize the arrest and detention of people on grounds that are vague and overboard. The provision allows the military to take a person into custody and before a military commission if the President states that he has "reason to believe" that the individual took part in "acts of international terrorism" against the United States. Because the Order fails to define "international terrorism" or to specify the nature of the proscribed conduct, it plainly constitutes an extreme derogation of the Article 9 prohibition against arbitrary arrest and detention. The provision of the Order authorizing military commissions for violations of the laws of war and "other applicable crimes," is flawed for the same reason. This open-ended category would permit the Executive to try persons for virtually any criminal offense.

The Military Order vests in the Secretary of Defense such unfettered authority to determine the place and length of detention—without any judicial oversight—that it directly undermines Article 9 guarantees. Under Article 9 of the Covenant, an individual detained on a criminal charge must be brought promptly before a judge or officer and is generally entitled to bail pending trial. Under this Article, trial must be held within a reasonable time, and anyone who is detained pending trial has the right to have the lawfulness of the detention determined by a court. But under the President's Military Order, there is no requirement that persons detained be told the reason for their arrest or the charges against them or that they be brought before a judicial authority to determine the lawfulness of their detention. In fact, the Order goes several steps further and expressly negates the right of a detainee to challenge the lawfulness of his or her detention, makes no provision for bail, and does not mandate that trials be held within a reasonable period of time after the commencement of detention.

The Military Order violates the ICCPR's Article 14 Guarantees of the Right to Due Process and to a fair and public hearing by a competent, independent and impartial tribunal

Although the Military Order states that trials held by the commissions should be "full and fair," the absence of key due process requirements in the Order indicate that this will not likely be the case. The Order does not provide for a trial by an independent and impartial judge or for a public trial. There is no requirement of a presumption of innocence, or of proof beyond a reasonable doubt. There is no privilege against self-incrimination, nor is there any guarantee that defendants will have access to the evidence submitted against them. An individual brought before a military commission will not be entitled to his counsel of choice. These shortcomings plainly run afoul of the Covenant's Article 14 guarantees by jeopardizing an accused's right to be informed of the charges against him or her and to properly prepare a defense.

Equally troubling is the fact that the Military Order does not provide for any appellate review, or even for review by a separate military commission pane. The accused's only recourse is for a review by the President of the Secretary of Defense as the President's designate. All judicial appeals are precluded, including those that might be made to international tribunals. Prominent human rights groups have noted that this denial of the right to appeal under international law is "especially troubling" because the Order expressly contemplates that the commissions will hand down death sentences.

Not only does the Order breach Articles 9 and 14, it also undermines several other provisions of the Covenant. In contravention of Article 18's non-derogable guarantee for the right to freedom of religion, Section 3(d) of the Military Order states that detainees will be able to exercise their religion only to the extent "consistent with the requirements of such detention." Similarly, in violation of the non-discrimination requirements of Articles 2 and 26 of the Covenant, the Order specifies that the military commission system will be applied only to non-United States citizens. This discrimination on the basis of national origin violates Article 4 as well.

In sum, an analysis of the provisions of the Military Order in light of binding international law reveals that the Order sacrifices the fundamental human rights to personal liberty and a fair trial in ways that far exceed what is permitted under international law even in times of crises. The Order plainly and unlawfully permits the President to violate our country's binding treaty obligations.

America's Foreign Policy with regard to the use of Military Tribunals.

In virtually every instance in which another country has used military tribunals to try civilians, the United States State Department has strongly criticized the practice, and has done so on the specific ground that the elimination of due process guarantees undermines the basic human right to a fair, public trial. Examples of U.S. pronouncements on this issue are abundant.

> China: Recently, in its annual Country Report on Human Rights Practices, the State Department recently criticized the Chinese justice system in part because defendants in China are not provided with certain specific due process guarantees, including the presumption of innocence, proof of guilt beyond a reasonable doubt, and habeas corpus relief. In particular, the State Department has identified as problematic the facts that the Chinese government has broad authority to define crimes that endanger :state security," that trials involving national security may be conducted in secret, that police can monitor attorney-client meetings, and that defendants are not always permitted to confront their accusers. Most recently, the State Department concluded that "the lack of due process is particularly egregious in death penalty cases."
>
> Egypt: In its last two Country Reports, the State Department severely criticized the manner in which military tribunals were used in Egypt to try offenses ranging from non-violent political dissent to acts of terrorism. Specific objections noted by the State Department included the same aspects of military tribunals that are causing concern here: civilians may be tried by the military tribunal, the judges are military officers appointed by the Ministry of Defense; and verdicts may not be appealed. The year 2000 annual Country Report issued by the State Department expressly

> noted that "this use of military courts...has deprived hundreds of civilian defendants of their constitutional right to be tried by a civilian judge." The 2000 Report also stated that "military courts do not ensure civilian defendants due process before and independent tribunal" and that the judges "are neither as independent nor as qualified as civilian judges in applying the civilian penal code.
>
> Peru: The State Department has continually criticized Peru's use of military tribunals to try civilians for treason and terrorism on the grounds that the "proceedings in these military courts-and those for terrorism in civilian courts do not meet internationally accepted standards of openness, fairness, and due process." Among the specific practices deemed objectionable by the State Department are the holding of treason trials in secret, the prohibition on access to state's evidence files by defense attorneys, and the prohibition on questioning of military and police witnesses. Some of the State Department's strongest language condemning Peru's military trial system was issued during the secret military trial of American citizen Lori Berenson. The State Department protested that the proceeding was not held in "open civilian court with full rights of legal defense, in accordance with international judicial norms."

Just as the United States has repeatedly refused to accept the rationalizations offered by foreign governments for dispensing with due process rights and convening secret military tribunals to try civilians, many political leaders and human rights advocates from inside and outside of the United States have begun to call us to account for putting forth the same unconvincing justifications. The Administration's rationale for its breathtaking disregard of official foreign policy pronouncements in this area has been threefold. According to the President, Attorney General Ashcroft, and Vice President Cheney, the military tribunal system is necessary because it will: (I) ensure swift and uncomplicated justice; (ii) allow the government to "use intelligence information that could not be used in a regular court proceeding" due to concerns about the safety of sources and the confidentiality of intelligence measures; and (iii) ensure the safety of jurors and witnesses. However, none of these justifications warrant our abandonment of the constitutional court system of which we are all rightly proud. The State Department has noted time and again in its criticisms of military tribunals held by other countries that none of the justifications it asserts now can demonstrate the need for such dramatic departure from constitutional guarantees in order to preserve national security. The record plainly demonstrates that our federal courts are completely capable of handling cases involving acts of terrorism against the United States. Following public trials which conformed to all constitutional requirements, federal courts convicted the individuals charged with the 1998 bombings of the American embassies in Kenya and Tanzania as well as those charged with the 1993 attack on the World Trade Center towers. The Administration's argument concerning the necessity of creating military commissions is belied by the fact that Congress has recently expanded the criminal jurisdiction of our federal courts in a deliberate effort to cover a broader range of terrorism offenses. The fact that there have been successful prosecutions of terrorists in our civilian courts lends weight to the growing outcry against the Administration's call for the use of extrajudicial proceedings. Moreover, because federal courts are authorized by law to restrict public disclosure of sensitive information, and have the power to hold defendants without bond pending trial if their release might cause harm to the national security or endanger the community, neither of these prosecutions jeopardized our intelligence sources or put at risk those serving as jurors witnesses. Similarly, the Speedy Trial Act ensures that there will not be unreasonable delays in bringing those accused of terrorist acts to justice.

Now What?

Our court system has been acknowledged as the world's model for transparent justice in a democratic society. But we need not, and indeed we must not, sacrifice out constitutional principles and abandon our commitment to the rule of law in order to punish those responsible for the acts of September 11th. If we implement the commissions contemplated by the Military Order, we will surely undermine our most noble accomplishments in the service of several extremely dubious objectives. First, we will demonstrate that in the tug of war between secrecy and democracy, secrecy must win. We will communicate to the world that it is acceptable in the name of expediency to replace a fair and open justice system with a system that permits one executive officer to play all of the roles- rule maker, investigator, accuser, prosecutor, judge, jury, sentencing court, reviewing court, and jailer or executioner-and makes no provision for accountability to any other branch of government or to the people. We will topple that exquisite balancing of powers achieved through many years of negotiation and governing. Second, we will create a model for military (and indeed even civilian) trials that is staggering in its departure from the principles of due process. We will create a system of secret proceedings in which the charges, the evidence, the verdicts, and the punishments never have to be revealed to the public. Indeed, we will have succeeded in erasing the rulebook of American justice that was painstakingly written during our nation's history, and replacing it with an unwritten code of vengeance. Third, by proclaiming our disdain for fundamental human rights principles in our own country, we will irrevocably damage our ability to exert leadership and champion human rights around the world. We will have advertised and exported to the world a model that gives license to the most repressive regimes to adopt policies and implement actions that will violate the human and civil rights of their citizens. With the use of these military commissions as contemplate, we will deal a tremendous blow to the institutions of international law. We will communicate to the world that United States will not comply with the international treaties that it has signed and ratified. We will have etched in bold relief for all to see our dismissal of the collaborative efforts of the world's countries, cultures, and peoples, and peoples, and our contempt for the results of these efforts. We must also consider the risks posed by the military commission policy to Americans living abroad. If we use these commissions, our government will be unable to protest effectively when other countries seek to use similar measures against American civilians, peace-keepers, diplomats, and soldiers abroad are accused of terrorist activities. In taking this most treacherous of steps, we will have announced that we reject our history as a country that was developed by and for immigrants seeking a better life. We will have announced that this country is no longer willing to be a haven-or even a way station-for those who seek refuge from oppression and violence around the globe. Even more startling to those of us who may remember our immigrant grandparents and parents, we will have announced to the world that any person who is not from this country is inherently suspect. Yet, contrary to what some would have the American citizenry believe, we remain a nation of courageous, open, and tolerant people. We have not forgotten how recently our own families, needing to make new lives because of persecution, drought, famine or disease, came to this country. And we are neither so ignorant or so blind as to confuse the word "terrorist" with the word "immigrant." We will not stray from the path of justice if we are brave and careful and wise in the steps that we take. We must embrace our responsibilities to our children, ourselves, and those struggling for freedom around the world. We cannot accept the devil's bargain that is being offered to us, for if we forfeit our commitment to civil and human rights in this campaign born of terror, we disprove the truth of our principles, we undermine our best in this country: justice, equality, and truth.

We should be concerned that the United States' double standard with regard to the treatment of POW's in Guantanamo Bay may endanger American soldiers and erode the United States' moral authority when we ask the Iraqi government to comply with the Geneva Conventions.

"Televising our soldiers violates the Convention's prohibitions on humiliating and degrading treatment and should not be done by any country," "Unfortunately, the United States is not in very good moral or legal position to make this a case. In its treatment of the Guantanamo detainees and others captured after 9/11 the U.S. has violated the Geneva Conventions in a wholesale fashion," he added. Among the violations cited by are:

- In January 2001, the United States released the famous picture of Guantanamo detaines kneeling, shackled and hooded. There was an outcry from other countries and the United States may have violated the Conventions by releasing the photo.
- Second, the United States has refused to treat captured Taliban fighters as Prisoners War-one of the most important requirements of the Conventions. Again, the Red Cross condemned the United States stating: "They were captured in combat [and] we considered prisoners of war."
- There are disturbing reports that "stress and duress" techniques are employed against detainees. These techniques would appear to violate the Conventions and may amount to torture.
- Most of you have seen the pictures of the abuse of the prisoners in Iraq. Naturally a picture speaks more than one thousand words.

First the government said it was an isolated case of a few soldiers. Then it was not a violation of the Geneva Convention because they were not war prisoners. Then they were called terrorists where the Geneva Convention did not apply.

We saw bits and pieces of sexual abuse, humiliation, physical and mental torture all in the name of freeing the Iraqis. How are we better than Saddam! There are thousands of pictures and video's that have not been shown because they are too horrible and too shocking, but they are shown on Arab television and on televisions all over the world.

Just read the Geneva conventions and make your own conclusions.

1. A prisoner must just state his name, serial number and date of birth.

2. Prisoners of war must at all times be protected against acts of violence of intimidation and against insults and public curiosity.

3. Neither physical or mental torture, nor any form of coercion may be inflicted on prisoners of war to secure from them information of any kind whatsoever. Prisoners of war who refuse to answer may not be threatened, insulted, or exposed to unpleasant or disadvantageous treatment of any kind

4. Beating people, forcing them to stand or kneel for hours, holding them in awkward painful positions, using bright light or loud noises to deprive them of sleep. Withholding medical attention or pain killers

It should be clear now and it should have been clear at the time the U.S. refused to apply the Conventions to the Guantanamo detainees: The U.S. has an immediate and long-term interest in upholding international conventions that establish universal rules of war and regulate the treatment of POW's. At the time of the Guantanamo captures, our own soldiers live in the threat of capture and that they, like all other combatants, deserve the protection of the Geneva Conventions. It is impossible to know whether U.S. violations of the Conventions led to Iraqi compliance, but U.S. compliance could have certainly make its current complaints more real and less hypocritical. Selective compliance with the law by the U.S. leads to selective compliance of others.

"The U.S. ought to remedy this double standard immediately and treat those detainees in Guantanamo in accord with the Geneva Convention will strengthen the moral authority of the U.S. complaint about the treatment of our soldiers.

Airport Terror

Since the air attack on the U.S.A on September 11, the main emphasis of the government has been to make air travel more safe.

Transportation Security Administration to act as a security force that can implement any rule it wants to frisk, detain, or otherwise infringe on the free travel of passengers that are not terrorists. From toddlers to nuns to senior citizens in wheel chairs. These Federal agents believe it is their duty to harass law abiding citizens who want to exercise their civil right to use an airplane to fly on business or for leisure.

Millions of nail files, lighters and sports articles have been confiscated on the premises that are not allowed onto the plane without any real analysis that a match or a shoe lace could be an equal weapon as could be a myriad of other items that at this time are perfectly legal.

Take off your shoes, your belt, your belly button jewelry. Even bra hooks set off the "You are a terrorist bells". Speak a word of dissent and you can get arrested. Ask one of the TSA (Terrorist Support Agency) as to why the need to see your camera, they will immediately think you are a terrorist.

On a recent trip I tried to be a gentlemen and while waiting in line, I gave my travel companion my two pound computer to hold while I carried her carry on. Just before we were directed to the search station, I tried to give her back her carry on while she tried to give me back my computer. Out of the air flying was a TSA agent that screamed that we were not allowed to switch our weapons of mass destruction once we were in the line and it almost had us arrested.

Where is the common sense that a two or three year old who just had to wait twenty minutes in line knows not to take his favorite toy is subjected to the same critical search as an adult. Where is the common sense that an eighty year old man in a wheel chair has to take off his shoes and belt and get out of his chair to subject himself to the criminal search of the TSA. No other country in the world treats travelers with such distasteful arrogance as in the U.S. We tolerate this on the belief that allowing our underwear to be searched will make us more safe. Okay, yes, a plastic knife is less dangerous then a steel fork.

Below is a list issued by the TSA to make us feel great while being searched.

TSA Issues Guidelines to Help Passengers

Through Security and Expands List of Prohibited Items

The Transportation Security Administration (TSA) issued some reminders to help travelers pass through security checkpoints at airports and an updated list of items that passengers may not bring into the aircraft cabin.

Allow extra time: Heightened security measures require more time to properly screen travelers.

Check-in:

A government-issued ID (federal, state or local) will be requested. Each traveler must be prepared to show ID at the ticker counter and subsequent points, such as at the boarding gate, along with an airline-issued boarding pass.

E-ticket travelers should check with their airline to make sure they have proper documentation. Written confirmation, such as a letter from the airline acknowledging the reservation, may be required to pass through a security checkpoint.

Screener Checkpoints: Only ticketed passengers are allowed beyond the security checkpoints. Each traveler will be limited to one carry-on-bag and one personal bag (such as a purse or briefcase.) Travelers and their bags may be subject to additional screening at the gate.

All electronic items (such as laptops and cell phones) are subject to additional screening. Be prepared to remove your laptop from its travel case so that each can be X-rayed separately.

Limit metal objects worn on your clothes or your body.

Remove metal objects (such as keys, cell phones, change, etc.) prior to passing through the metal detectors to facilitate the screening process.(putting metal objects in your carry-on bag will expedite the process of going through the metal detector.)

At all times:

- Control all bags and personal items
- Do not accept any items to carry onboard a flight from anyone unknown to you.
- Report any unattended items in the airport or on an aircraft to the nearest airport, airline or security personnel.

Items permitted in aircraft cabins:

Pets (if permitted by airline, check with airline for procedures)

Walking canes and umbrellas (once inspected to ensure prohibited items are not concealed)

Nail clippers with files attached

Nail files

Tweezers

Safety razors (including disposable razors)

Syringes (with medication and professionally printed label identifying medication or manufacturer's name)

Insulin delivery systems

Eyelash curlers

Items prohibited from aircraft cabins:

Ammunition

Automatic weapons

Axes

Baseball bats

BB guns

Billy clubs

Blackjacks

Blasting caps

Bows and arrows

Box cutters

Brass knuckles

Bull whips

Cattle prods

Compressed air guns

Corkscrews

Cricket bats

Crow bars

Disabling chemicals or gases

Dog repellent spray

Dynamite

Fire extinguishers

Flare pistol

Golf clubs

Gun lighters

Gunpowder

Hammers

Hand grenades

Hatchets

Hockey sticks

Hunting Knives

Ice axe/Ice pick

Knives (any length)

Kubatons

Large, heavy tools (such as wrenches, pliers, etc.)

Mace

Martial arts devices

Meat cleavers

Metal scissors with pointed tips

Numchucks

Pellet guns

Pen knives

Pepper spray

Pistols

Plastic explosives

Pool cues

Portable power drills

Portable power saws

Razor blades (not in a cartridge)

Religious knives

Revolvers

Rifles

Road flares

SCUBA knives

Sabers

Screwdrivers

Shotguns

Ski poles

Spear guns

Starter pistols

Straight razors

Stun gun/shocking devices

Swords

Tear gas

Throwing stars

Toy transformer robots

Toy weapons

Passengers should be aware that there are no provisions for returning banned items to them when they are left at the security checkpoint. In addition, those who attempt to bring banned items through the checkpoints are subject to civil penalties of up to $1,100 per violation in addition to criminal penalties.

Now tell me, how my tennis racket, golf club or toy robots can be a weapon of mass destruction.

I would write a book itself on the idiotic behavior of TSA personnel, which I have personally observed in my two years of travel since September 11. Yes, I have seen an inspector hold up ladies thong underwear, a vibrator and the taking away of a child's GI-Joe doll all which must look like weapons of mass destruction

Our Airport Gestapo At Work
Willkommen in Amerika

"They just keep passing it around—there were eight or nine or ten of them who handled it before it was over," he said.

"They had found it in my pocket at the airport, and they thought it was suspicious. It's shaped like a star, and they were looking at the metal edges of it, like it was a weapon. I asked for it back, but they kept handling it to each other and inspecting it. I was told to move to a separate area.

"I told them—just turn it over. The engraving on the back explains everything. But they thought they must have something potentially dangerous here.

"I told them exactly what it was-I said, 'That's my Congressional medal of Honor."

The man relating that story is retired General Joe Foss, 86. His experience in Arizona-at the international airport in Phoenix-may be the ultimate symbol of the out-of-kilter times we are going through. We are so afraid of terrorists in our midst that what happened to Foss is not only believable, but perhaps even inevitable: The Congressional Medal of Honor will be taken from its recipient because it looks vaguely ominous.

Foss said he holds no animosity about the incident. "I'm just as interested in defeating the terrorists as anyone is, I promise you that"—and that he is mostly sad that no one knew what the Medal of Honor was.

Foss was awarded the medal by President Franklin D. Roosevelt during World War II after shooting down 26 enemy planes as a Marine fighter pilot in solo combat in the Pacific. He grew up in South Dakota-after the war he would become governor of that state—and took flying lessons as a young man, then went to war.

He lives in Scottsdale, Arizona and when he travel, he is patted down in airports instead of going through metal detectors, because of a heart pacemaker. At the airport in Phoenix, he said, he was being searched manually and he put his jacket through the X-ray machine.

A couple of things caught the attention of the screeners-rightly so. Foss has a keychain made out of a dummy bullet, with a hole drilled through it to make it evident it is harmless; he also carries a small knife/file with the Medal of Honor Society's insignia on it. The screeners took both of them from Foss-traveling during these nervous days with items that look like bullets, or with even a small knife, will, and should, invite scrutiny. Even if you're 86 years old. Even if you're a war hero.

That's not what frustrated him. The screeners, he said, allowed him to mail the keychain and the little knife back to his home from the airport. But for 45 minutes, he estimated, he was passed from person to person, made to remove his boots and tie and belt and hat three different times, and prevented from boarding his flight because the security personnel, he said, had misgiving about his Medal of Honor.

"I want you to know," Foss said, "that I don't go around wearing my Medal of Honor, or carrying it with me. The only reason I had it with me on this flight was that I was supposed to give a speech to a class at the United States Military Academy at West Point, and I thought the medal was something the cadets might be interested in seeing." When asked what he remembered about being presented the Congressional Medal of Honor.

"I was right fresh out of combat when I was called to the White House," he said. "FDR was behind his desk, and he pinned the medal on my uniform. He said it was for actions above and beyond the call of duty.

"I was nervous, being in the presence of the president. I think I may have been more nervous there than I was in combat. My wife and mother were with me-it was quite a day. I think President Roosevelt called me 'young feller."

After the White House ceremony, Foss had his photograph taken with the medal-the nation's highest military honor for valor in action-on his uniform. That photo was the full front cover of Life magazine, the issue of

June 7, 1943; the cover caption was: "Captain Foss, U.S.M.C. America's No. 1 Ace."

And now, almost 60 years later, the Medal of Honor was being handed from one skeptical security screener to another in the Phoenix airport, while Foss, at 86, took his boots and belt off as ordered.

"I wasn't upset for me," he said. "I was upset for the Medal of Honor, that they just didn't know what it even was. It represents all of the guys who lost their lives-the guys who never came back. Everyone who put their lives on the line for their country. You're supposed to know what the Medal of Honor is."

Air Travel ID Requirement Challenged

San Francisco-civil libertarian John Glimmer challenged as Unconstitutional a secret federal rule that requires domestic US travelers to identify themselves.

"United States Courts have recognized for more than a century that Honest citizen has the right to travel throughout America without Government restrictions. Some people say that everything changed on 9/11, but patriots have stood by our Constitution through centuries of conflict and uncertainty. Any government that tracks its citizens' movements and associations, or restricts their travel using secret decrees, is violating the Constitution," said Gilmore, "With this case, I hope to redirect government anti-terrorism efforts away from intrusive yet useless measures such as ID checks, confiscation of tweezers, and database surveillance of every traveler's life."

At issue is a series of secret security directives issued by the Federal Aviation Administration and/or the Transportation Security Administration (TSA), in consultation with the Department of Justice and the Office of Homeland Security. The directives appear to require US airlines to demand identification before allowing customers to travel. Because the directives are secret, no citizen actually knows what they require.

Southwest Airlines staff prevented Gilmore from Boarding a pre-paid flight from Oakland to Washington, D.C, where he intended to petition the government to alter the ID check. He then went to San Francisco International Airport and tried to purchase a similar ticket on United

Airlines. Both airlines, though unable to identify any actual regulation requiring him to identify himself, prevented him from flying. United states that they were following an unwritten regulation that had only been communicated to them orally, and which changes frequently.

"History shows many abuses when government agents can demand 'your papers, please!'" said Bill Dimpich, an Oakland civil rights lawyer, and lead attorney in Gilmore's suit. "TSA plans to deploy "CAPPS II' later this year. This will use your ID to search in a stew of databases like credit card records, previous travel history, criminal record, motor vehicle records, banks, web searches, and companies that collect personal information from consumer transactions. Your life history will be gathered and scanned, using secret criteria, whenever you book a flight or arrive at an airport. If the machines decide you're at risk, the airline will not let you fly, and federal cops will show up to interrogate you. They will probably tell you that you were 'randomly' selected for all this attention, but they will be lying.

Gilmore V. Ashcroft filed in Federal Court for the Northern District of California, challenges every secret regulation that demand identification from innocent citizens, or restricts their domestic travel. Such regulations are unconstitutional because they are unpublished; require government agents to search and seize citizens who are not suspected crimes; burden the rights to travel, associate, and petition the government; and discriminate against those who choose anonymity. The case also argues that because the regulations are secret, they violate the Freedom of Information Act.

The No Secrets Card

The federal government has decided to test a "trusted traveler" card at America's airports as a means of speeding up lines at security checkpoints. In exchange for giving up certain biometrics information, such as fingerprints or retina scans, plus a lot of other as-yet-undefined personal information, trusted travelers would enjoy express check-in service rather than having to line up and wait with the riffraff. The airlines also have been contemplating a similar card, according to new accounts.

If the government was only honest with us telling us that they want control over all of our activities, it would be simpler than trying to use the September 11 incident to claim national security when in fact it was the government incremental taking of our freedom that started years before and September 11, allowed the accelerations which will continue until all of our activities are recorded on our No Secrets Card.

The answer in the endless search for both safety and convenience in the post 9/11 era is to stop worrying so much and recognize the potential of a benevolent, protective federal government using the latest technology.

Once you're comfortable with trusting the authorities, there are numerous solutions, if you've got a little imagination. Two that I've considered and rejected as rather extreme are a personal bar code that could be disguised as a designer tattoo on your cheek or forehead, and a microchip implanted in your belly button. They conjure images of branded cattle being led to slaughter. A more reasonable solution is a "No secret" card. An embedded chip in the card would hold key information about you and link to a federal database containing virtually every other scrap of information about you ever recorded in any form. The logic is impeccable: The more the authorities know about each and every one of us, the easier it will be for them to decide which of us are the bad guys.

With the No Secrets card, you could get rid of your credit cards, your driver's license, your voter registration, social security and club membership cards and all other forms of identification. If you hung the card around your neck on a chain – highly advisable, because you'd use it dozens of times a day – you could darn near get rid of your wallet. And you'd still be able to take it off at night in the privacy of your bedroom. The DNA code would be entered as well as your date and place of birth. Then we'd need your legal history, such as speeding tickets, incarceration records, overdue – library fines, parking tickets, civil judgements, etc. We'd need your complete medical files and all of your financial records, including your credit history and income-tax returns for the past seven years. We'd need your work, educational and travel history and, finally, your genealogy, specifically a complete family free descending from your great- grandparents. The card would be required at all security checkpoints, anywhere, any time.

The really neat feature about the No Secrets card would be that most of the information going forward would accumulate automatically. The authorities would keep a rolling record of all purchases you've made in the past five years. All cash registers, vending machines and other points of sale would be fitted with a device to record your every transaction, and no product or service could be legally sold, rented or leased without the card.

The No Secrets card would also stimulate the economy, because we'd need to create a new federal agency.

The manufacture and sale of millions of No Secrets card-access machines to the wholesale, retail and service industries as well as law-enforcement agencies would further stimulate the economy, and you would probably want to buy a card read-only machine at home. (no, you would not be allowed to edit your data.)

If there is an error you would have to deal with a government agency similar to the IRS to convince them it was not you who bought a nail file just before you bought a plane ticket.

Some initial opposition to the card could be expected because it would be mandatory for all U.S. citizens, green-card holders and foreign visitors.

George Orwell is laughing in his grave.

Threat of a national ID card

A device is now available to help pet owners find lost animals. It's a little chip implanted under the skin in the back of the neck; any animal shelter can quickly scan lost dogs or cats and pick up the address of the worried owner.

That's a good side of identification technology. There's a bad side: Fear of terrorism has placed Americans in danger of trading our "right to be let alone" for the false sense of security of a national identification card.

All of us are willing to give up some of our personal privacy in return for greater safety. That's why we gladly suffer the pat-downs and "wanding" at airports, and show a local photo ID before boarding. Such precautions contribute to our peace of mind.

However, the fear of terror attack is being exploited by law enforcement sweeping for suspect as well as by commercial marketers seeking prospects.

It has emboldened the zealots of intrusion to press for the Holy Grail of snoopery a mandatory national ID.

Police unconcerned with the sanctity of an individual's home have already developed heat sensors to let them look inside people's houses. The federal "Carnivore" Surveillance system feeds on your meatiest e-mail. Think you can encrypt your way to privacy? The Justice Department is proud of its new "Magic Lantern": All attempts by computer owners to encode their messages can now be overwhelmed by an electronic bug the FBI can plant on your keyboard to read every stroke.

But in the dreams of Big Brother and his cousin, Big Marketing, nothing can compare to forcing every person in the United States——under penalty of law——to carry what the totalitarians used to call "papers."

The plastic card would not merely show a photograph, signature and address, as driver's licenses do. That's only the beginning. In time, and with exquisite refinements, the card would contain not only a fingerprint, description of DNA and the details of your eye's iris, but a host of other information about you.

Hospitals would say: how about a chip providing a complete medical history in case of emergencies? Merchants would add a chip for credit rating, bank accounts and product preferences, while divorced spouses would lobby for a rundown of net assets and yearly expenditures. Politicians would like to know voting records and political affiliation. Cops, of course, would insist on a record of arrests, speeding tickets, E-Z pass auto movements, and links to suspicious Web sited and associates.

All this information and more is being collected already. With a national ID system, however, it can all be centered in a single dossier, even presses on a single card-with a copy of that card in a national databank, supposedly confidential but available to any imaginative hacker.

If you refuse you will not be able to travel, buy anything, get credit or live a normal life in the future.

Soon enough, police as well as employers will consider those who resist full disclosure of their financial, academic, medical, religious, social and political affiliations to be suspect.

The universal use and likely abuse of the national ID card—will trigger questions like: When did you begin subscribing to these publications and why were you visiting the spicy or seditious Web site? Why are you afraid to show us your papers on demand? Why are you paying cash? What do you have to hide?

Today's diatribe will be scorned as alarmist by the same security-mongers who shrugged off our attorney general's attempt to abolish habeas corpus. But the lust to take advantage of the public's fear of terrorist penetration by penetrating everyone's private lives—-this time including the lives of U.S. citizens protected by the Fourth Amendment—is gaining popularity.

Beware: It is not just an efficient little card to speed you through lines faster or to buy you sure-fire protection from suicide bombers. A national ID card would be a ticket to the loss of much of your freedom. Its size could then be reduced for implantation under the skin in the back of your neck.

U.S. to Weigh Computer Chip Implant

A Florida technology company is poised to ask the government for permission to market a first-ever computer ID chip that could be embedded beneath a person's skin.

For airports, nuclear power plants and other high security facilities, the immediate benefits could be a close-to-foolproof security system. But privacy advocates warn the chip could lead to encroachment on civil liberties.

The implant technology is another case of science fiction evolving into fact. Those who have long advanced the idea of implant chips say it could someday mean no more easy-to-counterfeit ID cards nor dozing security guards.

Just a computer chip—about the size of a grain of rice—that would be difficult to remove and tough to mimic.

Other uses of the technology on the horizon, from an added device that would allow satellite tracking of an individual's every movement to the storage of sensitive data like medical records, are already attracting interest across the globe for tasks like foiling kidnappings or assisting paramedics.

Applied Digital Solutions' new "VeriChip" is another sign that Sept. 11 has catapulted the science of security into a realm with uncharted possibilities- and also new fears for privacy.

The company states that in reality you can be tracked through the Internet, e-mail, credit cards and the cellular phone. If you have a vehicle that uses "on star" or "lo jack" your whereabouts are known anyway. So if you have a tollway pass you can be tracked and certain vehicles are steps ahead if having a chip built in that can be activated at will.

When a child is born, the skull is composed of three separate sections for easier passage through the birth canal. Why not have a chip implanted directly into the cranium. When the bones fuse in a few months, the chip will become a permanent fixture in your children.

Of course, this will be done "for their own good." And since these chips are already being researched for modification to RECEIVE and not just transmit data, who knows what it can be used for. Our founding fathers would turn in their graves to see how sheep-like their inheritors of liberty have become.

Pilots could be chipped and scanned before they entered the cockpit, to ensure the person sitting at the controls was indeed an airline employee. Violent criminals and known terrorists should be routinely chipped as a matter of policy.

What's Next?

Rats controlled by implant at current ranges of up to 500 yards have been announced today and the concept of a national ID chip implant takes on more ominous tones.

Now rats with an implant can be made to run, climb, jump or turn left and right through electrical probes, the width of a hair, implanted in their brains. Control movements are transmitted from a computer to the rat's brain via a micro radio receiver strapped to its back. Eventually, the receiver can be made the size of an implantable ID chip such as being developed by VeriChip.

One of the electrodes stimulates the "feelgood" center of the rat's brain, to reward proper actions with a "feelgood" impulse.

Two other electrodes activate the cerebral regions which process signals for mind control. In training, a shot of euphoria rewarded the rats for responding correctly, but after that they turned on cue without any need for reward.

Soon we will be the rats controlled by the government. So are you ready for an implant or maybe soon you will not have a choice.

A British company has developed a system of seat-based body sensors that measure passenger anxiety levels. Locked into a control panel, it signals the aircraft cabin crew. At that point, the crew would make decisions on whether or not to subdue the passenger.

The rationale for this system of emotion and thought monitoring is based on stopping "air rage" or potential terrorists.

"The thin-film sensors could aid cabin crew in monitoring passengers for things like anxiety or high stress or someone who has been motionless for some time," said the British government-owned company behind the sensors.

Airlines and governments are becoming increasingly strident in controlling the actions and words of passengers. By hooking passengers up to what is essentially a polygraph built into each seat, they will be making subjective decisions on whether to restrain an anxiety ridden passenger who just might be upset over visiting relatives or going on a business trip.

Upon landing the passenger under restraint could be met and interrogated by government agents. No mention has yet been made of combining this system with either auto restraints or something triggered by a flight attendant pressing a button on a control panel.

Happy flying we are there to serve you.

The war on terror is in whose hands?

George Soros in his book "The Bubble of American Supremacy" states that the invasion of Iraq was the first practical application of the pernicious

Bush doctrine of pre-emptive military action, and it elicited an allergic reaction worldwide- not because anyone had a good word to say about Saddam Hussein, but because we insisted on invading Iraq unilaterally without any clear evidence that he had anything to do with September 11 or that he possessed weapons of mass destruction.

The gap in perceptions between America and the rest of the world has never been wider. Abroad, America is seen as abusing the dominant position it occupies; opinion at home has been led to believe that Saddam posed a clear and present danger to national security. Only in the aftermath of the Iraq invasion are people becoming aware they have been misled.

Even today, many people believe that September 11 justifies behavior that would be unacceptable in normal times. The ideologues of American supremacy and President Bush personally never cease to remind us that September 11 changed the world. It is only as the untoward consequences of the invasion of Iraq become apparent that people are beginning to realize something has gone woefully wrong.

We have fallen into a trap. The suicide bombers' motivation seemed incomprehensible at the time of the attack; now a light begins to dawn: they wanted us to react the way we did. Perhaps they understood us better than we understand ourselves.

And we have been deceived. When he stood for election in 2000, President Bush promised a humble foreign policy. I contend that the Bush administration had deliberately exploited September 11 to pursue policies that the American public would not have otherwise tolerated. The US can lose its dominance only as a result of its own mistakes. At present the country is in the process of committing such mistakes because it is in the hands of a group of extremists whose strong sense of mission is matched only by their false sense of certitude.

This distorted view postulates that because we are stronger than others, we must know better and we must have right on our side. That is where religious fundamentalism comes together with market fundamentalism to form the ideology of American supremacy.

We may have more difficulty in perceiving the absurdity of pursuing supremacy by military means, because we have learned to rely on military power and we particularly feel the need for it when our very existence is threatened. But the most powerful country on earth cannot afford to be consumed by fear. To make the war on terrorism the centerpiece of our national strategy is an abdication of our responsibility as the leading nation in the world. The US is the only country that can take the lead in addressing problems that require collective action: reserving peace and economic progress, protecting the environment and so on.

Whatever the justification for removing Saddam, there can be no doubt that we invaded Iraq on false pretenses. Wittingly or unwittingly, President Bush deceived the American public and Congress and rode roughshod over our allies' opinions.

The gap between the administration's expectations and the actual state of affairs could not be wider. We have put at risk not only our soldiers' lives but the combat readiness of our armed forces. We have overstretched our ability to project our power has been compromised. Yet there are more places where we need to project our power than ever. North Korea is openly building nuclear weapons; Iran is doing so clandestinely. The Taliban is regrouping the Pashtun areas of Afghanistan. The costs of occupation and the prospect of permanent war weigh our economy, and we are failing to address festering problems both at home and globally. If we ever needed proof that the neo-cons' dream of American supremacy is misconceived, Iraq has provided it.

It is hard to imagine how the plans of the defense department could have gone more awry. We find ourselves in a quagmire that is in some ways reminiscent of Vietnam. Having invaded Iraq, we cannot extricate ourselves. Domestic pressure to withdraw is likely to build, as in the Vietnam War, but withdrawing would inflict irreparable damage on our standing in the world. In this respect, Iraq is worse than Vietnam because of our dependence on Middle East oil.

Nobody forced us into it; on the contrary, everyone warned us against it. Admittedly, Saddam was a heinous tyrant and it was a good thing to get rid of him. But at what cost? The occupying powers serve as a focal point for attracting terrorists and radicalizing Islam. Our soldiers have to do police work in full combat gear.

And the cost of occupation is estimated at a staggering $160 billion for the fiscal years 2003-2004- $73 billion for 2003 and $87 billion in a supplemental request for 2004 submitted at the last minute in September 2003. Of the $87 billion, only $20 billion is for reconstruction estimated at $60 billion. For comparison, our foreign aid budget for 2002 was $10 billion. Just recently, the President asked for another $25 billion for 2004.

There is no easy way out. The Bush administration is eager to get the United Nations more involved but is unwilling to make the necessary concessions. We have no alternative to sticking it out and paying the price for our mistake. Eventually a different president with a different attitude to international cooperation may be more successful in extricating us.

The US is not the only country at the center of the global capitalist system, but it is the most powerful and it is the main driving force behind globalization. The European Union may equal the US in population and gross national product, but it is far less united and far less comfortable with globalization. In military terms, the EU does not even qualify as a power, because members make their own decisions.

Insofar as any nation is in charge of the world order, it is the US. That is not to suggest that other countries are exempt from having to concern themselves with the well being of the world. Their attitudes are not without consequence, but it is the US that matters most.

If Bush is rejected in 2004, his policies can be written off as an aberration and America resumes its rightful place in the world. But if he is re-elected, the electorate will have endorsed his policies and we will have to live with the consequences. But it isn't enough to defeat Bush at the polls. The US must examine its global role and adopt a more constructive vision. We cannot merely pursue narrow, national self-interest. Our dominant position imposes a unique responsibility.

Imagine what the government with all of the new powers we gave it will do.

Where is the public outcry to the passing of the Patriot act?

...Sadly, we have become the frogs and the warm water feels good... HMMM.

Chapter IV
Citizen Spying

The USA was founded in the name of democracy, equality and individual freedom, but is failing to deliver the fundamental promise of protecting rights for all.

-Amnesty International, 19 Jan 2001

"The cost of liberty is less than the price of repression."

-W.E.B. Du Bois

Spying on You and Me

You may have noticed the signs on the street corner where you live showing the "Neighborhood Crime Watch Symbol".

More and more of the public are asked to spy on their neighbors or anyone in the neighborhood who looks suspicious to them.

In some villages and towns, ordinary citizens have been given a speed-measuring gun to take down license numbers or call them in to a law officer of anyone speeding past them.

It won't be long before there will be a requirement of everyone living in each home to display who lives on the premises. As is now required from a visitor, just to get access in a high rise or where there is a guard on duty is screened and if you are not on the list access is denied.

Any visitor to your home will have to provide proper identification and nothing stops anyone from building a data base of who visited you and when. Does this not get as close to pre-1989 Russia where each citizen kept record of the coming and going in their building or worse is in the NAZI Era where similar records were kept to establish that people were having meetings with others that were not related that could be for anti-government purposes.

Become the Neighborhood Snitch.

Uncle Sam wants you. He wants you to spy on your customers, to spy on your co-workers, and perhaps even to spy on your neighbors and family members.

The Terrorist Information and Prevention System, benignly dubbed. "TIPS", represents the latest Bush's Ashcroft assault on civil liberty and just plain civility. Under the TIPS plan being set up by the Justice Department, the government will start recruiting millions of citizen-volunteers across the country to become domestic spies for the federal government.

When the plan goes into effect, UPS drivers, movers, repair personnel and amateur busybodies may be snooping around your home or office for signs of "suspicious" activity. And it gets worse. "All it will take," explains the FBI, "is a telephone or access to the Internet tips can be reported on the toll-free hotline or online." Once received, information may be entered into government database and will be "referred electronically" to local law-enforcement authorities.

You can rest assured that means that thousands of Americans can expect to find the police knocking on their doors—or breaking them down –simply because a person with no law-enforcement training grew suspicious about something they thought they saw or heard. And tens if not hundreds of thousands of Americans, particularly those in immigrant communities, may find their good names in some terrorist database that will be used for who know what purposes.

It is an entirely different matter, however, for the federal government to establish a cadre of private citizens for the specific purpose of spying on the rest of us, particularly when that spying may extend to the home. And the Justice Department's new suggestion that the TIPS hotline number will "not be shared" with certain types of workers with access to homes is meaningless, as the number of course will be widely disseminated by the press and members of the public.

The attacks of September 11th have placed enormous strains on our society and on our government. Unfortunately, the compelling need for enhanced security has spawned many proposals by the Bush Administration that offer few security benefits but strike at some of our most cherished values. TIPS is one of those proposals and should be abandoned.

History is replete with citizens spying on each other. In the German city of Wuerzburg in 1598 citizens turned in other citizens as witches and warlocks only to be burned on the stake.

Pretty much, is that if you're accused of witchcraft, you're a witch. Torture is an unfailing means to demonstrate the validity of the accusation. There are no rights of the defendant. There is no opportunity to confront the accusers. Little attention is given to the possibility that accusations might be made for impious purposes-jealousy, say, or revenge, or the greed of the inquisitors who routinely confiscated for their own private benefit the property of the accused. This technical manual for torturers also includes methods of punishment tailored to release demons from the victim's body before the process kills.

In the murky territory of bounty hunters and paid informers, vile corruption is often the rule—worldwide and through all of human history. To take an example almost at random, in 1994, for a fee, a group of postal inspectors from Cleveland agreed to go underground and ferret out wrongdoers; they then contrived criminal cases against 32 innocent postal workers.

The Neighborhood Watch Program

The Neighborhood Watch Program is touted as a highly successful effort which has been in existence for some thirty years in cities across America. It provides a unique infrastructure that brings together local officials, law enforcement and citizens for the protection of communities.

In cities around the country, neighbors for three decades have banded together to create these "watch" programs. They understand that the active participation of neighborhood residents is a critical element in community safety-not through vigilantism, but simply through a willingness to look out for suspicious activity in their neighborhood, and report that activity to the police and to each other. In doing so, residents take a major step toward reclaiming high-crime neighborhoods, as well as making people in all areas of a city or town feel more secure and less fearful.

In the aftermath of September 11, 2001, the need for strengthening and securing our communities has become even more critical. President Bush has announced that, with the help of the National Sheriffs' association, the Neighborhood Watch Program will be taking on a new significance. Community residents will be provided with information which will enable them to recognize signs of potential terrorist activity, and to know how to report that activity, making these residents a critical element in the detection, prevention and disruption of terrorism.

They will be publishing information which will assist citizens in organizing Neighborhood Watch Programs, knowing what to look for in the community, and understanding what to do if they observe suspicious activity. Under the umbrella of the newly-created citizen preparedness Councils, the Neighborhood Watch Programs will help to distribute useful information circulated by the Councils and other agencies.

Many neighborhoods already have Neighborhood Watch programs, which are vibrant and effective. For those that do not, this new initiative may provide the incentive for them to participate in an important new effort on behalf of their friends and neighbors, as well as the nation as a whole.

At what point does the Neighborhood Watch Programs step over the line and take away our freedom. Imagine a jealous neighbor who wants to get even with you.

Operation TIPS.

Administered by the U.S. Department of Justice and developed in partnership with several other federal agencies, is one of the five component programs of the Citizen Corps. Operation TIPS will be a national system for reporting suspicious, and potentially terrorist-related activity. The program will involve the millions of American workers who, in the daily course of their work, are in a unique position to see potentially unusual or suspicious activity in public places.

The Department of Justice is discussing participation with several industry groups whose workers are ideally suited to help in the anti-terrorism effort because their routines allow them to recognize unusual events and have expressed a desire for a mechanism to report these events to authorities.

These workers will use their common sense and knowledge of their work environment to identify suspicious or unusual activity. This program offers a way for these workers to report what they see in public areas and along transportation routes.

All it will take to volunteer is a telephone or access to the Internet as TIPS can be reported on the toll-free hotline. Information received will be entered into the national database and referred electronically to a point of contact in each state as appropriate. This is not a national 911 center, and callers are expected to dial 911 for emergency local response.

Industries that are interested in participating in this program will be given printed guidance material, flyers and brochures, about the program and how to contact the Operation TIPS reporting center. This information can be distributed to workers or posted in common work areas. The goal of the program is to establish a reliable and comprehensive national system for reporting suspicious, and potentially terrorist-related, activity. By establishing one central reporting center, information from several different industries can be maintained in a single database. Operation TIPS will be phased in across the country to enable the system to build its capacity to receive an increasing volume of tips.

The next time your meter reader looks into your living room, just smile. I am sure the postman and the UPS delivery person will report all of your purchases that are being delivered to you. Remember not to have new vehicles in your driveway unless you want to be considered a money launderer. Plan no trips to exotic locations unless you want your travel agent to report you as a drug dealer. Do attend the neighborhood crime watch meetings regularly and buy night vision goggles so you can see what your neighbors are up to.

Our Friends to Protect us?

Look at the web-site for USA on Watch.org and it is enough to get scared. Under the suspicion of serving the people, a whole bunch of organizations have joined being the policeman in you driveway.

Neighborhood Watch Programs and Partners.

For over 60 years, The National Sheriffs' Association (NSA) has been dedicated to raising the bar of professionalism for those practicing in the criminal justice field. At the heart of this objective are collaborative programs designed to help enable sheriffs, their deputies, chiefs of police, and others in the field to perform their jobs to the best of their ability and to most effectively serve the people in their jurisdictions.

As a result of the events that took place on September 11, 2001, these collaborations have become even more important and serve as a vital component in securing our homeland. National Sheriffs' Association values the alliances it has formed with the organizations listed below. The partnerships National Sheriffs' Association has formed with these groups indeed play an essential role in keeping America safe.

Citizen Corps: The mission of Citizen Corps is to harness the power of every individual through education, training, and volunteer service to help make communities safer, stronger, and better prepared to respond to the threats of terrorism, crime, public health issues, and disasters of all kinds. Volunteers in Police Service: Volunteers in Police Service (VIPS) provides support for resource-constrained police departments by incorporating civilian volunteers so that law enforcement professionals have more time for frontline duty. Medical Reserve Corps: The Medical Reserve Corps (MRC) coordinates volunteer health professionals, as well as other citizens with an interest in health issues, to provide ongoing support for community public health needs and resources during large-scale emergencies. Community Emergency Response Team: The Community Emergency Response Team (CERT) trains people in neighborhoods, the workplace, and schools in basic disaster response skills, such as fire suppression, urban search and rescue, and medical operations, and helps them take a more active role in emergency preparedness. Community Oriented Policing Services: The Office was created as a result of the Violent Crime Control and Law Enforcement Act of 1994. As a component of the Justice Department, the mission of the Office is to advance community policing in jurisdictions of all sizes across the country.

National Association of Town Watches (NATW): The National Association of Town Watches is a non-profit organization dedicated to the development and promotion of organized, law enforcement-affiliated crime and drug prevention programs. National Crime Prevention Council (NCPC): Famous for its famous dog's motto, "Take a Bite out of Crime," The National Crime Prevention Council is a national non-profit organization dedicated to educating individuals and communities about crime prevention.

It sure is scary to have all of those organizations watch whether I wash my car once or twice a week.

Snitch on Your Girlfriend, earn $1000.00.

A new school program will pay students up to $1,000 to snitch on classmates who tote weapons, drink alcohol or use drugs around school.

The paid-informant program will operate similar to a crime stopper hotline that's been around for 23 years. But the new telephone number is exclusively for pupils who want to call the school police anonymously.

Similar programs have been started on school campuses nationwide, from Charleston, S.C., to Thousand Oaks, California.

Some people would never report it no matter what, because they are in a gang or something, but if people knew they could get money for it, that might outweigh (the risk). Imagine how easy it would be to get even with someone you don't like, how easy to go after the friend of a girl or boy you want to get rid of, how easy it is to lie just for making money or getting recognized.

Soon We will have a New National Hymn.

"Oh say can you see, by the dawns early light,

Your neighbor's in your tree, with your bedroom in sight.

He's not interested in rockets red glare, he just wants to know who's in there

To give proof to the right that they're exercising their might

O say can you see, can you still see our flag wave

For we were once the land of the free, and the home of the brave"

Who Does the Government Care For?

The concept of maintaining continuity of government during and after an emergency is not a new idea.

During the Cold War, Congress established elaborate and rather luxurious survival facilities in the mountains of West Virginia. Presumably, while the American "common folk" would be incinerated, the privileged could survive and guarantee the continuity of government and civilization based on their own criteria for human survival.

It was on this premise that in 1964, the great film Director Stanley Kubrick created the classic "Dr. Strangelove."

According to the Washington Post, the operation was re-activated after the September 11 attacks. It is reported to involve officials drawn from all departments, depending on the perceived level of threat.

Those taking part, live and work underground for long spells at secret fortified locations on the East Coast. The core group of federal managers would be drawn from the same bureaucratic minions whose self pre-occupation, negligence and apathy caused the deaths of thousands in the World Trade Center.

The plan for a shadow government has been implemented now because of heightened fears that Osama Bin Laden's Al-Qaeda network might obtain portable nuclear weapons.

While US intelligence had no specific knowledge of such weapons, the risk was great enough to warrant activation of the plan.

President George W. Bush did not foresee ever needing to turn over government functions to the secret operation, but believed it was prudent to put the plan into action in the light of the war against terrorism and persistent threats of future attacks.

The back-up government consisted of anything from 70 to 150 people at two principal locations on the East Coast. They are suspected to be living and working in heavily fortified mountain bunkers, carved out under Pennsylvania's Raven Rock Mountain and Weather Mountain in Virginia during the Cold War in the 1950's.

These underground cities are home to government officials who rotate through on three-month stints. Their identities and even their titles are kept secret. As with all budding bureaucracies, it is not unreasonable to assume that this number will increase, as will the funding and lavishness of accommodations.

Once activated for what some call "bunker duty", they live and work underground 24 hours a day, away from their families. No formal mention was made relative to having families join them as accommodations grow larger.

Those deployed for the operation are not allowed to tell anyone where they are going or why. "They're on a 'business trip', that's all," one official was quoted as saying.

Although it does not identify the exact location of these sites, they make use of geological features to render them highly secure. They are well stocked with food, water, medicine and other supplies and are capable of generating their own power. There are video links, computers and other connections to the unprotected and totally vulnerable civilian populace.

Only the executive branch is represented in the full-time shadow administration. Other branches-such as Congress and the judiciary-have separate continuity plans.

The Bush Administration is following a script that was maintained during every administration, up through the Clinton years. But at the

Pentagon, at the Federal Emergency Management Agency (FEMA) and at the new Office of Homeland Security (Now being elevated to a 170,000 strong super Agency), officials have been busy updating those plans, particularly the way they relate to using the military as a kind of domestic national police for "continuity of government." For those unaware of fed-speak, this means the protecting of elected officials and bureaucrats from the rest of us, who are viewed as the potential enemy.

Many people feel that the Posse Comitatus act of 1878, might protect them from a police state combining the military and civil law enforcement, with heavy managerial input by the US Department of Justice. But laws are already on the books authorizing martial law, including Section 32CFR 501.4** of the Code of Federal Regulations. These are the rules written by unelected bureaucrats that govern our lives.

In broad based terms, the CFR simply states: "Martial law depends for its justification upon public necessity."

With constitutional government "temporarily" placed in the garbage heap, the American people would be subject to direct control by unelected bureaucrats scrambling to destroy the dreams of our Founding Fathers.

40 Years of Executive Orders Trashes Our Constitutional Guaranty of Liberty.

A Presidential Executive Order, whether Constitutional or not, becomes law simply by its publication in the Federal Register Congress is bypassed.

Here are just a few Executive Orders that would suspend the Constitution and the Bill of Rights. These Executive Orders could be enacted by the stroke of a Presidential pen.

It should be noted that over time some of the following Executive Orders have been rescinded or replaced by others. But the true terror to our liberty rests with the ease in which they can be issued how earlier orders are frequently replaced by those of a more draconian nature:

*Executive Order 10990 allows the government to take over all modes of transportation and control of highways and seaports.

*Executive Order 10995 allows the government to seize and control the communication media.

*Executive Order 10997 allows the government to take over all electrical power, gas, petroleum, fuels and minerals.

*Executive Order 10998 allows the government to take over all forms resources and farms.

*Executive Order11000 allows the government to mobilize civilians into work brigades under government supervision.

*Executive Order 11001 allows the government to take over all health, education and welfare functions.

*Executive Order 11002 Designates the Postmaster General operate a national registration of all persons.

*Executive Order 11003 allows the government to take over all airports and aircraft, including commercial aircraft.

*Executive Order 11004 allows the Housing and Finance Authority to relocate communities, build new housing with public funds, designate areas to be abandoned, and establish new locations for populations.

*Executive Order 11005 allows the government to take over all railroads, inland waterways and public storage facilities.

*Executive Order 11051 specifies the responsibility of the Office of Emergency Planning and gives authorization to put all Executive Orders into effect in times of increased international tensions economic or financial crisis.

*Executive Order 11310 grants authority to the Department of Justice to enforce the plans set out in Executive Orders, to institute industrial support, to establish judicial and legislative liaison, to control all aliens, to operate penal and correctional institutions, and advise and assist the President.

*Executive Order 11049 assists emergency preparedness function federal departments and agencies consolidating 21 operative Executive Orders issued over a fifteen year period.

*Executive Order 11921 allows the Federal Emergency Prepared Agency to develop plans to establish control over the mechanisms of production and distribution, of energy sources, wages, salaries, credit and the flow of money in financial institution in any undefined national emergency. It also provides that when a state of emergency is declared by the President, Congress cannot review the action for six months.

*Executive Order 12148 creates the Federal Emergency Management Agency (FEMA) that is to interface with the Department of Defense or civil defense planning and funding. An "emergency czar" was appointed. FEMA has only spent about 6 percent of its budget on national emergencies, the bulk of their funding has been used for the construction of secret underground. Facilities to assure continuity of government in case of a major emergency, foreign or domestic.

*Executive Order 12656 appointed the National Security Council as the principal body that should consider emergency power. This allows the government to increase domestic intelligence and surveillance of U.S. citizens and would restrict the freedom of movement within the United States and granted the government the right to isolate large groups of civilians. The National Guard could be federalized to seal all borders and take control of U.S. air space and ports of entry.

The Federal Emergency Manager Agency has broad powers in all aspect of the nation. The chief of FEMA's Civil Security Division stated in a conference that he saw FEMA's role as a "new frontier in the protection individual and government leaders from assassination, and of civil army military installations from sabotage and/or attack, as well as preventing dissident groups from gaining an audience to U.S. opinion, or a global audience in times of crisis."

The Violent Crime Control Act provides additional powers to the President of the United States, allowing the suspension of the Constitution and Constitutional Law of Americans during a "drug crisis" provides for the construction of detention camps, seizure of property and military control of populated areas.

When the Constitution of the United States was framed it placed the exclusive legislative authority in hands of Congress and with the President. Article I, section 1 of the United States Constitution is clear in it's language. "All legislative powers herein granted shall be vested in a Congress of the United States, which shall consist of a Senate and House of Representatives." That is no longer true. The Bill of Rights protected Americans against loss of freedom. That is no longer true. The constitution provided for a balance and separation of powers. That is no longer applicable.

Since the enactment of Executive Order 11490, the only thing standing between us and dictatorship is the good character of the President, the lack of a crisis severe enough that the public would stand still for it."

...It feels so good in the warm pot, a little more heat would feel great...

Chapter V
Government Rights

" If you will not fight for right when you can easily win without bloodshed; if you will not fight when your victory will be sure and not too costly; you may come to the moment when you will have to fight with all odds against you and only a precarious chance of survival. There may be even a worse fate, you may have to fight when there is no hope of victory, because it is better to perish then to live as slaves. "

-Winston Churchill

For the sake of safety and security, we are losing all of our personal freedom that we were trying to preserve in the first place.

The Government, knowing what is best for us, has taken away our rights and we let them be taken away.

I hear people saying "They can search my house, I have nothing to hide."

A metal detector used to be present when entering a prison. Now our whole nation has become prisons, Schools, courts, airports, public buildings, sporting events, and private buildings. We are not far away from having a chip implanted to keep track of our whereabouts. Whatever happened to our constitutional rights under the 4th and 10th amendments?

Our U.S. Constitution

Everyone including Congress and the police should have to read these amendments on a yearly basis. We should ask our judges to keep these on their desks.

Bill of Rights.

Amendment I

Congress shall make no law respecting an establishment of religion, or prohibiting the free exercise thereof; or abridging the freedom of speech, or of the press; or the right of the people peaceably to assemble, and to petition the government for a redress of grievances.

Amendment II

A well regulated militia, being necessary to the security of a free state, the right of the people to keep and bear arms, shall not be infringed.

Amendment III

No soldier shall, in time of peace be quartered in any house, without the consent of the owner, nor in time of war, but in a manner to be prescribed by law.

Amendment IV

The right of the people to be secure in their persons, houses, papers, and effects, against unreasonable searches and seizures, shall not be violated, and no warrants shall issue, but upon probable cause, supported by oath or affirmation, and particularly describing the place to be searched, and the persons or things to be seized.

Amendment V

No person shall be held to answer for a capital, or otherwise infamous crime, unless on a presentment or indictment of a grand jury, except in cases arising in the land or naval forces, or in the militia, when in actual service in time of war or public danger; now shall any person be subject for the same offense to be twice put in jeopardy of life or limb; nor shall be compelled in any criminal case to be a witness against himself, nor be deprived of life, liberty, or property, without due process of law; nor shall private property be taken for public use, without just compensation.

Amendment VI

In all criminal prosecutions, the accused shall enjoy the right to a speedy and public trial, by an impartial jury of the state and district wherein the crime shall have been committed, which district shall have been previously ascertained by law, and to be informed of the nature and cause of the accusation; to be confronted with the witnesses against him; to have compulsory process for obtaining witnesses in his favor, and to have the assistance of counsel for his defense.

Amendment VII

In suits at common law, where the value in controversy shall exceed twenty dollars, the right of trial by jury shall be preserved, and no fact tried by a jury, shall be otherwise reexamined in any court of the United States, than according to the rules of the common law.

Amendment VIII

Excessive bail shall not be required, nor excessive fines imposed, nor cruel and unusual punishments inflicted.

Amendment IX

The enumeration in the Constitution, of certain rights, shall not be construed to deny or disparage others retained by the people.

Amendment X

The powers not delegated to the United States by the Constitution, nor prohibited by it to the states, are reserved to the states respectively or to the people.

Teach Your Children

I think it is very important that we teach our children about the true nature of government. Now, at last, there is a way to give your children a basic civics course right in your own home.

Teach your child to play a card game called WAR. In this game, each player gets an equal amount of cards. Each player throws down one card every round. The highest ranking card beats the lower ranking card. The higher card takes all cards played in that round. The game is over when one person has all the cards, and this person, obviously, is the winner.

Then create a new game called GOVERNMENT. In this game, whoever is the government wins every trick regardless of who has a better card. Soon your child will lose interest in the game, but I believe you will have taught your child a valuable lesson of dealing with the government.

When your child is a little bit older, you can teach him about our tax system in a way that is easy to grasp and will allow him to understand the benefits. Offer him, say, $10 to mow the lawn. When he has mowed it and asks to be paid, withhold $5 and explain that this is their income tax. Give $1 of this to his younger brother, who has done nothing to deserve it, and tell him this is "fair" because the younger brother 'needs money too'. Also, explain that you need the other $4 yourself to cover the administrative costs of diving up the money.

Make him place his $5 in a savings account over which you have authority. Explain that if he is ever naughty, you will remove the money from the account without asking him. Mention that if he tries to hide the money, this, in itself, will be evidence of wrongdoing and will result in you automatically taking all of the money from him.

Conduct random searches of his room in the small hours of the morning. Burst in unannounced. Go through all of his drawers and pockets. If he questions this, tell him you are acting on a tip-off from a friend of his who casually mentioned that he had earned cash last week without reporting it to you. If you find it, confiscate all of that money and also take his stereo and television. Tell him you are selling these and keeping the money to compensate you for having to make the raid. Also, lock him in his room for a month as further punishment.

When he cries injustice of this, tell him he is being "selfish" and "greedy" and only interested in looking after his own happiness. Explain that he should learn to sacrifice his own happiness for other people and that since he cannot be relied upon or trusted to do this voluntarily, you will use force to ensure he complies. Later in life, he will thank you.

Make as many rules as possible. Leave the reasons for them obscure. Enforce them arbitrarily. Accuse your child of breaking rules you have never told him about and carefully explain that ignorance of your rules is not an excuse for breaking them. Keep him anxious that he may be violating commands you haven't yet issued. Instill in him the feeling that rules are utterly irrational. This will prepare him for living under a democratic government.

Tell him he is too young to understand the benefits of democracy, so explain this wonderful system as follows. You, your wife and his brother get together and vote that your son should have all privileges removed, and confined to his room for a week. If he protests that you are violating his rights, patiently explain his error and tell him that the majority has voted for his punishment and nothing matters except the will of the majority. When your child has matured sufficiently to understand how the judicial system works, set a bedtime for him of, say, 10 p.m. and then send him to bed at 9 p.m. When he tearfully accuses you of breaking the rules, explain that you made the rules and you can interpret them in any way that seems appropriate to you, according to changing conditions.

Promise often to take him to the movies or the zoo, and then, at the appointed hour, recline in an easy chair with a newspaper and tell him you have changed your plans. When he screams, "but you promised!" explain to him that it was a campaign promise and hence meaningless. Every now and then, without warning, slap your child. Then explain that this is self-defense. Tell him that you must be vigilant at all times to stop any potential enemy before he gets big enough to hurt you. This, too, your child will appreciate, not right at that moment, maybe, but later in life.

If he finds this hard to accept, you can further illustrate the point as follows. Take him on a trip across town with you, to a strange neighborhood. Walk into any random house you choose and start sorting out their domestic problems, using violence if that is what is required.

Make sure you use overwhelming force to crush the family into submission, this avoids a protracted visit and becoming involved for long periods of time. Explain to your son that only a coward stands idly by whilst injustice is happening across town. Tell him we are all brothers and problems left to fester will eventually spill over into your neighborhood. Use some of the $5 you took from your son as bus fare and to purchase a baseball hat.

Drink a bottle of whisky and then lecture him on the evils of smoking dope. If he points out your hypocrisy, remind him that the majority of people drink and that, as already explained, the needs of the majority are the only moral standard.

Break up any meeting between him and more than three of his friends as being an 'unlawful gathering.'

If he strokes the cat without the cat giving its express permission, slap him for feline harassment.

Mark a designated spot in the yard where he can leave his bike. If he leaves it anywhere else, padlock it and demand $50.00 to release it. If he offends more than three times, confiscate the bike, sell it, and keep the money.

Install a CCTV system in your son's bedroom and also record all his telephone conversations. If he protests, accuse him of having something to hide. Explain that only criminals seek privacy and that good, dutiful children relinquish their privacy in exchange for the advantages which protective parenthood offers. Remind him of the boy across town who was caught smoking dope in his bedroom by just such a CCTV system, and explain that this case justifies installing CCTV in all teenager's bedrooms.

Lie to your child constantly. Teach him that words mean nothing-or rather that the meanings of words are continually "evolving," and may be tomorrow the opposite of what they are today.

Have a word with his teachers at school and ask them to share any merit marks your son achieves, with any ethnic minority students who did not get any merit marks. If he questions this policy, explain that long ago, we abused the ancestors of these people, and so it is only fair that he shares the merits around to compensate their descendants.

This is also probably a good time to tell him that his energy, talent and enthusiasm will not secure him a job if the quota of such 'abused' people has not yet been filled. Tell him talent stands for nothing, it is fairness and sharing which are important. Remind him that his primary duty is the happiness and welfare of people he does not know, and will never meet.

Ban cutlery from your home and make your son eat with his fingers. If he asks why, remind him of the youth who stabbed a cat to death last week with a fork. Explain that if just one cat is saved by the banning of cutlery, then this prohibition will be worthwhile. If he protests, question him closely about why he is intending to kill innocent cats, or accuse him of being a cat hater.

Issue him with a pass card, which he must show before he can enter the house. Stand guard at the front door. When he comes home, politely but firmly take him into the spare room and question him about his movements. Ask him how much cash he has on his person. If in excess of $50, confiscate the lot as it exceeds the house rule for maximum cash allowed. Then search his backpack and pockets. To keep him guessing, do the occasional strip search. If he protests, detain him for longer and make the search more thorough. If he gets really angry at this, hold him in a locked room until he misses his next outing or party.

If these methods sound harsh, I am only being cruel to be kind. I think it is important for children to understand the nature of society in which we live.

I hope you found that amusing. I did when I wrote it, but on second reading, I feel a bit sick. It makes the point too plainly to avoid.

Real Patriots ask questions

"Now it's no good to have such rights if they're not used. A right of free speech when no one contradicts the government, freedom of the press when no one is willing to ask the tough questions, a right of assembly when there are no protests, universal suffrage when less than half the electorate votes, separation of church and state when the wall of separation is not regularly repaired. Through disuse they can become no more than votive objects, patriotic lip service. Rights and freedoms: Use 'em or lose 'em.

The Bill of Rights decoupled religion from the state, in part because so many religions are in an absolutist frame of mind, each convinced that it alone had a monopoly on the truth and therefore eager for the state to impose this truth on others. Often, the leaders and practitioners of absolutist religions were unable to perceive any middle ground or recognize that the truth might draw upon and embrace apparently contradictory doctrines.

The framers of the Bill of Rights had before them the example of England, where the ecclesiastical crime of heresy and the secular crime of treason had become nearly indistinguishable. Many of the early Colonists had come to America fleeing religious persecution, although some of them were perfectly happy to persecute other people for their beliefs. The Founders of our nation recognized that a close relation between the government and any of the quarrelsome religions would be fatal to freedom.

Its first and most immediate purpose rested on the belief that a union of government and religion tends to destroy government and degrade religion.

In his celebrated little book On Liberty, the English philosopher John Stuart Mill argued that silencing an opinion is "a peculiar evil." If the opinion is right, we are robbed of the "opportunity of exchanging error for truth;" and if it's wrong, we are deprived of a deeper understanding of the truth in "its collision with error." If we know only our own side of the argument, we hardly know even that; it becomes stale, soon learned only by rote, untested, a pallid and lifeless truth.

When we consider the founders of our nation-Jefferson, Washington, Samuel and John Adams, Madison and Monroe, Benjamin Franklin, Tom Paine and many others-we have before us a list of at least ten and maybe even dozens of great political leaders. They were well educated. Products of the European Enlightenment, they were students of history. They knew human fallibility and weakness and corruptibility. They were fluent in the English language. They wrote their own speeches. They were realistic and practical, and at the same time, motivated by high principles. They were not checking the pollsters on what to think this week. They knew what to think. They were comfortable with long-term thinking, planning even further ahead than the next election. They were self-sufficient, not requiring careers as politicians or lobbyists to make a living. They were able to bring out the best in us. They were interested in and, at least two of them, fluent in science. They attempted to set a course for the United States into the far future, not so much by establishing laws as by setting limits on what kinds of laws could be passed.

Jefferson had little to do with the actual writing of the U.S. Constitution; as it was being formulated, he was serving as American minister to France. When he read its provisions, he was pleased, but with two reservations. One deficiency: no limit was provided on the number of terms the President could serve. This, Jefferson feared, was a way for a President to become a king, in fact if not in law. The other major deficiency was the absence of a bill of rights. The citizen-the average person-was insufficiently protected, Jefferson thought, from the inevitable abuses of those in power.

He advocated freedom of speech, in part so that even wildly unpopular views could be expressed, so that deviations from the conventional wisdom could be offered for consideration. Personally, he was an extremely amiable man, reluctant to criticize even his sworn enemies. Nevertheless, he believed that the habit of skepticism is an essential prerequisite for responsible citizenship. He argued that the cost of education is trivial compared to the cost of ignorance, of leaving the government to the wolves. He taught that the country is safe only when the people rule.

Part of the duty of citizenship is not to be intimidated into conformity. I wish that the oath of citizenship taken by recent immigrants, and the pledge that students routinely recite, included something like "I promise to question everything my leaders tell me." That would be really to Thomas Jefferson's point. 1984 was not just for engaging political fantasy; it was based on the Stalinist Soviet Union, where the rewriting of history was institutionalized. Soon after Stalin took power, pictures of his rival Leon Trostsky, a monumental figure in the 1905 and 1917 revolutions began to disappear. Heroic and wholly anhistoric paintings of Stalin and Lenin together directing the Bolshevik Revolution took their place, with Trotsky, the founder of the Red Army, nowhere in evidence. These images became icons of the state. You could see them in every office building, on outdoor advertising signs sometimes ten stories high, in museums, on postage stamps.

New generations grew up believing that was their history. Older generations began to feel that they remembered something of the sort, a kind of political false-memory syndrome. Those who made the accommodation between their real memories and what the leadership wished them to believe exercised what Orwell described as "doublethink." Those who did not, those old Bolsheviks who could recall the peripheral role of Stalin in the Revolution and the central role of Trotsky, were denounced as traitors or unreconstructed bourgeoisie or "Trotskyites" or "Trotsky-fascists," and were imprisoned, tortured, made to confess their treason in public, and then executed. It is possible, given absolute control over the media and the police to rewrite the memories of hundreds of millions of people, if you have a generation to accomplish it in. Almost always, this is done to improve the hold that the powerful have on power, or to serve the narcissism or megalomania or paranoia of national leaders. It throws a monkey wrench into the error-correcting machinery. It works to erase public memory of profound political mistakes, and thus to guarantee their eventual repetition.

In our time, with total fabrication of realistic stills, motion pictures and videotapes technologically within reach, with television in every home, and with critical thinking in decline, restructuring societal memories even without much attention from the secret police seems possible. What I'm imagining here is not that each of us has a budget of memories implanted in special therapeutic sessions by state appointed psychiatrists, but rather that small numbers of people will have so much to work major changes in collective attitudes.

The Sedition Act made it unlawful to publish "false or malicious" criticism of the government or to inspire opposition to any of its acts. Some two dozen arrests were made, ten people were convicted, and many more were censored or intimidated into silence. The act attempted, Jefferson said, "to crush all political opposition by making criticism of Federalist officials or policies a crime."

As soon as Jefferson was elected, indeed in the first week of his presidency in 1801, he began pardoning every victim of the Sedition Act.

Under the threat of war with France, Congress in 1798 passed four laws in an effort to strengthen the Federal government. Known collectively as the Alien and Sedition acts, the legislation sponsored by the Federalists was also intended to quell any political opposition from the Republicans, led by Thomas Jefferson.

The first of the laws was the Naturalization Act, passed by Congress. This act required that aliens be residents for 14 years instead of 5 years before they became eligible for U.S. citizenship.

Congress then passed the Alien Act, authorizing the President to deport aliens "dangerous to the peace and safety of the United States" during peacetime.

The third law, the Alien Enemies Act, was enacted by congress on July 6. This act allowed the wartime arrest, imprisonment and deportation of any alien subject to an enemy power.

The last of the laws, the Sedition Act, passed on July 14 declared that any treasonable activity, including the publication of "any false, scandalous and malicious writing," was a high misdemeanor, punishable by fine and imprisonment. By virtue of this legislation twenty-five men, most of them editors of Republican newspapers were arrested and their newspapers forced to shut down.

One of the men arrested was Benjamin Franklin's grandson, Benjamin Franklin Bache, editor of the Philadelphia Democrat-Republican Aurora. Charged with libeling President Adams, Bache's arrest erupted in a public outcry against all of the Alien and Sedition Acts.

The Alien and Sedition Acts, 1798

An Act concerning aliens

Sec. 1. Be it enacted by the Senate and House of Representatives of the United States of America in Congress assembled, That it shall be lawful for the President of the United States at any time during the continuance of this act, to order all such aliens as he shall judge dangerous to the peace and safety of the United States, or shall have reasonable grounds to suspect are concerned in any treasonable or secret machinations against the government thereof, to depart out of the territory of the United States, within such time as shall be expressed in such order, which order shall be served on such alien by delivering him a copy thereof, or leaving the same at his usual abode, and returned to the office of the Secretary of State, by the marshal or other person to whom the same shall be directed.

And in case any alien, so ordered to depart, shall be found at large within the United States after the time limited in such order for his departure, and not having obtained a license shall not have conformed thereto, every such alien shall, on conviction thereof, be imprisoned for a term not exceeding three years, and shall never after be admitted to become a citizen of the United States.

Provided always, and be it further enacted, that if any alien so ordered to depart shall prove to the satisfaction of the President, by evidence to be taken before such person or persons as the President shall direct, who are for that purpose hereby authorized to administer oaths, that no injury or danger to the United States will arise from suffering such alien to reside therein, the President may grant a license to such alien to remain within the United States for such time as he shall judge proper, and at such place as he may designate.

And the president may also require of such alien to enter into a bond to the United States, in such penal sum as he may direct, with one or more sufficient sureties to the satisfaction of the person authorized by the President to take the same, conditioned for the good behavior of such alien during his residence in the United States, and not violation his license, which license the President may revoke, whenever he shall think proper.

Sec.2. And be it further enacted, That it shall be lawful for the President of the United States, whenever he may deem it necessary for the public safety, to order to be removed out of the territory thereof, any alien who may or shall be in prison in pursuance of this act; and to cause to be arrested and sent out of the United States such of those aliens as shall have been ordered to depart therefrom and shall not have obtained a license as aforesaid, in all cases where, in the opinion of the President, the public safety requires a speedy removal.

And if any alien so removed or sent out of the United States by the President shall voluntarily return thereto, unless by permission of the President of the United States, such alien on conviction thereof, shall be imprisoned so long as, in the opinion of the President, the public safety may require.

Sec.3. And be it further enacted, That every master or commander of any ship or vessel which shall come into any port of the United States after the first day of July next, shall immediately on his arrival make report in writing to the collector or other chief officer of the customs of such port, of all aliens, if any, on board his vessel, specifying their names, age, the place of nativity, the country from which they shall have come, the nation to which they belong and owe allegiance, their occupation and a description of their persons, as far as he shall be informed thereof, and on failure, every such master and commander shall forfeit and pay three hundred dollars, for the payment whereof on default of such master or commander, such vessel shall also be holden, and may by such collector or other office of the customs be detained.

And it shall be the duty of such collector or other officer of the customs, forthwith to transmit to the office of the department of state true copies of all such returns.

Sec.4. And be it further enacted, That the circuits and district courts of the United States shall respectively have cognizance of all crimes and offences against this act.

And all marshals and other officers of the United States are required to execute all precepts and orders of the President of the United States issues in pursuance or by virtue of this act.

Sec.5. And be it further enacted, That it shall be lawful for any alien who may be ordered to be removed from the United States, by virtue of this act, to take with him such part of his goods, chattels, or other property, as he may find convenient; and all property left in the United States by any alien, who may be removed, as aforesaid, shall be and remain subject to his order and disposal, in the same manner as if this act had not been passed.

Sec.6. And be it further enacted, That this act shall continue and be in force for and during the term of two years from the passing thereof.

Approved June 25, 1798

An act for the punishment of certain crimes against the United States.

Sec.1. Be it enacted by the Senate and House of Representatives of the United States of America in Congress assembled, That if any persons shall unlawfully combine or conspire together, with intent to oppose any measure or measures of the government of the United States, which are or shall be directed by proper authority, or to impede the operation of any law of the United States, or to intimidate or prevent any person holding a place or office in or under the government of the United States, from undertaking, performing or executing his trust or duty; and if any person or persons, with intent as aforesaid, shall counsel, advise or attempt to procure any insurrection, riot, unlawful assembly, or combination, whether such conspiracy, threatening, counsel, advice, or attempt shall have the proposed effect or not, he or they shall be deemed guilty of a high misdemeanor, and on conviction, before any court of the United States having jurisdiction thereof, shall be punished by a fine not exceeding five thousand dollars, and by imprisonment during a term not less than six months nor exceeding five years; and further, at the discretion of the court may be holden to find sureties for his good behaviour in such sum, and for such time, as the said court may direct.

Sec.2. And be it further enacted, That if any person shall write, print, utter, or published, or shall knowingly and willingly assist or aid in writing, printing, uttering or publishing any false, scandalous and malicious writing or writings against the government of the United States, or either house of the Congress of the United States, or the President of the United States, with intent to defame the said government, or either house of the said Congress, or the said President, or to bring them, or either of them, into contempt or disrepute; or to excite against them, or either or any of them, the hatred of the good people of the United States, or to excite any unlawful combinations therein, for opposing or resisting any law of the United States, or any act of the President of the United States, done in pursuance of any such law, or of the powers in him vested by the constitution of the United States, or to resist, oppose, or defeat any such law or act, or aid, encourage or abet any hostile designs of any foreign nation against the United States, their people or government, then such person, being thereof convicted before any court of the United States having jurisdiction thereof, shall be punished by a fine not exceeding two thousand dollars, and by imprisonment not exceeding two years.

Sec.3. And be it further enacted, That if any person shall be prosecuted under this act, for the writing or publishing any libel aforesaid, it shall be lawful for the defendant, upon the trial of the cause, to give in evidence in his defense, the truth of the matter contained in the publication charged as a libel. And the jury who shall try the cause, shall have a right to determine the law and the fact, under the direction of the court, as in other cases.

Sec.4. And be it further enacted, That this act shall continue to be in force until March 3, 1801, and no longer....

The Abyss

A man cannot call himself a man
Until he has jumped into the Abyss
Without any assurance of survival.

There is a great deal of truth to this statement. It takes courage to face a bottomless pit, rhetorical speaking, and jump into it not knowing what lies ahead. What dangers will be encountered? Will one survive the unknown? Only those who have taken extreme risks because of their beliefs know.

People who have had goals of starting their own businesses with very little money and no other incomes know. It is a frightening action to take as all could be lost or, conversely, all could be gained. It takes dedication and the willingness to forego all else along with the willingness to make sacrifices, regardless of the cost.

Our forefathers knew this when they wrote the Declaration of Independence and declared the colonies separate from England, and created a viable country in and of itself. They did so with the willingness sacrifice their lives, if necessary, to assure liberty. And many did make the ultimate sacrifice.

Our forefathers also knew it when drafting the Constitution. It took great dedication and courage for those who went against the Federalists, the rich and powerful who wanted the government to hold all the power over the people. Those who believed the strongest in the human will to be free along with the great value and necessity of the unalienable rights of the individual while limiting the central government fought for their beliefs while facing the potential of death.

And they did overcome with the result the central government established was extremely limited in its powers. The Constitution ratified by the States assured that the rights of the individual would never be infringed upon; our Constitution guaranteed it.

These great men had faced the abyss, jumped into it, and did so without any assurance of their survival. They surely lived their lives in great fear but went ahead anyway. That is courage. It doesn't take courage if the outcome is known, such as a bully beating up on some little person, or a government agency breaking into someone's home and scaring the holy devil out of them and their families.

We, the people of this nation, meaning the 50 states of the United States now face an abyss whether most are aware of it or not. Those that are trying to make all people aware of the corruption of the federal government, who are trying to make all people aware of the abuses to the

Constitution that have or are taking place by the people we have placed in government, are now on the very brink of the abyss.

No one outside of the government most noteworthy for its "hidden agendas" can really be sure of what lengths the federal government will go to in order to insure its robbing us of our unalienable rights. No one can be certain when speaking out against the government that actions will not be taken against them in some form or another.

The one certainty is the federal government has the will and the potential to do whatever is necessary to assure its complete control over the people.

It is gaining complete control by taking little steps. Prior to the last few years, the steps were spread apart and rather timidly taken (although that is not the case now). It has been nearly four decades since driver's licenses, as an example, became required to have pictures on them.

Then, between two and three decades later, social security numbers became 'required'.

When I began driving, one could drive anywhere without worrying about getting stopped unless one committed a traffic violation or suspected of committing a crime. Then, a law, was passed giving law enforcement the right to stop anyone they wished with a blanket search warrant, so to speak. The result is citizens may be stopped for no reason and checked out.

Recently, the Supreme court of the United States voted to uphold a law requiring you to identify yourself if you fail you can be arrested, then I believe you have the right to remain silent.

Soon, your fingerprints will be demanded at spot checks. If you refuse the law persons demanding it, you may be imprisoned up to two years and/or heavily fined.

Thus, when you are subjected to fingerprints, guess what, you are being treated as a common criminal without any protection of your rights. You may be thrown on the ground, beat up, belittled, humiliated, and maybe even shot for resisting arrest.

Banks send private information to the government, which is also unconstitutional. No person other than those you wish to know, have any right to any information about you, not your full name, your address, your social security number, your date of birth, interest earnings, investments, whether you own or rent your home, where you work, and so on. All of these was privileged information protected by the Constitution.

The second amendment is in the Constitution in order that the people always have a means of defense. Defense against criminals, you might think. Not hardly. Our forefathers knew the dangers associated with putting power in the hands of a few.

They knew corruption would be probable if the people didn't keep constant vigilance over the members of government put in office. They knew the failings of people that power creates greed and greed creates corruption. Corruption was certain unless the people could always defend themselves against the tyranny of a centralized government.

Think about it. The people of the newly formed union of States had just fought a war, a war won because of the people being armed, not because of a well-organized army. The people had the means to fight for liberties held dear by them.

Thus, the Second Amendment guarantees the people must always have the right to keep and bear arms in order to protect itself against the federal government, not criminals which is a secondary benefit. Of course, as our government now is, there is very little difference between government and criminals.

The U.S. Government is demanding personal information, credit card numbers and what meal you ordered when you fly on a plane and they also require the same of any foreigner visiting the U.S. In addition to fingerprints, a picture and an Iris scan.

There are literally dozens of examples of governmental control that is far in excess of the power given to the government by the people. Actual government control is very limited, as was intended by our forefathers. Above all else, this nation's forefathers knew the rights of the individual must be protected. The rights are unalienable and not granted by government but, instead, by our maker. The government had never had, nor does it have, the power to interfere with those rights in any way.

But, it has interfered, it is interfering, and it will continue to interfere until all rights of the individuals making up this nation are done away with. Already the majority of the Bill of Rights, the first ten amendments, have been violated by the government.

One day all of us are going to have to face the abyss and demand what is ours and not the government's right to take. In accomplishing this, we may have to completely replace the current government with the limited government that was intended.

You also do not have to take what the government does to your rights. We have legal recourse-it is called the Constitution of the United States of America and its purpose is to protect our rights.

With rights, we also have an obligation, though. The obligation is that we also do what is necessary to protect the Constitution. That is our failing. We have not done so.

We have allowed elected people to government, appointed people to government and those who are wealthy and easily corrupt the corruptible, to get by with removing rights or infringing upon those rights.

Our citizenship in each of our resident states making up the union are protected by the Constitution guaranteeing us we may exercise our rights in our pursuit of happiness as long as we don't infringe upon the rights of others. The government must be made to operate the same.

A classic example of Government Bureaucracy at work is demonstrated when out of the blue, three tickets (citations) arrived from the City of Chicago at my office citing me with violations for not cutting the weeds, leaving abandoned vehicles and abandoned appliances on a lot in Chicago that the city insists is owned by me.

Twice I had to prove that I am not the owner of this property, never was and still another set of citations were issued to me.

If I would not appear in court, a judgment against me for money and possible arrest will be issued. The notice for arrest will be entered into the government computer and if I intend to leave the country, I will be stopped because the mistake the city made is holding me responsible for property I never had any interest in. So off to court I will go for the third time to clear my name without having done anything that would cause this problem.

Imagine the mix up in your personal file that you would not have access to and you would be stopped from flying, opening a bank account or getting a loan. You just cannot trust the government not to make mistakes.

This is our nation made up of individual states, joined in a union of aid in the defense of our beliefs. The Union does not belong to the federal government-the federal government exists only because we allow it to exist. Without the states, the government is nothing. It constitutionally has no functions other that protecting the Constitution that protects the people, to provide for the common defense, and to assure that all citizens of the states have their rights to liberty protected, their general welfare not interfered with by a Big Brother type, totalitarian government.

Be afraid of it (the government) but have the courage to stand up for your rights and jump into the abyss. Otherwise, resign yourself to living in Nazi America. You cannot believe how other nations look at us.

Be that as it may, right at this moment, we do have a constitution that we might be able to use but the day is not far off that the Constitution will not provide any protection as the government arms its agencies to a greater and greater extent while de-arming the population to a greater and greater extent. The potential of peaceful resolution will soon be gone, as dissenters against government expansion will be swatted down like flies should a protest of any nature be made. Have you seen the expansion of SWAT Teams in your area?

As I write, the government is probably monitoring me even though I am essentially a nobody. The government does so regularly to people who write against them. Now, in order to be more efficient at monitoring home computer users, the government is trying to pass legislation that will allow them to break into your home, go through your computer, put a chip in it, with the result that even allows monitoring of encrypted personal files.

Of course, this is supposedly to tap in on illegal activities, but, if the truth be known, the illegal activity the government is concerned with isn't individuals conducting illegal activities; its concern will be to pinpoint those who may act against the government. It goes along with the government wanting to know who has what weapons, where they go, what they spent their money on, who they correspond with, and so on.

In other words, it is allowing the government to violate your home while you aren't there and do whatever they want in order to monitor your activities. Cameras computer taps, and phone taps, we should vote out of office every congressmen who has had even an iota of involvement in any legislation removing or affecting our liberties. I thank the thousands upon thousands who have died in the name of freedom.

Don't allow this nation to get to the point that millions of us must jump into the abyss not knowing whether we will live in order to re-establish this nation as it was originally intended. For God's sake and your own, don't allow it to get to the point that millions will have to die in order to keep unalienable rights and to prove to the government once and for all time that those liberties must be preserved if mankind is to progress as a self actualizing being.

We have become the Guinea Pigs.

Public Law 95-79. Title 50, Chapter 32, Section 1520.
Chemical and Biological Warfare Program.

"The use of human subjects will be allowed for the testing of chemical and biological agents by the U.S. Department of Defense, accounting to Congressional committees with respect to the experiments and studies."

"The Secretary of Defense [may] conduct tests and experiments involving the use of chemical and biological [warfare] agents on civilian populations [within the United States]."

These utterly appalling and frightening words I have taken from the actual wording of Public Law 95-79.

I have attached in the appendix at the end of the book, the law authorizing the poisoning of you and your family. When you and I become stricken by their bacteria from the sky, or when we fall ill from their poisoning of our water supply, it will be too late to prevent harm to us.

Title 50-War and National Defense
Chapter 32-Chemical and Biological Warfare Program.

Sec.1520: Use of human subjects for testing of chemical or biological agents by Department of Defense; accounting to Congressional committees with respect to experiments and studies; notification of local civilian officials.

Not later that thirty days after final approval within the Department of Defense of plans for any experiment or study to be conducted by the Department of Defense, whether directly or under contract, involving the use of human subjects for the testing of chemical or biological agents, the Secretary of Defense shall supply the Committees on Armed Services of the Senate and House of Representatives with a full accounting of such plans for such experiment or study, and such experiment or study may then be conducted only after the expiration of the thirty-day period beginning on the date such accounting is received by such committees.

The Report Explains That Operations During the Three-month Periods in Minneapolis Involved:

'Eighty-one field experiment hours and eleven thousand one-hundred and seventy man hours, including full-time and part-time personnel in the field and laboratory.'

Experiments were conducted between 8:00 P.M. and Midnight, and between 1:30 P.M. and 5:00 P.M. Thus, hundreds of personnel were carrying out the experiments for months, when people were sleeping, at work, or commuting, when children were at school or playing outdoors. No time, no location, no segment of the population, whether old, young, sick or poor, were exempt from exposure to the zinc cadmium sulfide particles.

Couple charged after Clinton visit.

A husband and wife upset by the terrorist bombing of a U.S. Military installation in Saudi Arabia were arrested on disorderly conduct charges after shouting obscenities at President Clinton and Secret Service.

Glenn and Patricia Mendoza were charged with misdemeanors. Police said they arrested Patricia Mendoza for "verbalizing threats to the president." Both were charged with disorderly conduct. "To be railroaded for no cause it's like a nightmare to us," Glenn Mendoza said. Police said Clinton approached the couple amid a crowd of festivalgoers. Patricia

Mendoza extended her hand to him, then pulled it back and yelled, "You Suck, and those boys died." Police said Secret Service men who descended on the couple responded because they treat "everything as a threat." According to police, the two were given orders to stop, but continued yelling obscenities. Both claimed to be "expressing freedom of speech," apparently the police thought otherwise.

No Child For You.

A bill in Illinois House would allow the government to meddle in family matters.

So, ma'am, you're having a baby. Let me ask some questions so that the government can decide if you'll be a fit parent. Have you seen a shrink? Do you have a phone? Does your husband work? Are you married? What's your income?

If you think these are bold questions for the government to be asking, there's more under state legislation designed to find out whether parents need government help to avoid becoming abusive or neglectful. Pregnant or new mothers also could be asked: Have you abused drugs or alcohol? Got any marital problems? Ever been depressed?

Wait, it gets better.

Have you ever put up a child for adoption? I guess that means that putting a child up for adoption makes you capable of committing child abuse or neglect.

Finally, there's this: How many abortions have you had? Have you unsuccessfully sought an abortion? For all the times abortion-rights advocates have proclaimed that a woman's reproductive choices are no one else's business, here are their liberal friends pushing legislation that enables government to inquire and make value judgements about women's abortions. Where are pro-choicers when you need them?

Apparently not opposing a package of bills that allows government to butt into family matters. House bill 1301, the Early Childhood Education Collaboration Law, would provide "a continuum of early childhood education opportunities in community settings to prepare children from birth through 5 years of age for school." In other words, it puts the State

Board of Education at the top of an unprecedented pyramid of government-licensed, supervised and funded childcare networks.

The state could screen potential mothers on a weekly basis to determine if the mothers are fit to have children.

The programs own rhetoric talks about its "powerful interventions" directed at "women, infants, preschoolers and their parents." It says it is in the business of creating a "coordinated, continuous system of care" and a "permanent infrastructure."

Private agencies will be hired by the state to perform this function. Now, what is at stake here is the institutionalization of childhood by professional busybodies who believe that many, maybe even most, parents are incapable of or unwilling to raise healthy children. These busybodies should take their nanny bills and go mind their own business.

Masses yearn for courtesy.

Everyone in Downtown Chicago on a weekday morning notices the long line of people that starts at 10 W. Jackson, the district headquarters of the Immigration and Naturalization Service. The line, which snakes around the building and around the corner, is the most visual example of a Government Agency who culture is "the customer is always wrong."

The hundreds of people in line are indeed customers. They pay handsomely for every service—$325 to be eligible for naturalization-not including the cost of fingerprints, photos, transportation or time off from work. The cost of aggravation is incalculable.

Every person in line had their own horror story. Some had been waiting since 5 a.m. to be among the 600 who would be served that day. Many waited for hours simply to get a form, never told that forms were available on the internet or by phone. Others were spending their second or third consecutive day in line. There was a 12-year-old girl whose green card said she was born in 1972 instead of 1992. Clearly, this was a mistake made by an INS employee. Instead of receiving an apology, the family was ordered to submit a new application, pay more fees and stand in more lines. She was one of the many there because of an INS mistake.

About 10:30 a.m., an INS officer came out, and told the hundreds still waiting that the doors were shut and no one else would be taken that day. She then barked at them to "move or go to jail."

As people left, some in utter disbelief, they were given a piece of paper with phone numbers and told they could get their questions answered on the telephone instead of waiting in line. Why wasn't that paper distributed at 7:30 a.m.? Because "people wouldn't leave anyway," the officers told condescendingly, "Besides," she added, "many of these people have tried those numbers and they haven't worked for them."

The Department of Immigration and Naturalization Service represents how inefficient our government can be. How shameful that new residents, many of whom faced persecution in their home countries and took great risks and made great sacrifices to come to the "Land of the free," are treated with astonishing disrespect by the very agency mandated to help them become American citizens.

The line is the tip of the iceberg. One should look into the way in which people who are seeking asylum are treated, the way that the citizenship test is administered, and the arbitrary manner in which disability waivers are granted.

You can trust your Government Agency.

Have you had dealings with the IRS, have you asked them a question on your taxes. Recent reports show that over 80% of the questions they answer is wrong. Have you tried to stop them collecting a wrongful debt? The IRS can freeze your bank accounts, garnish your wages and even put you in jail wrongfully and there is little, if anything you can do. This is the future of dealing with governmental agencies that all of us face.

Where is my money?

Clair Smith got a big surprise when she tried to withdraw $70,000 she says she deposited some time ago into a savings account at a bank. The money had grown to nearly $100,000 with interest, was gone.

There was no big mystery. The bank explained to Smith because she had never touched the account in the last five years, the money had been turned over to the State under a law governing dormant bank accounts.

All she needed to do was file a claim to prove the money was hers. But nearly one year later, the state still has the $100,000. Smith sued the Circuit Court to force the state to give the money back.

But state officials say there are enough discrepancies in Smith's claim to justify their decision to hang on to the money until she can get a court order.

"We want to make sure the right person gets the money," said the supervisor of the State's Unclaimed Property Division. The person who opened the account used the name Smith Clair, not Clair Smith, even signing the name that way. He also said Smith's Social Security number doesn't match the Social Security number listed by the person who opened the account.

Smith said in court papers that he gave the state documentation that includes a deposit slip from the account, and Smith's birth certificate.

Banks are required to turn over funds from any savings account that has not had owner-generated activity for five years.

● ● ● ●

Pursue Your Dreams

Dale Brown was a poster boy for the American dream, an athletic former Eagle Scout whose start-up company near the Johnson Space Center outside Houston hustled contracts with NASA.

Brown worked seven days a week, 18 hours a day getting his company started in the late 1980's, trying to pair clients and their promising technologies with niches in the billion-dollar needs of the U.S. space program.

Like most small companies, Brown's Terraspace Technologies Inc. sometimes struggled to make ends meet. A man who bragged about his Mississippi roots and his ability to make things happen promised to change that in 1992. John Clifford told Brown he had developed a product that NASA might use and he was prepared to spend big money to get it noticed.

It was called a miniature lithotripter, an ultrasound device whose technology might one day be used to improve the medical monitoring of astronauts in space.

Brown checked out Clifford and his companies with Dunn & Bradstreet, the Better Business Bureau and the banks that worked with him. All gave the Mississippi man a thumbs-up.

"I came to believe this guy was our savior, our knight in shining armor," Brown said.

Brown, though, was wrong. John Clifford was actually Hal Francis, an agent for the FBI. His new device was phony, though legitimate companies had agreed to help the FBI by pretending to manufacture it. It was part of an FBI sting operation aimed at trapping Brown and several others who worked in the space program or on its periphery.

Francis and dozens of other federal agents and prosecutors had set their sights much higher: Key employees at NASA and a few of its contractors were suspected of giving and taking bribes, but the feds had failed to snare these high-placed managers.

Millions already had been spent on Operation Lightning Strike including enormous bills for luxury hotel suites, gourmet meals, deep-sea fishing trips and booze-filled nights at Houston strip clubs. Federal agents needed something to show for their effort. So they went to work trying to lure minor space agency players into doing something illegal. Brown would be one of these consolation prizes.

It was a scenario similar to dozens of other failed government stings that the Pittsburgh Post-Gazette uncovered in a two-year investigation of federal law enforcement officers' misconduct.

S.W.A.T. Nation

Though the raid on the King/Garvey project was brutal and audacious, it was not unusual. Paramilitary or tactical policing-law enforcement that uses the equipment training, rhetoric, and tactics of warfare is on the rise nationwide. According to a study by sociologist Peter Drasda, there are more than 30,000 heavily armed, military trained police units in the United

States and the number of paramilitary police "call-outs" quadrupled since 1995.

The tactical buildup has been fueled by fattened drug-war budgets and a wave of federal largesse. Between 1995 and 1997 the Department of Defense gave local police 1.2 million pieces of military hard-ware, including more than 3,800 M16 automatic assault rifles, 2,185 Rugar M14 semiautomatic rifles, 73 M79 Grenade launchers, and 112 armored personnel carriers (APC.). One tactical outfit calls its APC, "mother"; another, in east Texas, has named its APCs "Bubba One" and "Bubba Two".

Military gear given to the SFPD (San Francisco Police Department) includes two helicopters, several electrical generators, vehicles, and office furniture, according to tactical officer Dino Zografos. Several years ago the department acquired two APCs from the United Kingdom.

The Department's 45-officer tac-squad buys its own AR 15 and MP53 assault rifles. Most of the SFPD's tactical training is done in-house, though SWAT officers have received special instruction from FBI, military, and private instructors.

Nationwide, tactical units have metastasized from emergency response teams into a standard part of everyday policing. SWAT teams that would once have been called in only to handle the occasional barricaded suspect now conduct routine drug raids like the one on the King/Garvey co-op. In Fresno, Indianapolis, and San Francisco, they even patrol high-crime areas.

Critics of SWAT-style policing say militarized training, weaponry, and organization cause cops to over-react and treat ordinary policing situations as military operations. "The fundamental problem with the SWAT model is that if police become soldiers, the community becomes the enemy," says Sacramento State University sociologist Tony Platt, one of the first scholars to analyze the rise of tactical policing. "paramilitary policing erodes the idea of police as public servants subordinate to community needs."

And Kraska says, "The more paramilitary police units exist, the more all policing will be militia rized." Considering what's happening around the country, those charges don't seem farfetched. According to a CBS News

Survey of SWAT encounters, police use of deadly force has increased 34 percent in the past three years.

Tactical Future

For a look at the future of American law enforcement, travel south on Highway 99 from San Francisco to Fresno, and tun off on one of the city's southern exits. On the packed side streets of southwest Fresno's sprawling ghetto, among fading stucco bungalows and dying rail yards, massive paramilitary police operations take place almost every night.

It's a cold October night; 30 police officers (three squads of 10) don black jumpsuits, military helmets, and bulletproof vests, lock and load their Heckler and Koch MP5 submachine guns, and fan out for a routine patrol. Meet Fresno's Violent Crime Suppression Unit (VCSU), the Fresno P.D.'s "special forces" and America's most aggressive SWAT team.

The VCSU has patrolled the city's and suburbs in full military gear, with automatic assault rifles (the same model used by Navy SEALS). The unit is backed by two helicopters with infrared scopes and an army-surplus APC; it's equipped with attack dogs, flash-bang grenades, smoke bombs, tear gas, pepper spray, metal clubs, and "blunt trauma ordinance," essentially beanbags fired form shotguns, designed to daze rather that kill.

"It's a war,' Sgt. Margaret Mims of the Fresno Sheriff's Department says. In the name of crisis management, the VCSU is free to use aggressive and unorthodox tactics. Sometimes the unit quietly deploys troops on foot to surround targeted corners or sweep through neighborhoods. At other times, like this autumn night, agents move in a fleet of regular patrol cars "like a wolf pack" looking for "contact," as a VCSU officer put it. "Contacts" generally involve swooping onto street corners, forcing pedestrians to the ground, searching them, running warrant checks, taking photos, and entering all the new "intelligence" into a state database from computer terminals in each patrol car. The area of operation is a poor and desolate African American neighborhood Fresno residents call the Dog Pound.

As the patrol makes a routine traffic stop, a man is standing on the sidewalk talking to the driver. When the VCSU pull up, he flees into a nearby house. The VCSU immediately surround the area. Officers with

AR 15's and H&K MP5's "hold the perimeter," some watching the house, others looking out at the neighborhood. Five officers rush to the door.

The VCSU are not, technically, in "hot pursuit." They have no legal right to enter the premises. But the elderly woman behind the black metal door is confronted with five SWAT-style officers with submachine guns, and they want to search her house. She consents. Five big, white cops move into the living room and grab a young African American man. They demand to know his name; it's David, "What?" he says. "Man, I didn't do anything!" As he protests, his voice cracks and a tearful grimace clouds his face.

With consent from David's trembling grandmother, three cops search the little bungalow. For all the agents' science fiction-esque uniforms and state-of-the-art gear, they call up an awful specter from the past. More than anything else, the robocops of the VCSU resemble the "patrollers" of the Old South, the slave-catching militias that spent their nights rousting plantation shacks looking for contraband, weapons, and signs that slaves were planning to escape north.

"Are you on parole, probation? Hub?" a VCSU officer demands. "Let's go outside David." The suspect is cuffed, searched, interrogated, and forced to the ground. His name is fed into a computer. A flashlight is continuously pointed at his face. No drugs are found. But David lied, saying he wasn't on parole, and he is. "That's a violation of parole, David." The cops send another man off to jail.

For much of the rest of the night, a standoff occupies 30 cops from three different agencies and two from three different agencies and two helicopters. The target is a teenager who hasn't been charged with anything; he's just wanted for questioning. "If you're 21, male, living in one of these neighborhoods, and your not in our computer, then there's definitely something wrong," VCSU officer Paul Boyer says.

Widespread Abuses

Fresno's is the only police department in the country that deploys its tactical units for routine patrol work. But big, aggressive SWAT operations like the one at the King/Garvey co-op are becoming more common. From Albuquerque to Miami, tactical teams have repeatedly shot and killed unarmed civilians in the course of botched drug raids. In a recent case in

Bethlehem, Pa., a SWAT team killed a suspect, then burnt his house down. And thanks to confusion and the overzealous use of flash-bang grenades, tactical officers are increasingly shooting one another; a case in Oxnard, Calif., is the most recent example.

Perhaps the most infamous police tactical operation took place several years ago in Chapel Hill, N.C. In "Operation Ready-Rock," police received a blanket warrant allowing them to search every person and vehicle on the 100 block of Graham Street.

"We believe that there are no 'innocent' people at this place," the police department's warrant request stated. "Only drug sellers and drug buyers are on the described premises." Forty-five heavily armed commandos from local and state law enforcement agencies sealed off the street and made what police would describe as a "dynamic entrance" into a pool hall by smashing in the front door and holding occupants at gunpoint. Whites were allowed to leave the area, more than 100 African Americans were searched. Agents found only minor quantities of drugs.

It's not every municipal agency that can afford equipment that's too powerful for the task at hand. Elsewhere in North Carolina, the Greensboro public library's bus-sized "bookmobile" was recently retired for lack of funds. Shortly thereafter, the police department bought the bookmobile and converted it into a mobile command and control center for its elite 23 member Special Response Team.

The cops were delighted: a six-foot-five SRT officer had trouble standing up in the previous van. "It's a great piece of equipment," police spokesperson M.C. Bitner said, "It's really much better than what we had."

How vivid is the picture in your mind of a SWAT soldier in Miami said pointing a gun at little Elijah The Cuban boy that President Clinton and his Attorney General sent back to Cuba at gunpoint.

The U.S.A loves its citizens

"They that can give up essential liberty to purchase a little temporary safety deserve neither liberty or safety." - Ben Franklin

The Center for Constitutional Rights (CCR) has filed suit in the United States District in Washington on behalf of an elderly couple from Michigan who's lawyers say were unfairly penalized by Cuba embargo regulations. Lawyers also say the two were not informed of their Fifth Amendment rights protecting them from self incrimination.

Under the existing economic embargo against Cuba, Americans are allowed to travel to Cuba but are prohibited from spending any money. Travelers are presumed to have spent money in Cuba unless they prove otherwise and can face large monetary travel fines.

The couple, Kip, 73 and Patrick, 58 Taylor of Traverse City, MI, sailed to Cuba on a boating trip in April, knowing that U.S. law prohibited spending money in Cuba, they stocked their sailboat with enough food to last for the duration of their three-month trip. While sailing back to Florida from Cuba, their boat was in a storm and struck by lightning that destroyed the mast.

The Cuban Coast Guard rescued them in international waters, and the boat was towed back to port. When they applied to the Treasury Department for permission to repair it, they were told to abandon the boat and their two dogs-in Cuba and fly back to the U.S. After weeks of attempting to negotiate, unwilling to abandon. The Taylors had the boat fixed. Many of the repairs were done by the Taylors themselves with the help of visiting sailors who donated parts.

After their return, the Taylors responded openly to every question asked by government officers. The Taylors were never told about their Fifth Amendment privilege to stay silent, their right to counsel and any statements or evidence produced by them could be used against them in court.

Remarkably, after disclosing that they gave band-aid to a local cook who had burned his finger. The Taylors were charged with provision of "nursing services to a Cuban national" a transaction forbidden by the embargo. For the next four and a half years, the Taylors' who are on a fixed income-requested a reconsideration of the penalty or a hearing, without success. In April, 2001, Patrick Taylors' tax refund was needed to pay for urgent medical expenses, but it became frozen and applied to the Taylors' debt.

"The Center has long believed that the embargo is ill advised, illegal and unconstitutional in that it infringes the right of every American to travel freely, said Ron Daniels, Executive Director, Center for Constitutional Rights. "The way the embargo regulations are worded makes it very difficult to figure out what the law is and how to comply with it. Nonetheless, the Taylors made exceptional efforts to comply despite an incredible amount of bad luck. The Taylors' experience is a glaring example of how the rights of American citizens can be disregarded.

Trust Your Government

A couple with two grown children sold a building and they went to a bank to deposit their money. They wanted to make sure that their deposit was insured and were handed a brochure issued by the FDIC (Federal Deposit Insurance Corporation) that showed that they could have up to $700,000 insured. It showed that each parent could shelter $100,000 insured, thus they could have a joint account and then each of them could have a joint account with each child therefore totaling $700,000 insured. But wait- when the bank went under, they only paid on $300,000. The Governments argument stated that the money that each parent had on deposit with each child was not insured since the money was really the parents and the joint deposit between the child and the parent an amount equal to $400,000 was only deposited to circumvent the law and therefore it was not insured.

... Nothing needs to be done it feels so good to be taken care of in this warm womb-like atmosphere... I am a happy frog...

Chapter VI
War on Drugs

"I tried marijuana once. I did not inhale."

-Bill Clinton

"Those who steal from private individuals spent their lives in stocks and chains; those who steal from the public treasury go dressed in gold and purple."

-Marcus Porcius Cato-(Roman Statesman-190 BC)

Them vs. Us

The statistics alone are staggering four thousand AIDS cases could be prevented if the US had a needle trade program. Governments spent over fifty billion dollars per year on the war on drugs. Every twenty seconds someone is arrested for a drug violation.

On the average one hundred seventeen people are put in prison for drug violation everyday. Of the over two million people incarcerated in America, eighty percent are imprisoned because of some involvement with drug law violations. The equation that follows is frightening-there are as many as 2.5 million "orphans" of the drug war. Women are now the fastest growing population within the prison system, first time offenders, and the majority are young parents, forced to leave their children behind without a mother. Truly a national disgrace.

The so-called "War on Drugs" is a grave threat to individual liberty, to domestic order and to peace in the world; furthermore, it has provided a rationale by which the power of the state has been expanded to restrict greatly our right to privacy and to be secure in our homes.

In New York.

Members of a Brooklyn family say they were terrorized by narcotic cops who broke down their door, lobbed a concussion grenade into their apartment and kept them handcuffed for more than an hour while searching for drugs and guns. No contraband was found in the Shorter family home, but police officials staunchly defended the raid.

"This was not a wrong apartment search," Police Commissioner Howard Safir said. "Very often we execute search warrants where drugs are not found because drugs are mobile, and I don't know if this was a drug location or not."

And In California

Just before dawn law-enforcement officers wearing black masks and fatigues and armed with assault rifles stormed an apartment complex. They used special "shock-lock" shotgun rounds to blow apartment doors off their hinges and cleared people out of rooms by throwing "flash-bang grenades," which produce non-lethal explosions that terrify and disorient people.

A few days later at a police commission meeting, a train of furious and sobbing residents from the raided housing complex- all of them African American- described how officers slapped them, stepped on their necks and put guns to their heads while other officers ransacked their homes. Weeping and terrified children, some as young as six, were handcuffed and separated from their parents. Some urinated in their pajamas.

Residents of the complex say the raid was a violation of their civil rights. Scores of people with no charges against them and no criminal records were put in disposable plastic "flex-cuffs." Civil servants and grand mothers were held at gunpoint. One woman was hospitalized after a fit of seizures; other people were so distraught they couldn't return to work for days.

And a pit bull named Bosco-which many residents described as well liked and friendly-was shot inside an apartment, dragged bleeding outside and shot again. The Deputy chief told police commissioner that, according to police intelligence gathered during covert operations, "the dog was "known for its jumping ability and was shot in midair."

The squad that raided the housing complex included agents from the San Francisco Police Department's tactical squad and narcotics division, the District Attorney's office, the FBI, the Drug Enforcement Agency, and the Bureau of Alcohol, Tobacco and Firearms. According to SFPD narcotics lieutenant, who initiated the planned operation, the action was designed to "put fear in the hearts" of a gang. "The raid went off, more or less, without a hitch," the Lieutenant said. "I feel bad for the innocent women and children that were there, but in a way they do bear some responsibility for harboring drug dealers."

Agents made eleven arrests and netted a pound of what the lieutenant described as "high-grade" marijuana, almost four ounces of crack cocaine, seven pistols, and four thousand dollars cash. Residents say that money was not drug money, but that it had been collected to help pay for the funeral of Germain Brown, a recently deceased friend. Thanks to state and federal asset forfeiture laws, the SFPD may get to keep and spend the seized money.

The US Subsidizes Terrorists

Shortly after the September terrorist attacks, House Speaker Dennis Hastert unveiled a new panel: the Speaker's Task Force for a Drug Free America. "The illegal drug trade is the financial engine that fuels many terrorist organizations around the world, including Osama bin Laden," he explained. "By going after the illegal drug trade we reduce the ability of these terrorists to launch attacks against the United States."

We subsidize the terrorists. "Going after the illegal drug trade" is what allows terrorist to fund their operations with profits inflated by prohibition. In that sense, the $40 billion or so the US spends on drug law enforcement each year represents a subsidy for murderers. Banning a product that people want creates an opportunity for criminals, who can earn big profits because they are willing to risk producing, transporting and selling contraband.

This "risk premium" means cocaine and heroin sell for 20 to 40 times as much as they otherwise would. Prohibition thus delivers to armed thugs a handy stream of revenue, which they can dip into by selling drugs or by taxing producers and traffickers. Bin Laden's organization seems to have benefited from the drug trade indirectly: Opium money supports his Taliban hosts in Afghanistan.

Stronger enforcement, Hastert's favored solution, would tend to increase the risks of drug trafficking, eliminate competitors, and raise profits. So it hardly makes sense to fight terrorism by cracking down on drugs.

In fact, the events of September 11 highlighted how the War on Drugs has skewed the government's priorities and compromised our security. The cost of focusing on traffickers instead of terrorists was illustrated by the announcement that federal drug agents would be trained to protect travelers because there aren't enough sky marshals.

How many of you have entered the United States whether it is by vehicle through Canada or by plane at any airport. You cannot even have a shoe or belt buckle on to go through customs yet apparently thousands of pounds of drugs enter the USA. In my opinion being a frequent traveler there has to be collusion with the government or main Government officials to get their drugs into the country.

It will not simply say that the War on Drugs and the War on Terrorism must be waged simultaneously. Aside from the problem that one war generates the black-market profits that help support our enemies in the other, we have to face the fact that our resources are finite. Every dollar spent intercepting drugs is a dollar that could be spent intercepting bombs. Every agent infiltrating a drug cartel is an agent who could be infiltrating a terrorist cell.

We have to ask ourselves which is scarier: a dealer who sells an intoxicant to a willing buyer or a terrorist who murders people at random. Confronting the question does not necessarily mean repealing prohibition, but it does mean taking into account the trade-offs associated with the drug war.

Banks' 'War on Drugs' An Invasion of Privacy

In response to a proposal under review by the banking industry and the federal government known as "know your customer." The concept is to allow the banking industry to forward confidential, personal monetary information to the federal government. This would be done to find money-laundering schemes typically used by drug dealers.

This idea is utterly ludicrous! To put this under the guise of a "war on drugs" is basically insulting the intelligence of the public. Please tell me where the upstanding drug dealers are that will put hundreds of thousands of dollars in a bank! Are they doing it for the wonderful gifts? If they are, then the government should search houses to see who has an abundance of toaster, blenders and wall clocks.

Why would any corrupt individual send up a flag to the establishment, "Hey, I've got tons of money! I put it in a safe place, a bank." If the money were in a bank to begin with, then it is reportable income to the IRS. The IRS should be able to track "discrepancies" by auditing tax returns.

I really believe that this is a further attempt to subject people who have legitimately earned money to scrutiny. To subject hard-working, security-minded individuals to another government microscope will only harm the future of the country.

I want to voice my extreme and unequivocal rejection of this idea of having the banking industry act as "DEA agents" and government spies. This is another "feel good" act by the government. If I want to live in a socialist country, I will move.

Annual drug deaths: tobacco: 395,000, alcohol: 125,000, 'legal' drugs: 38,000, illegal drug overdoses: 5,200, marijuana: 0. "Considering government subsidies of tobacco, just what is our government protecting us from in the drug war?" -Ralph Nader

Just Say No
To the War on Drugs

"Clearly, we're losing the war on drugs in this country [and] it's insanity to keep doing the same thing over and over again."

We know the terrible things drugs can do. We've seen the despair, the sunken face of the junkie. No wonder those in government say that we have to fight drugs. And polls show most Americans agree. Drug use should be illegal. Or as former "drug czar" Bill Bennett put it: "it's a matter of right and wrong."

But when "right and wrong" conflict with supply and demand, nasty things happen. The government declaring drugs illegal doesn't mean people can't get them. It just means they get them on the black market, where they pay much more for them.

"The only reason that coke is worth that much money is that it's illegal," argues Father Joseph Kane, a priest. "Pure cocaine is three times the cost of gold. Now if that's the case, how are you gonna stop people from selling cocaine?"

Kane has come to believe that while drug abuse is bad, drug prohibition is worse- because the black market does horrible things to his community. "There's so much money in it, it's staggering," he says.

Besides luring kids into the underworld, drug money is also corrupting law enforcement officers, he argues.

Cops are seduced by drug money. They have been for years. "With all the money, with all the cash, it's easy for [dealers] to purchase police officers, to purchase prosecutors, to purchase judges," says Oliver, the Detroit police chief.

The worst unintended consequence of the drug war is drug crime.

The violence happens because dealers arm themselves and have shootouts over turf. Most of the drug-related violence comes from the fact that it's illegal, argues Kane. Violence also happens because addicts steal to pay the high prices for drugs.

An Alternative to Prohibition

There's no question that drugs often wreck lives. But the drug war wrecks lives too, creates crime and costs billions of dollars.

Is there an alternative? Much of Europe now says there is.

In Amsterdam, using marijuana is legal. Holland now has hundreds of "coffee shops" where marijuana is officially tolerated. Clients pick up small amounts of marijuana the same way they would pick up a bottle of wine at the store.

The police regulate marijuana sales shops may sell no more than about five joints worth per person, they're not allowed to sell to minors, and no hard drugs are allowed.

What has been the result of legalizing marijuana? Is everyone getting stoned? No. In America today 38 percent of adolescents have smoked pot in Holland; it's only 20 percent.

What Amsterdam police did was take the glamour out of drug use, explains judge Gray. The Dutch minister of health has said, "We've succeeded in making pot boring."

The DEA has said legalizing cannabis and hash in the Netherlands was a failure an unmitigated disaster. Not so, say people in Amsterdam. And Rotterdam Police Superintendent Jur Verbeek says selling the drug in coffee shops may deter young, curious people who will try marijuana one way or another, from further experimentation with harder drugs.

"No drug, not even alcohol, causes the fundamental ills of society. If we're looking for the sources of our troubles, we shouldn't test people for drugs, we should test them for stupidity, ignorance, greed and love of power." -P.J. O'Rourke

Don't Ask, Don't Tell

Still, in America, there's little interest in legalizing any drug. President Bush says "drug use threatens everything." And officials talk about fighting a stronger war. Some say it shouldn't even be talked about.

What the Dutch are doing makes sense to Gray. "They're addressing it as managers," he says. "We address it as moralizers. We address it as a character issue, and if you fail that test, we put you in prison."

Experiments with being more permissive of drugs have spread beyond the Netherlands. Today, police in most of Europe ignore marijuana use. Spain, Italy and Luxembourg have decriminalized most drug use.

Hopeless Fight?

Still, how many wars can America fight? Now that we're at war against terrorism, can we also afford to fight a drug war against millions of our own people? Is it wise to fight on two fronts?

The last time America engaged in a war of this length was Vietnam, and then, too, government put a positive spin on the success of war.

Why not sell drugs like we do alcohol, though maybe with more restrictions. Let's make it available to adults. Brown packaging, no glamour, take the illegal money out of it and then furnish it, holding people accountable for what they do. These drugs are too dangerous not to control.

"Reality is a crutch for people who can't cope with drugs."

-Lily Tomlin

Is It Time to End the War on Drugs?

Legalize drugs- that's a frightening thought. Maybe more people would try them.

Gray says even if they did, that would do less harm than the war we've been fighting for the past 30 years.

"What we're doing now has failed. In fact it's hopeless," he argues. "This is a failed system that we simply must change."

Since the days of "Just Say No," this domestic quagmire has lasted longer than the Vietnam War. It has killed, detained and bullied innocent citizens and non-violent offenders in a futile campaign to vacuum every last cannabis seed from America's streets. This fool's errand isn't cheap. Between 1990 and 1999 alone, federal anti-drug law-enforcement activities have cost taxpayers $181 billion. States and cities have spent even more. Meanwhile, illegal drugs have become even more plentiful.

The War on Drugs burns through innocent human lives, tax dollars and civil liberties more swiftly than a joint at a jazz festival. Cops certainly should prevent those on illegal drugs or legal alcohol from operating cars and heavy machinery. Beyond that, government should do little more than counsel moderation. That's sound advice for adults who seek mind expansion, from either marijuana or martinis. As for the War on Drugs, it's high time to hoist a white sheet up the nearest flagpole.

The United Nations Universal Declaration of Human Rights

The Universal Declaration of Human Rights (UDHR) was adopted by the UN in 1948 as a response to the Nazi holocaust and to set a standard by which the human rights activities of all nations, rich and poor alike, are to be measured.

Preamble: Whereas recognition of the inherent dignity and of the equal inalienable rights of all members of the human family is the foundation of the freedom, justice and peace in the world.

Whereas it is essential that human rights should be protected by the rule of law.

Whereas the people of the United Nations have in the Charter reaffirmed their faith in fundamental human rights, in the dignity and worth of the human person and in the equal rights of men and women and have determined to promote social progress and better standards of life in larger freedom.

Whereas Member States have pledged themselves to achieve, in cooperation with the United Nations, the promotion of universal respect for and observance of human rights and fundamental freedoms.

Now, therefore The General Assembly proclaims this Universal Declaration of Human Rights as a common standard of achievement for all peoples and all nations, to the end that every individual and every organ of society, keeping this Declaration constantly in mind, shall strive by teaching and education to promote respect for these rights and freedoms and by progressive measures, national and international, to secure their universal and effective recognition and observance.

And American civil rights as put forth by the United States Constitution & Bill of Rights

The Promise of the American Republic

"We hold these truths to be self-evident, that all men are created equal, that they are endowed by their Creator with certain unalienable Rights, that among these are Life, Liberty and the pursuit of Happiness. That to secure these rights, Governments are instituted among Men, deriving their just powers from the consent of the governed. That whenever any Form

of Government becomes destructive of these ends, it is the Right of the People to alter or to abolish it, and to institute new Government, laying its foundation on such principles and organizing its powers in such form, as to them shall deem most likely to effect their Safety and Happiness."

-American Declaration of Independence, 1776

Article 5

"No one shall be subjected to torture of to cruel, inhuman or degrading treatment or punishment."

The Eighth Amendment to the United States Constitution also protects prisoners against cruel and unusual punishment, specifically banning excessive bail and fines.

The Drug War has created Draconian prison sentences and asset forfeitures that are disproportionate to the offense. Federal mandatory minimum sentences put first-time, nonviolent, low-level drug offenders in prison for five, ten, twenty years or even life, without parole-often for longer terms than violent criminals convicted of murder, rape or robbery, felons who are eligible for parole. Urine testing without probable cause is an insidious example of degrading treatment that has become a familiar routine in American schools and the corporate work place.

Universal Declaration of Human Rights

Article 10

" Everyone is entitled in full equality to a fair and public hearing by an independent and impartial tribunal, in the determination of his rights and obligations and of any criminal charge against him."

The Constitution guarantees a jury trial, both in criminal cases (Sixth Amendment) and in common law civil suits involving a value over twenty dollars (Seventh Amendment).

Sentencing guidelines and mandatory minimum penalty laws tie judges' hands when it comes to dispensing justice. Physical evidence is replaced with exaggerated estimates. In a group offense, each person is liable for the whole amount instead of their actual level of involvement. Back room plea-bargaining has replaced public hearings. Furthermore, under federal civil asset forfeiture law, a person's entire life savings can be seized, without a prior hearing, and without even being charged with a crime. If the property has a value of less than five hundred thousand dollars it can be forfeited administratively, without any judicial proceedings unless the owner posts a cost bond. Even if he pays the cost bond, the owner can still be deprived of the right to a jury trial through summary judgment, if the judge is not satisfied with the amount of proof he submits on paper. Since most judges have come up the ranks as hard-nosed prosecutors, they are often biased against the accused.

Universal Declaration of Human Rights

Article 11.1

"Everyone charged with a penal offense has the right to be presumed innocent until proven guilty according to the law in a public trial at which he has all the guarantees necessary for his defense."

The Fifth Amendment further adds the right to a speed trial and right to legal counsel and forbids the use of secret witnesses by requiring their testimony in court.

In Drug War criminal cases, anonymous informants can reduce or work off charges and even receive payment and commissions to provide "evidence" for search warrants, and lawyers refer to a de facto "drug war exception" to the Bill of Rights. Police use entrapment to lure people to break the law under a system that creates a conflict of interest due to the seizure of property for law enforcement use. These problems are compounded by prosecutorial misconduct, vague and overly board conspiracy charges, changes of venue, biased judicial instructions, limits placed on defense evidence and motivation, etc.

Universal Declaration of Human Rights

Article 12

"No one shall be subjected to arbitrary interference with his privacy, family, home, or correspondence, nor to attacks upon his honor and reputation. Everyone has the right to the protection of the law against such interference of attacks."

The Fourth Amendment protects the people from "unreasonable searches and seizures" by requiring that "no Warrants shall issue, but upon probable cause supported by Oath or affirmation, and particularly describing the place to be searched, and the persons or things to be seized."

In recent years, people in the US have suffered increasing intrusions on their privacy, including phone taps, invasive urine testing, infrared scanning of homes, garbage and mail searches, computer searches of bank records and utility bills. Employees are routinely subjected to random urine testing, with neither probable cause nor warrant, as a job requirement. Police sweep neighborhoods and block public roadways to search people, sometimes with dogs. If your appearance fits one of the stereotypical "profiles," you may be singled out for special harassment. Having one hundred dollars cash on your person is all it takes for police to seize your money as suspected drug income, even when you can prove otherwise. And when warrants are still issued, they are often based on hearsay evidence, high-tech surveillance and monitoring systems even the amount of electricity a home or business uses in a month or gauge the amount of heat it gives off.

Universal Declaration of Human Rights

Article 16.3

"The family is the natural and fundamental group unit of society and is entitled to protection by society and the state."

The Fourth Amendment lists "The right of the people to be secure in their persons, houses, papers and effects."

What happens to the children when narcotics police take the family car and home, and send mommy and daddy to prison for decades at a time under mandatory minimum sentences? How does it affect children to see their parents tied up face down on the floor while armed men in dark suits tear the house apart? How can a person support their family from prison, financially or emotionally? How can an inner city community survive with a quarter of its adult male population stigmatized by a criminal record? Indeed, the family is a primary target of the Drug War.

Universal Declaration of Human Rights

Article 17.2

"No one shall be arbitrarily deprived of his property."

The US Constitution Fifth Amendment also promises that no American shall be "deprived of life, liberty or property, without due process of law."

Under US civil asset forfeiture laws, police agencies and informants get to keep the proceeds of their confiscations. Inherent conflicts of interest arise from forfeiture laws. Property of innocent parties has often been seized by police agencies without even a conviction. Forfeiture victims do not have to be charged with a crime to lose their right to trial. Although the US Supreme Court held in 1993 that disproportionate forfeitures are unconstitutional, the abuses continue. Arbitrary selection of suspects based on appearance (racially and culturally discriminatory drug courier profiles, such as ethnicity, hair length, political bumper stickers, etc.) Buying your garden supplies from a store under surveillance by police agencies can lead to a search of your home. In addition, the lines separating legal from illegal drugs is not based on scientific criterion (like demonstrable health effects) or objective standards (such as impairment or likelihood of inducing violent behavior), but rather on the arbitrary moralistic and political attitudes of elected officials and appointed bureaucrats. Anyone who enjoys the wrong kind of flowers or intoxicants may well find their property seized by the government, along with their children and personal liberty.

Universal Declaration of Human Rights

Article 18

"Everyone has the right to freedom of thought, conscience and religion: This right includes freedom to change his religion or belief, and freedom, either alone or in community with others and in public or private, to manifest his religion or belief in teaching, practice, worship and observance."

The US Constitution First Amendment begins the Bill of Rights: "Congress shall make no law respecting an establishment of religion, or prohibiting the free exercise thereof."

The government has prosecuted every effort to formulate and establish new religions that involve the use of mind expanding drugs. When Drug War zeal even infringed on the Native American Church by forbidding the use of peyote in its ceremonies, Congress created a special, narrow exemption for its practitioners through the Religious Freedom Restoration Act of 1993, but the Supreme Court in 1997 overturned the law. And what about other religions? The Drug War has effectively outlawed traditional cannabis-based religions such as Rastafari, Coptic Christians, Sufi Moslem, Sadhu Hindu, etc. Members of these churches are singled out and prosecuted for practicing their religions by partaking of their sacraments. Frequently they are targeted for harassment, surveillance and entrapment, and courts routinely exclude any testimony or reference to their religious motives when "the facts" of a case are presented to a jury. Once members of a congregation are convicted felons, as a condition of parole after serving a prison sentence, they are forbidden to associate, congregate or worship together, or even remain in contact.

Universal Declaration of Human Rights

Article 25.1

"Everyone has the right to a standard of living adequate for the health and well-being of himself and of his family, including food, clothing, housing and medical care and necessary social services."

US Constitution Ninth Amendment stipulates: "The enumeration in the Constitution, of certain rights, shall not be construed to deny or disparage others retained by the people."

Hemp is a raw material used for at least ten thousand years for making food, clothing, housing, paper and other consumer goods. The US once had laws requiring farmers to grow hemp, and Presidents Washington and Jefferson, among others, would today be sentenced to death for growing their acreage of this rugged and versatile crop. Every President since Franklin Roosevelt, including Bill Clinton in 1994, has listed hemp as an essential strategic material for the national defense. But it is illegal to grow here and all hemp must be imported. Banning hemp suppressed domestic jobs and enterprise in the hemp industries, at an estimated cost of a million jobs and tens of billions of dollars in business. The Drug War deprives patients of medical marijuana, an effective, natural healing agent. The Drug Enforcement *Administration forbids* health care professionals from administering or even recommending cannabis, even when they know it will help.

Universal Declaration on Human Rights

Article 26

26.2: "Education shall be directed to the full development of the human personality and to the strengthening of respect for humans rights and fundamental freedoms. It shall promote understanding, tolerance and friendship."

26.3: "Parents have a prior right to chose the kind of education that shall be given to their children."

Federal drug policy is categorized as "zero tolerance"; to be achieved through the stigmatization and criminalization of targeted individuals and lifestyles. The D.A.R.E. (Drug Abuse Resistance Education) anti-drug program brings police officers into grammar schools to talk to children about the private activities of parents and friends. Students are instructed not to take their workbook home. Plainclothes police infiltrate high schools and college campuses, engaging in sting operations.

Universal Declaration of Human Rights

Article 27.1

"Everyone has the right freely to participate in the cultural life of the community, to enjoy the arts and share in scientific advancement and its benefits."

"Congress shall make no law abridging the freedom of speech, or of the press; of the right of the people peaceably to assemble," states the US Constitution First Amendment.

The Drug War targets specific subcultures identified as having an interest in illicit substances. The Rastafari, hippies, and musical fans of jazz, reggae, hip-hop, the Grateful Dead (known as Deadheads), and certain other persuasions are singled out for persecution. Police barricade the roadways leading to political rallies and annual events, such as the Rainbow Family Gathering. Participants are systematically harassed, intimidated and provoked by authorities instigating trouble. Similarly, political groups are infiltrated by police provocateurs who try to incite violence and undermine the legitimated activities of these organizations. People who take advantage of scientific advancements in the medical use of cannabis face criminal prosecution. The same bureaucrats who insist we need more research are the very ones who block such studies. Federal agencies such as National Institute on Drug Abuse (NIDA) substitute propaganda for science to manipulate research data. They publish biased reports to prop up prohibition. Researchers who produce accurate data tend to have their funds cut and permits revoked. Those who support the Drug War with unsubstantiated theories of bizarre risks are likely to receive funding increases and gain easy access to news media and lawmakers. Long after spurious claims have been proven false, such as marijuana inducing "brain damage" and "male breasts", or LSD causing "chromosomal mutation", these hysterical charges continue to appear in government publications.

Universal Declaration of Human Rights

Article 8

"Everyone has the right to an effective remedy by the competent national tribunals for acts violating the fundamental rights granted him by the constitution or by law."

The US Constitution First Amendment promises the right to "petition the Government for a redress of grievances."

The Drug War violates many of the most fundamental tenants of human rights, and call on the US government and all international human rights agencies to review this record with an unbiased and objective eye on the human rights issued involved. There should be as an immediate remedy the release of those wrongly or unfairly imprisoned and the full restoration of human rights to all Americans.

High Schoolers can get $1,000 Bounty Under New Drug "Snitch" Program

A plan by three Oregon high schools to pay $1,000 bounties to teenagers who anonymously turn in other students on drug charges is a morally reprehensible program that will turn high schools into "schools for snitches".

"This is the first step towards turning America's teenagers into paid informants for the government."

Students in three high school districts in Portland, Oregon, will be paid up to $1,000 for snitching on fellow students who use drugs or alcohol on school property.

Under the new Crime Stoppers program, students will be given a direct, anonymous hotline to school police.

"This turn-in-your-friends-for-cash scheme at Judas Iscariot High School is a stark example of how Drug Prohibition has warped the morals of this nation. Instead of treating drug abuse as a medical problem that requires concern and compassion, this program treats drug abuse as an opportunity to earn thirty pieces of silver by ratting on your schoolmates."

"How many high school grudges will be settled by calling 1-800-BE-A-SNITCH?" "How strong will the lure of a $1,000 reward be to a student who suffered from a broken romance-and wants revenge? For every honest report of drug abuse, how many anonymous calls will be made to settle a score?"

It will create a climate of fear and distrust. "Programs like this will cause every student to wonder: Who will be turned in next? Betrayal, snitching and anonymous informants are not the proper recipes for creating school spirit, respect and trust."

It will funnel teenagers with drug problems into the criminal justice system instead of the medical system.

Civil Asset Forfeiture

Kleptocracy (klep-toc-ra-ci) – n. government by thievery

Between 1985 and 1995, the federal government through the Departments of Justice and Treasury, has seized over $4,000,000,000.00 (four billion) from US citizens, many of whom have never even been charged with a crime. In a single year, fiscal year 1994, the DEA alone made 13,631 seizures with a total value of $646,786,850.00. "Civil asset forfeiture laws are being used in terribly unjust ways, are depriving innocent citizens of their property, with nothing that can be called due process. You never have to be charged with any crime. If fact, even if you are acquitted by a jury on criminal charges, your property can be seized."

-US Rep. Henry Hyde (R, IL)

Are you next?!?

What is Civil Forfeiture?

Search and Seizure Fever

Federal and many state forfeiture laws empower governments to take people's private property without ever charging a crime. Legally, the property is accused of a crime, not the owner. Lawyers call that in rem-Latin for "against the thing." One odd result is case names such as US vs. $2,452" or "US vs. A Parcel of Land Known as 4492 South Lavonia Road."

Civil asset forfeiture laws allow the government to seized property without charging anyone with a crime, and then keep it without ever having to prove a case. Seized property is presumed guilty and may be forfeited based upon mere hearsay, or even a tip supplied by an informant who stands to gain up to 25% of the forfeited assets. Since police get to keep nearly all the proceeds from forfeited property, officers often succumb to budget pressures and the temptation of bounty in the form of seized assets for their departments. Beyond the Drug War and following in its wake, over two hundred federal forfeiture laws are attached to non-drug offenses.

What's Wrong With Asset Forfeiture?

"A law designed to give cops the right to confiscate and keep the luxury possessions of major drug dealers mostly ensnares the modest homes, cars and hard-earned cash of ordinary, law-abiding people. This was not the way it was supposed to work."

-US Rep. John Conyers (D, MI)

The corrupting influence of unbridled greed has led to many personal tragedies. Innocent rancher Donald Scott killed by police when a forfeiture grab for his two hundred fifty-acre ranch went awry. Byron Stamate lost his forty-four-acre ranch when he was caught growing medical marijuana for his wife, who committed suicide in remorse rather than testify against him in court.

What property can the government seize?

Property can be seized if the police claim that it was:

-Bought from the profits of illegal activity

-Instrumental in committing a crime.

Who gets to keep the seized assets?

In federal forfeiture cases, law enforcement gets to keep the assets. Some states provide that a portion goes into their General Fund.

How much evidence do they need to seize property?

No hard evidence; just probable cause – the same standard required for a search warrant or arrest. Police can use hearsay evidence, such as a tip from an informant whose name is not revealed. Hearsay is not allowed in criminal trials, where a defendant has a right to question his accuser.

Can seized property be reclaimed?

You must file a "claim" that you are the owner of the seized property and, except for real estate or property worth more than $100,000.00, post a cash bond equivalent to 10% of the value of the seized property.

At trial, the burden of proof is on you, not the government. You must prove that your property is innocent by a "preponderance of the evidence" – a higher standard than the "probable cause" standard used by police to seize the property.

What if a person is found innocent in a criminal case?

It might help. Until recently, it was held irrelevant to the forfeiture case (where you must prove your money or property was legally obtained or is innocent of facilitating a crime).

Thought Crimes: Conspiracy Law

You never have to touch any drugs or money to be prosecuted in the Drug War. It's what you know; it's whom you know, and it's what you don't know. That's the idea behind conspiracy laws. In 1988, the Omnibus Anti-Drug Abuse Act added a significant dimension by including conspiracy convictions in the mandatory sentencing scheme.

People with no active participation in a drug offense are penalized for "aiding and abetting" simply for knowing about a situation and not reporting it to the police. Sometimes even for not knowing about a plan or situation prosecutors say they should have know about, and even for trying to talk someone else out of committing a drug crime! Wives and girlfriends of offenders have suffered the brunt of this law.

With that logic, no one is safe – except, of course, government agents and spies, who are paid to go out into society and manufacture, buy, sell, and use drugs, arrange deals, etc., to entrap and betray others.

In criminal cases such as murder, proof is required that an "act to effect the object of the conspiracy" has occurred. However, in 1994, Sandra Day O'Connor wrote a US Supreme Court decision ruling that just talking about breaking a law is enough.

Rather than requiring drug laws to be Constitutional or even consistent with other criminals codes, the Court ruled that "Congress appears to have made the choice quite deliberately" and cited as precedent an English case from 1705, which held that "the very assembling together was an overt act." These are exactly the kind of Orwellian laws that the Bill of Rights was written in 1781 to prevent

" The Nazis said they had a Jewish problem. We say we have a drug abuse problem. Actually, 'Jewish problem' was the name the Germans gave to their persecution of the Jews; 'drug abuse problem' is the name we give to our persecution of people who use certain drugs." -Thomas Szasz, M.D.

What Are Mandatory Minimum Sentences (MMS)?

Federal mandatory minimum sentences (MMS) are determined solely by the weight of the drugs, or the presence of a firearm during a felony offense. The prisoner must serve at least 85% of this sentence, and there is no parole available. The only way to get a sentence reduction is through acting as an informant against others, including one's confidants, friends and family.

The sentences are mandatory in that judges must impose them, regardless of the defendant's role in the offense, his culpability, likelihood of rehabilitation, or any other mitigating factors.

Many states have adopted similar mandatory minimum sentences.

How Did We Get Into This MMS?

This is America's second experience in fifty years with mandatory minimum sentences for drug law violators.

> **-1951** Congress passed the Boggs Act, which imposed MMS.
> **-1956** The Boggs Act was modified to further toughen these sentenced, including terms of five, ten and fifteen years for drug offenses.
> **-Late 1960s** By this time it became manifestly clear that the mandatory minimums were failing. Congress found that drug use was increasing, prisons were overflowing, and the judicial branch was ineffective because of its inflexibility.
> **-1970** Almost all MMS were repealed.

Unfortunately, that was not the last we heard of MMS. In the 1980s the drug issue became a media epidemic. In the election year of 1986, crack was in the headlines of All-American papers, and a top rated TV show about chasing drug traffickers, Miami Vice. The cocaine-related deaths of athletes Len Bias and Don Rogers within one week was the final impetus to set Congress into motion.

> **-1986** Despite the fact that a separate commission was developing standard sentencing guidelines, Congress passed a new set of MMS to prove it was "tough on crime" and "tough on drugs".
> **-1994** Congress enacted a "Safety Value" provision that allows federal judges to exempt certain non-

> violent, first-time offenders from mandatory minimum penalties. This provision is no retroactive. Therefore, it did not change sentences imposed before its effective date.

These are roughly the same MMS that we have today. In an eerie parallel to the late 1960s, the Sentencing Commission found in 1991 that the judiciary has been weakened by MMS and that prison overcrowding is rising. But Congress seems as unable to learn from its own mistakes, as it is to learn from history.

Federal Mandatory Minimums (MMS) for First-Time Drug Offenders

Drug	5 Years	10 Years
Drug	*5 Years*	*10 Years*
Type of substance	*No parole*	*No parole*
LSD	*1 gram*	*10 grams*
Marijuana	*100 plants or 100 kilos*	*1000 plants or 1000 kilos*
Crack Cocaine	*5 grams*	*50 grams*
Powder Cocaine	*500 grams*	*5 kilos*
Heroin	*100 grams*	*1 kilo*
Methamphetamine	*10 grams*	*100 grams*

Other Mandatory Minimum Sentences

Offense	Length of Sentence
Possession of a gun	**5 years (added to drug sentence) during a drug offense**
Armed Career Criminal Act	**15 years (Felon in possession of a gun)**
Continuing Criminal Enterprise	**20 years**

MMS Are Costly Socially

The Less calculable costs of the Drug War are in human damage caused to those imprisoned for unduly long periods of time, and to their families. Women and children truly bear the brunt of the Drug War. Women are the "hidden body count" and children are the "unseen victims." Children of prisoners lose one or both of their parents, forcing them to fend for themselves, to be taken in by relatives, or to live in foster homes. Brothers and sisters are often separated from each other in the breakup of their families.

Asset forfeitures seize family homes, cars, and savings, leaving many families homeless with no transportation and no money.

Too often, young children watch in terror as DEA agents break down the front door of their family home, throw their parents to he floor an aim guns at their heads, shouting curses at them. The children themselves are frequently kept at gunpoint for hours.

> -In 1978, the number of imprisoned parents was 21,000 (twenty one thousand). By 1990, it had risen to 1,000,000 (one million).
> -Since mandatory minimums were enacted, the number of women inmates has tripled. The majority of these women are first-time, non-violent, low-level offenders.
> -Over 80% of the female prisoners in the Unites States are mothers, and 70% of these are single parents.

These kinds of incarcerations may be sowing the seeds of a new generation of inmates. Studies show that, relative to the general population, inmates are more than twice as likely to have grown up in a single parent family and that half the juveniles in state and local jails have an immediate family member who is a felon.

With so much talk in Congress about "Family Values," one might expect to see some concern about the destruction of the family unit, which is caused by the Drug War, its mindless escalation.

MMS Are Costly Financially

> -The average cost of incarcerating a federal inmate is **$33,000 per year.**
> **-About 60%** of federal inmates – 65,697 people are dug offenders. Half of these are first time, non-violent offenders.
> -To feed, clothe, house and guard these 65,697 prisoners cost taxpayers **$6.14 million per day**, or $2.21 billion annually.
> -Each year, the portion of your tax dollars that goes to support federal prisoners grows faster than any other federal

expenditure, including education, defense, the environment, transportation and social security.
-The federal Bureau of Prisons budget has grown 1,400% since the enactment of mandatory minimums in 1986. The budget jumped from $220 million in 1986 to **$3.19 billion in 1997.**
-It costs more to send a person to prison for four year than to pay for college including tuition, fees, room and board, books and supplies.

Mandatory Minimums Are Arbitrary

Possession of 4.99 grams of crack is punishable with no more than one year in prison; possession of 5.01 grams of crack is subject to a mandatory minimum of five years. These "sentencing cliffs", as they are known, create absurd disparities in sentencing, yet there is no way for judges to circumvent them.

Furthermore, because of the way the law is written, a drug is defined as any mixture, which contains a drug, which can result in even more absurd sentencing. For instance, mandatory minimums for LSD are calculated using the weight of the carrier medium, such as blotter paper. Hence, the accused may face more time in prison for the paper than for the actual drug.

Mandatory Minimums Are Unjust

Mandatory minimum sentences undermine the basic tradition of justice that Americans have enjoyed for 200 years – that the punishment fit the crime.

Judges are only allowed to consider the weight of the drug in sentencing. Judges are not allowed to consider any of the following factors:

- The nature and circumstances of the offense
- The history and character of the defendant
- The need for the sentence to deter further criminal conduct
- The need for the sentence to protect the public
- Alternative sentencing options

- The need to avoid sentence disparities with similar defendants

By preventing judges from considering these factors MMS straightjackets the judge, forcing him or her to tear the "just" out of "criminal justice".

...It's getting a little warm in here, but it feels good...

Chapter VII
Our Court System

"Without free speech, no search for truth is possible...no discovery of truth is useful...Better a thousandfold abuse of free speech than denial of free speech. The abuse dies in a day, but the denial slays the life of the people, and entombs the hope of the race."

-Charles Bradlaugh-(English reformer-1890)

Recent court decisions have questioned the viability of the U.S. Justice System. The obvious guilty go free and the non-guilty are coerced into make a deal pleading guilty to save lawyer's costs and potentially serious penalties for minor infractions sometimes with serious consequences.

A petty thief pleads guilty for stealing from a store and the third time is incarcerated for the rest of his life under the "Three strikes you are out", laws in some states.

A nineteen-year-old honor student madly in love with a girl whom he had been dating in a small Iowa town goes to the house of another boy knowing she is with him. He knocks-gets no answer, calls for her to come out and is rebuffed. He pushes in the door and confronts her. The police show up, he is arrested for forcible entry. The states attorney offer a deal on a guilty plea. The boy, feeling he is not guilty, does not accept the deal. He brings witnesses but the Judge still finds him guilty and sentences him to twenty years in jail, the mandatory sentence in Iowa. No one was killed, on one was injured, and nothing was taken. This is the American Justice System.

Americans protest over the inhumane treatment of the Chinese legal system. Yet, Amenity International the worldwide group that tracks the legal systems of the world finds a disproportional number of young poor American people are sentenced to death of to life in prison without parole on a guilty plea to save them from the death penalty.

The court appoints any lawyer to defend in accused poor, even one that has never had any criminal court experience. In some states, their hourly rate is fixed at fifty dollars per hour with a defense budget of two thousand for a murder case. Other public defenders have a genuine paper mill. Their desks are stacked with cases for defendants with whom he may never talk to before meeting in the courtroom and being offered a deal.

Recently, Canada and some European countries had public hearings as to how to improve their court system. People from all walks of life wrote letters and appeared before panels citing problem with the court system in those countries. This would never happen in the United States. We think we are all above any review.

In most other countries in the world, you take courses in becoming a Judge and then Judges are appointed after passing a stringent exam working their way up to higher positions in the Judicial Branch.

In the United States, most Judges are elected. All they need is a political party affiliation and they run for office on a political party ticket.

Think of the lawyer who works for a law firm handling criminal cases with political ambitions. He or she asks for the prevailing political party for support. He or she holds a series of fund raisers where other lawyers and law firms, other special interest groups and businesses and other individuals make contributions expecting acknowledgment and maybe more in return. The lawyer wins the election and becomes a Judge. Nothing is required in expertise other than a popularity contest. Lawyers have comes Judges even if they never tried a case in court. Previous sports figures have become Judges simply on their name recognition.

Now this new Judge has sworn to uphold the law but do you think that the contribution to the fund-raisers are not known. Do you really think they made their contribution not expecting anything in return?

The new Judge may have severed the relationship with the old law firm but maybe their pension or profit sharing plan is still with the old firm and how do you sever a working and friendship relationship?

It is obvious that their law firm has special standing before this Judge. There is a built in bias that cannot be ignored.

Federal Judgeships are handed out by people in government as political favors. Wives of ex-governors and other politicians become appointed as Judges for favors rendered. In some instances, court administrators have tried to reduce the influence of a law firm appearing before the Judge of their choice by assigning cases to Judges on an at a random computerized system. A few dollars to the clerk or is has happened in Chicago the lawsuit filed, filling fees being paid as many times in a row until the "right" Judge is assigned and the other cases are withdrawn or dismissed. A well worth investment in order to get the right Judge.

Sadly a poor person does not have the same laws and procedures apply to them. They really are at the mercy of the law. The result of our system is court decisions that defy logic on both ends to the spectrum of harshness and leniency.

Don't Go on a Vacation

A couple leaves a ten-year-old and a fourteen-year-old for a week in their home while they take a vacation. They call daily to check on the children and a grandparent who lives nearby is to be notified in the event of an emergency. Somehow a neighbor finds out that the children are "alone". They are taken into foster care and the parents are arrested upon their arrival at the airport. One hundred thousand dollars in legal fees later (they had to sell their home). The couple have to agree to give up the children in exchange for not serving time in jail. Eventually, the pressure of the whole situation results in divorce. Is this what society expects from our court system?

Guilty as not charged

A young mother of four children received fifteen years in prison for pawning a pistol in Florida. Her boyfriend suggested pawning his gun when the family needed money. Since her friend did not have a valid driver's license, the young mother offered to use hers. So for thirty dollars she pawned the gun. Three years earlier, she was convicted of selling three twenty dollar chucks of crack cocaine, about the size of a pencil eraser to an under cover police officer. Her prior conviction made the pawning of the gun a felony requiring her to serve fifteen years in jail without any parole, just for signing a pawn slip for her boyfriend.

● ● ● ●

The question on the fairness of the American Judicial System for someone who will be away from her four children for fifteen years for a crime when she's hurt no one, and someone committing armed robbery, murder or rape can be sentenced to two to seven years.

Our American court system has even given the death sentence to individuals who failed to have the mental capacity to understand their actions nor their accusations. In addition, children as young as eight years old face being tried as an adult and may be jailed for life without any chance for parole. This is our court system. It consists of laws that you may not even be aware of. Laws that impose sentences that for the ordinary person do not make sense. Judges who get elected or become judges as a favor for political services. Judges with little or no court experience. Judges with built in biases who run on a political party platform and must raise funds to win elections.

Defense attorneys that have no criminal experience are appointed to defend the rights of the accused without a budget to properly defend. Public defenders who are overworked and make deals to get rid of cases. Sentences that defy explanations or harshness and the finding of not guilty or obvious guilt. Think of the O.J. Simpson decisions. Most of us believe that he was guilty of killing his ex-wife yet the jury decided that if the glove does not fit he should be not guilty.

In matters of criminal justice, the Bill of Rights recognized the temptation that may be felt by police, prosecutors and the judiciary to intimidate witnesses and expedite punishment. The criminal-justice system is fallible: innocent people might be punished for crimes they did not commit; governments are perfectly capable of framing those who, for reasons unconnected with the purported crime, they do not like.

Guilty and more guilty

Zeal for convictions leads government to accept tainted tips, testimony.

The bullet that tore into Don Carlson's thigh sent him sprawling across the hallway floor.

After he fired two shots at his from door in a vain attempt to stop the intruders, he dropped the gun. Carlson made it to his bedroom, punching 9-1-1 into a portable telephone as the men stormed into his house. He fell into a corner. Twice more he was shot-in the back. One bullet splintered and collapsed a lung. "Don't move or I'll shoot you again," a man yelled. Carlson didn't know it, but the man who shouted at him was a federal agent. The dozen or so other officers in his house represented the Drug Enforcement Administration, the U.S. Customs Service and the Sad Diego police department and sheriff's office. Carlson is still not sure when they realized their mistake. For 30 minutes on that sultry August night he lay bleeding, handcuffed and shackled, on his bedroom floor, barley able to breathe. "Why would they do this to me?" he recalled muttering. Agents raided Carlson's home in San Diego suburb of Poway in search of 2,500 pounds of cocaine. They based the search on information that an informant named Ronnie Edmond provided. Edmond was an ex-drug dealer whom the federal government paid $2,000.00 a month to inform on others in the drug trade. This informant frequently lied, a fact the agents knew, but they nonetheless used his story to get a search warrant for Carlson's house. He'd never been in trouble with the law.

Carlson was no drug dealer. There were no drugs in his house. He'd never been in trouble with the law. The informant picked Carlson's home because he thought it was vacant and figured he could cook up another lie when the agents found no drugs.

Carlson had recently divorced, and his wife got the furniture. That's why the house looked empty. If the consequences of Edmond's lie weren't so serious, the episode might have been comical. Instead, it illustrates a problem in the federal justice system that receives little attention but as profound impact, a two-year Pittsburgh Post-Gazette investigation found. Perjury has become the coin of the realm in federal law enforcement. People's homes are invaded because of lies. People are arrested because of lies. People go to prison because of lies. People stay in prison because of lies, and sometimes, bad guys go free because of lies. Lying has become a significant problem in federal court cases because the rewards to federal law enforcement officers can be so great and the consequences so minimal. Perjurers are seldom punished; neither are the law enforcement officers who ignore or accept their lies. Carlson believes some of the agents who stormed his house wanted to kill him to cover up the informant's lies but could risk it because so many agents from different jurisdictions were there. "The only thing that saved me was that there were too many agencies involved." Federal officers would not respond to requests for comment on the case.

Guilty, guilty – I said guilty.

More defendants on death row have been proved to be no guilty that people executed. Yet, Government officials such as a prior Illinois Attorney General who twice sent an innocent man to death row and then ever though the detectives admitted that they lied and had planted evidence. Seventeen years he was on death row and the ex-Attorney General says that he would still find him guilty because he was a liar.

Conveniently the ex-Attorney General forgets that another inmate had confessed to the crime, the person's DNA checked with the DNA found on the crime scene but somehow this person as of this date has not been charged with the murder. How could this happen in our time? Sadly the Bill of Rights that is to protect defendants is confidently swept under the carpet.

A detective testified that they used the defendants boots to put footprints in the snow and it was only after another detective testified that one specific date he heard the defendant make a comment when many years later it was found out that the detective was on that date on his vacation at Disney World.

In the first study of its kind, a Chicago Tribune analysis of thousands of court records, appellate rulings and lawyer disciplinary records from across the United States has found:

Since a 1963 U.S. Supreme Court ruling designed to curb misconduct by prosecutors, at least 381 defendants nationally have had a homicide conviction thrown out because prosecutors concealed evidence suggesting innocence or presented evidence they knew to be false. Of all the ways that prosecutors can cheat, those two are considered the worst by the courts. And that number represents only a fraction of how often such cheating occurs.

The U.S. Supreme Court has declared such misconduct by prosecutors to be so reprehensible that it warrants criminal charges and disbarment. But not one of those prosecutors had been convicted of a crime. Not one was barred from practicing law. Instead, many saw their careers advance becoming Judges or district attorneys. One became a congressman.

In Georgia, George "Buddy" Darden became congressman after a court concluded that he withheld evidence in a case where seven men, later exonerated, were convicted of murder and one was sentenced to death. In New Mexico, Virginia Ferrara failed to disclose evidence of another suspect in a murder case. By the time the conviction was reversed she had become chief disciplinary counsel for the New Mexico agency that policies lawyers for misconduct.

Bennett Gershman, a law professor at Pace University in White Plains, N.Y., has written extensively about misconduct by prosecutors and calls it a "serious cancer in our system of justice."

"There is no check on prosecutorial misconduct except for the prosecutor's own attitudes and beliefs and inner morality," he said.

In 1979, Isaac Knapper was accused of murdering a tourist. He was convicted, but more than a decade later the Louisiana Supreme Courts reversed his conviction because prosecutors didn't disclose a police report undercutting their case. The report documented the arrests of three men for a different robbery five blocks away using the same gun that killed the tourist.

After his conviction was reversed in 1991, Knapper was not retired. He was 16 when arrested, a gifted amateur boxer working to become a professional. He was 29 when freed. The years in between were spent at the penitentiary in Angola, one of the country's toughest prisons. After being freed, Knapper boxed professionally for awhile, but his best years were behind him.

"They wanted to get a conviction, they wanted to clear the books," he said recently. "They railroaded me."

Laurie White, the defense attorney who won Knapper's appeal, used to work for Connick but now refers to prosecutors as "those lying, cheating bastards." She has won new trials for five clients-four convicted of murder, one of rape-by showing that prosecutors suppressed evidence. In another case, a judge quashed a murder indictment because prosecutors withheld evidence.

When Ray Whitley ran for the reelection last year as the chief prosecutor in Sumner County, Tenn., Robert Spurlock spent months working for Whitley's opponent-making signs, handing out fliers and sharing his story with all who would listen.

Spurlock, a 32-year-old mechanic, served more than four years in prison for a crime he didn't commit.

Spurlock and Ronnie Marshall were convicted in 1990 of murdering a man and dumping him in a drainage ditch. But the appeals court reversed the convictions and lambasted Whitley, saying the concealed evidence that pointed to other suspects and discredited his star witness. He also allowed witnesses to lie, the court ruled.

The star witness, Henry "Skully" Apple, testified that he was with Spurlock and Marshall on the night of the murder. He told a story of hearing screams in the distance, then seeing Spurlock spattered with blood.

Apple denied he had been promised an early release from jail on an unrelated crime in exchange for testifying against Spurlock. A sheriff's deputy also testified that no such promise was made. But both those witnesses lied, the appeals court said. But Whitley failed to disclose those tapes, the court ruled.

After receiving new trials, Spurlock and Marshall were convicted again. But in 1996, they were freed after newly discovered evidence implicated the real killer, who later pleaded guilty.

The state's lawyer disciplinary agency investigated Whitley but cleared him of wrongdoing. Rick Halprin, a Chicago attorney representing Spurlock, called the investigation a "whitewash" and an "outrage."

Voters also approved of Whitley's work. Despite Spurlock's campaign efforts, residents reelected Whitley in August with 58 percent of the vote.

Have you noticed that the system of criminal justice in this country is shutting down, piece by piece by piece?

DNA identification, which had become more sophisticated by the years, is the greatest advance in criminal detection since the fingerprint. It has enabled the system to put away criminals who otherwise would have gotten off scot-free and to find matches years after the crime when their DNA shows up after an unrelated arrest. Short of a truth serum, this is the best thing that could happen for the criminal justice system.

The problem is, DNA evidence sometimes shows that the system messed up and nailed the wrong person for a crime. In fact, it happens depressingly often.

The notorious inability of prosecutors to admit that they are ever wrong is a fact of life. What is far more horrifying is the refusal of judges and courts to look at evidence that proves innocence. Can you imagine how that must feel – to be in prison for a crime you didn't commit and to finally be able to prove it, only to have a court refuse to consider the evidence?

Most of this is a consequence of a noxious law that Congress rushed through after the Oklahoma City bombing.

Called the Anti-Terrorism and Effective Death Penalty Act of 1996, the law was aimed at the ability of federal judges to second-guess state courts and at the ability of prisoners to file endless habeas corpus claims challenging the constitutionality of their convictions. ("Habeas corpus" is a Latin phrase meaning "you have the body" and goes back hundreds of years in common law as will as being in the Constitution. It means that if you can show you were unfairly tried, you have a remedy through the courts.)

True, the right has been abused for nit-picking purposes by some lawyers, but to effectively abolish the right is a dreadful abrogation of freedom. Where in the world are the militia folks now that we need them? Where are all those right-wingers who claim freedom as their most cherished possession?

The trouble with the '96 law is that it was poorly written and has been subject to conflicting interpretations by the lower courts. The law says that a federal judge can reverse a state court conviction only if it was contrary to federal law or if it applied federal law in an "unreasonable" way.

As Justice Ruth Bader Ginsburg pointed out, reasonable jurists always disagree on constitutional issues.

A recent film "The Hurricane," with Denzel Washington, is about a case in point. Rubin "Hurricane" Carter, a contender for the middleweight boxing title, was wrongfully convicted of a 1966 triple murder. He spent 19 years in prison before he was finally released.

The movie depicts the conviction as a frame-up by one racist cop, but as Selwyn Rabb, who originally covered the story for the New York Times, wrote: "The actual story is more harrowing because it exposes an underlying frailty in a criminal justice system that convicted Mr. Carter not once but twice. The convictions were obtained not by a lone, malevolent investigator but by a network of detectives, prosecutors and judges who countenanced the suppression and tainting of evidence and the infection of racial bias into the courtroom."

Under current interpretations of the 1996 law, Hurricane Carter would not be free today.

A "Frontline" documentary on PBS, "The Case for Innocence," gives the most chilling case histories in a stupid and tragic trend in criminal justice.

The most thoughtful comment in the documentary came form a law professor concerned about the criminal justice system's refusal to consider its own errors. He pointed our that in most other systems, when something goes horrible wrong – a plane falls from the sky, a type of car begins bursting into flames, a hospital patient dies from gross malpractice – there is a system in place to deal with the error. There are investigations, reports and ultimately corrections made to prevent recurrence.

In the criminal justice system, there are only denials and strenuous efforts to prevent the exculpatory evidence from being presented in court. The ease with which our criminal justice system can nail the wrong person has been painfully demonstrated time and again.

Perhaps the saddest and most terrifying finding in "The Case for Innocence" is that in the 60-some-odd cases in which innocence has been proved by DNA and the accused finally freed, none of the cases has been reopened.

The Chicago Tribune and many news broadcasts give us a vivid picture as to what has happened in the courts.

With impunity, prosecutors across the country have violated their oaths and the law, committing the worse kinds of deception in the most serious of cases.

They have prosecuted black men, hiding evidence the real killers were white. They have prosecuted a wife hiding evidence her husband committed suicide. They have prosecuted parents, hiding evidence their daughter was killed by wild dogs.

They do it to win.

They do it because they won't get punished.

They have done it to defendants who came within hours of being executed, only to be exonerated.

Couple Jailed for leaving baby outside restaurant

New York – A woman visiting from Denmark who left her child in a stroller outside a restaurant was jailed and the youngster placed in foster care.

Annette Sorenson, an actress visiting New York for a month, left her 14-month old daughter, Liv, next to the restaurant's plate glass window, amid outdoor tables and chairs.

She went inside with the baby's father, Exavier Wardlaw, a movie production assistant who lives in New York, and sat three tables from the window, 6 feet away.

Waiters and customers dialed 911. Officers charged the parents with endangering the welfare of a child. The father also was changed with disorderly conduct. The couple spent three days in jail.

Mayor Rudolph Giuliani said police intervened because "patrons in the restaurant were complaining that the baby was left alone, that the baby was crying and the baby was being neglected."

"I think we did the right thing, Giuliani said. If they acted out of an excess of caution, so be it."

He said a judge will decide what happens next, in Criminal Court.

Sorensen declined comment. "We're trying to help her obtain legal counsel and find out what this case is really about," said Danish consulate spokesman Kim Christiansen. He said a Dane would find it strange that "you could actually be charged here with leaving your child outside a place very near where you could see what was going on."

In Denmark, parents have children unattended while they shop or dine. But that rarely is done in New York, where people chain up outdoor garbage cans and flowerpots to prevent theft.

Wardlaw's lawyer, David Kirsch, said the parents "had no idea that there was anything wrong with what they were doing…They were on one side of a glass partition, and on the other side was the child."

Suburban 'cowboy' rides into wrong side of law

Ted Tanner came to court Monday wearing a black cowboy hat and black leather chaps-but the Addison resident said that doesn't mean he's a bad guy.

After all, he also rode up on his white horse, Thunder, which he left tied to a tree on the lawn at the DuPage County administration center in Wheaton.

Tanner, 35, a self-described "cowboy," made his distinctive appearance Monday in traffic court to fight three tickets that he was slapped with last year by DuPage County Forest Preserve police.

But to Tanner, the tickets were an attack on what he see as a harmless hobby that bother on one – riding his horse and sometimes camping in the woods and fields of the county's 22,500-acre forest preserve system.

"I'm just a cowboy," said Tanner, who actually works as an interior designer, riding instructor and entertainer. "I just want to be left alone to do what I've been doing for 23 years. I've been enjoying the woods ever since I was a kid."

Tanner was ticketed last March at Cricket Creed Woods in Addison for camping, carrying a machete and not having forest preserve registration tags required of horseback riders. He admits he didn't have the tags, but he insists he wasn't camping overnight, which was forbidden in county forest preserves.

"I had my bedroll out but people lay out blankets all the time," said Tanner, acknowledging that he sometimes camps in the backwoods of the forest preserves.

As for the machete, Tanner said he didn't know the weapon was illegal in forest preserves. It's just one of the camping tools he uses. Despite his arguments, he was found guilty on all three tickets by Judge C. Andrew Haton and ordered to pay up $75 fine on each charge. Hayton added his own spin on the case when Tanner first approached the bench.

"Nice pants," Hayton quipped, eyeing Tanner's chaps. Hayton offered Tanner some advice about where to pursue his horseback riding. "Go west, young man," he said.

Rebel Cancer doctor to go on trial for fraud

HOUSTON—a physician whose treatment of cancer patients led to a long-running legal battle over his use of an unapproved medicine went on trial on charges of fraud and violating federal drug regulations.

Stanislaw Burznski has become part of the debate over the U.S. Food and Drug Administration's handling of unconventional therapies for life-threatening illnesses.

Burzynski has maintained his innocence, saying the government and jealous colleagues are unfairly prosecuting him.

The 75-count indictment centers on Burzynski's patented "antineoplastons" treatment, which some cancer patients believe has saved their lives.

Burzynski, and his Burzynski Research Institute in Houston were charged in an indictment with mail fraud in the filing of insurance claims, contempt of a judge's order banning him from shipping his drug across state lines, and violations of federal laws against such shipments.

Federal law requires rigorous clinical trials to prove a drug works. However, the indictment says that Burzynski had treated just six patients under FDA-approved clinical trials.

Burzynski says antineoplastons, which he discovered in human urine and makes synthetically, serve as biochemical switches that "turn off" cancer genes by interrupting signals that instruct cells to multiply.

"The truth is that this treatment works," Burzynski said before a pre-trial hearing last week. "It should be brought to the jury's attention."

However, U.S. District Judge Sim Lake has ruled that whether He said that unless he is persuaded otherwise, such testimony will not be allowed.

One way to introduce such evidence might be through a "necessity" defense, which claims that laws were broken to save lives.

Burzynski has battled the FDA, state and federal courts, and the Texas Board of Medical Examiners since opening his clinic that Antineoplastons are effective is not relevant in the criminal trial.

He has described himself as a "revolutionary who's going to change the science" and contends that the government and medical establishment want to block alternative therapies.

He says many patients came to his clinic after chemotherapy and radiation treatments did not work. Cancer patients testified about Burzynski's treatments before a House subcommittee that held hearings on whether the FDA was blocking potentially lifesaving treatments.

In court documents, prosecutors say Burzynski refused to obey the order and "has defrauded insurance companies by tricking them into paying exorbitant fees for treating insured patients with this drug as thought it was ordinary, in-patient chemotherapy.

'79 Murder Conviction Thrown Out By Court

A federal appeals court Monday overturned the murder conviction of a Chicago man who has spent the last 20 years in prison, finding that the evidence against him was thin and that his defense attorney erred badly.

Ramior Hernandez, serving a 50-year sentence for this 1979 conviction in the murder of Jorge Orosco, must be released or granted a new trial within 120 days of the ruling, the U.S. 7th Circuit Court of Appeals in Chicago ruled.

Spokeswoman for Illinois Attorney General and Cook County State's Attorney declined to say whether prosecutors would seek a new trial.

The decision, written by the Chief Judge, said, "no reasonable jury could have convicted Hernandez" on the scant evidence presented at trial.

The Chief Judge also suggested that a key witness was the actual killer and got a sweetheart deal in return for implicating Hernandez. The Judge also said the prosecutor's closing argument in the case was "reprehensible," though not a factor in Monday's decision.

No 'right to die,' Scalia again states

WASHINGTON—Supreme Court Justice Antonin Scalie says there is no constitutional "right to die"—a question the high court soon will address in deciding whether states may ban doctor-assisted suicide.

Even though Scalia's views on the right-to-die issue have been known since 1990, experts on legal ethics suggested it was unwise for him to discuss the subject publicly while an assisted-suicide case is before the court.

It is "absolutely plain that there is no right to die." Scalia said at Catholic University's School of Philosophy. "There were laws against suicide" when the Constitution was drafted, he noted.

The high court agreed earlier to decide whether doctors can be barred from prescribing life-ending drugs for terminally ill patients who no longer want to live.

Most states forbid doctor-assisted suicide, but lower courts have stuck down bans imposed by New York and Washington state.

Scalia, one of the court's most conservative justices, did not mention the assisted suicide, according to a transcript of his speech.

Legal ethics expert Geoffrey Hazard, a University of Pennsylvania law professor, said he thought the justice's statement was "very poor form."

For those with a case coming before the court, "I think they would feel that his mind is closed to them and that is an unfortunate feeling to have when you're going before the court," Hazard said.

New York University law Professor Stephen Gillers noted that Scalia already wrote forcefully in a 1990 opinion that the Constitution doesn't recognize a right to die.

But Gillers added, "If he had called me, I would have said, 'You don't need this.' It will give the public less confidence in the objectivity of his vote."

Therefore it is illegal to take your own life.

The American Court System has been broken for a long time. Gone are the days when the Justice of Peace, a local person elected by the people to make decisions based on the facts. Now you need a lawyer for procedure and formality before you can even step foot into the courtroom door. It is no longer a matter of truth but a matter of technicalities. What is the definitions of "is" is more important then the facts "the truth".

Judges now rule the courtroom as if they were dictators. Defendants that are too outspoken are given a collar that can send 50,000 volts by the push of a button to incapacitate the defendant.

The United States is one of the few countries left in the world to have the death penalty. The United States has repeatedly refused to acknowledge the World Court in De Hague. The United States has more lawyers then the rest of the world combined. Finally, the legal system is based on who you can afford to hire rather then on the truth.

...Just a little more heat, we love it...

Chapter VIII
You will now Die

"An evil deed is not redeemed by an evil deed of retaliation. Justice is never advanced in the taking of human life. Morality is never upheld by legalized murder."

-Coretta Scott King

Which country in the world has more children under 19 years old on death row?

Which country has executed more proven innocent people in the last 10 years?

The United States.

Which country has attacked sovereign nations with the alleged aim to guarantee human rights and at the same time Amnesty International, the not for profit group that keeps track of the treatment of prisoners, has asked the United States to stop their executions.

For many people and nations the USA serves as a model, so it is difficult to imagine how we can persuade nations like Burma and China to respect basically human rights as long as the USA does not do so. We give China the most favored Nation status and preferential trading with the US as a reward for their abuse of human rights.

There are only six countries that execute children under 18 years old, Iran, Nigeria, Pakistan, Saudi Arabia, Yemen and the good old USA. More than 100 countries have abolished the death penalty in law or practice. The USA by contrast has increased its rate of executions and the number of crimes punishable by death. Thirty-eight states currently have the death penalty on their statute books.

More than 350 people have been executed in the USA since 1990. More than 3,300 others are on death row.

The application of the death penalty is racist. Black and white people are the victims of violent crime in roughly equal numbers, yet 82% of people executed since 1977 have been black. Ex- President Clinton who appears to have done everything for the children has done nothing to stop their executions.

Children have not reached a full understanding of their actions. No one should be sentenced to death for a crime they committed before the age of 18. However, in 24 US states people can be sentenced to death for crimes committed when they were children.

In 1989 the US Supreme Court ruled that it was not unconstitutional to execute mentally retarded people. Since then some 30 mentally impaired people have been executed.

Whether someone is sentenced to life or death can depend more on their lawyer than on the crime. A defendant who cannot afford an experienced and competent lawyer is more likely to be sentenced to death than someone who can.

One execution is one too many because, no matter how it's carried out, the death penalty is cruel, inhuman and degrading. It's an assault on human dignity and a violation of human rights.

I think it is embarrassing to watch how cynical politicians abuse the fear among their fellow citizens by using the death penalty in their campaigns and thereby sacrificing human lives in their struggle to gain political power. When governor Bill Clinton during his primaries campaign in New Hampshire in 1992 announced that he had to go back home to Arkansas to be there at the execution of Rickey Ray Rector, a black inmate who was so retarded that he asked the staff on death row to put the dessert from his last meal aside so that he could have it after his execution. And Rector is only one of many mentally retarded who have been sentenced to death.

Not to speak of the mentally ill. Emile Duhamel, a severely mentally ill death row inmate, died in the beginning of July 1998 on Texas death row. Duhamel could not understand where he was or what it meant to be executed.

Although almost all civilized nations agree that the execution of juveniles is completely out of the question a considerable number of American states are ready also to kill inmates who were children when they committed the crime.

One thing is that American politicians – in spite of all international laws and treaties and critics from the UN – claim the right to kill their fellow citizens.

It is also done without much effort to guarantee a fair trial for the defendant. Unless you are an O.J. Simpson and have the money to hire a dream-team you are in deep trouble if you are being charged with a capital crime as your risk of having an ineffective defense counsel are quite considerable.

And with new rules for review of death penalty cases the politicians have minimized your chances to have your sentence overthrown, even if you are able to provide new evidence demonstrating your innocence.

But not only money beats justice in the American court rooms. The color of skin also does; both the color of the defendant and the skin of the victim.

And if insufficient funding and racism is not enough to ensure a death penalty verdict there are other ways. There are numerous examples of miscarriage of justice, where police and prosecutors produce false evidence, suppress evidence in favor of the defendant and provide perjured testimony, not to mention "purchase" of evidence from so-called expert witnesses.

Of course this special kind of "justice" has sent a considerable number of persons to death row in spite of their innocence, and since 1976 seventy-five inmates have been released from death row after it was shown that they had been wrongfully convicted. Proponents of the death penalty claim that this only demonstrates that the system works. But the truth is than many of these releases are not due to the efficiency of the judicial system, but to the intervention of law students, journalists and others who care more than those who are supposed to defend the rights of the inmates.

And the rest of the four thousand inmates on death row do not have big chances to leave if alive. In recent years more and more has been done to deprive the inmates of their constitutional rights to a fair appeal or review of their case, and in some states not even new evidence of innocence is enough to cancel their appointment with the executioner.

For those inmates who are not so lucky to get off the death row the time until their execution is a life like human garbage where they are deprived of the most fundamental human rights and being subject to brutal treatment, no matter how humane it seems on paper.

And to fulfill this degradation of human life many states invite the relatives of the victim – whom many politicians and prosecutors try to convey the delusion that the execution will bring them closure – to come and witness and celebrate the execution, a perversion which the USA shares only with countries like China and a few Arabic nations.

A widespread pattern of misconduct and mistakes has landed at least nine innocent men on death row in Illinois. Fortunately, these men were able to prove their innocence before their irrevocable sentences were carried out. But how many of the one hundred sixty-five other condemned men and women in Illinois are innocent? How many of them were wrongfully convicted and sentenced to death? Unfortunately, no one knows.

•**Perry Cobb** and **Darby Tillis** were finally acquitted in 1987 after five trials and many years on death row for a murder they did not commit. By the sheerest of chance, a new witness came forward after reading a magazine article that established their innocence. This type of mistake also led to false convictions of **Dennis Williams** and **Verneal Jimerson** in Cook County, as well as **Joseph Burrows** in Iroquois County, **Gary Gauger,** in McHenry County, and **Carl Lawson** in downstate St. Clair County.

•**Rolando Cruz** was freed after spending twelve years on death row for a crime he didn't commit. His case points to the fact that dishonest police and prosecutors have shown an appalling willingness to break the law themselves in order to obtain murder convictions and death sentences against innocent persons.

•**Racism** still plays a significant role in the process, as studies show that the death penalty is far more likely to be sought by prosecutors, and imposed by juries, when the victim is white and the defendant is black.

•Some indigent defendants in Illinois end up on death row simply because they were represented by incompetent or underpaid lawyers who lacked the skills or resources to mount and effective defense.

Let me put some statistics into your head just to give you an idea of the way things are right now in the country. Currently there are thirty-six states that retain the death penalty: Twenty-seven states use lethal injection, twelve use the electric chair, seven use the gas chamber, four still use the old noose-and-rope technique of hanging, and Utah still uses the firing squad, though only once.

For members of society who are retentionists and want to keep the death penalty, its deterrent effects are one of their primary arguments. But there is no conclusive evidence that the death penalty deters would-be criminals from their act of violence.

But there is nothing that can shut a person up quicker than plain, hard facts. According to the death penalty information center, since the death penalty was reinstated in 1976, the executions per year have gone up, but so has the murder rate per 100,000. It's also shown that death penalty states often have a higher murder rate than their non-death penalty neighbors. Iowa, for example, has less than two murders per 100,000 people, while its retentionist neighbor Missouri has a murder rate of nine per 100,000. It's also shown that in some states the murder rate increases more during execution years than non-executioners do.

The fact is, that there is no deterrent value in the death penalty.

Many people seem to think that by killing a person we are saving the taxpayer's money. But in reality, holding a prisoner on death row is more expensive then holding them in prison without the possibility of parole.

It costs up to three times the amount to keep a prisoner on death row than it would be to keep them in prison for the rest of their lives. Capital cases cost at least $2.6 million more per execution in some states.

Speaking which, the poor and mentally ill are being sent to death row much quicker that the rich. Why? Because they cannot afford adequate council. They are sent to the court and usually end up with a court appointed attorney, who could usually care less what happens in the case. Most of them also have very little experience in capital cases.

The Constitution says everyone's entitled to the attorney of his or her choice. The Constitution doesn't say the lawyer has to be awake. Judge Doug Shaver, presiding over the trial of McFarland, who, who is now on Texas Death Row after a trial where his attorney fell asleep several times.

The majority of the appeal courts of the USA will not look at the simple question of whether a death row inmate is innocent of the crime for which he or she was sentenced to die. Their main concern seems to be whether the legal procedures and the constitution were followed.

This is not a perfect system. Yes, you are going to have mistakes. But with any system that's possible and (the execution of an innocent person) is an acceptable risk. Former Georgia Attorney General Michael Bowers, who ran for governor.

"It's kind of ironic that the man who signed a law speeding up the death penalty cases and undermining habeas corpus goes lecturing anyone on human rights." This former professor of constitutional law has signed into law more violations of human rights than any recent president. Leonard Weinglass, attorney on death penalty cases, commenting on Clintons visit to China.

"You always lose some soldiers in any war." Sen. David Jaye, R-Washington Township, commenting on the risk of executing an innocent.

I am not convinced that capital punishment, in and of itself, is a deterrent to crime because most people do not think about the death penalty before they commit a violent or capital crime. Willie L. Williams, Police Chief, Los Angeles, CA.

One area of law more than any other besmirches the constitutional vision of human dignity... The barbaric death penalty violates our Constitution. Even the most vile murderer does not release the state form its obligation to respect dignity, for the state does not honor the victim by emulating his murderer. Capital punishment's fatal flaw is that is treats people as objects to be toyed with and discarded...One day the court will outlaw the death penalty. Permanently. William J. Brennan, Jr., retired Supreme Court Justice, 1996.

The cop paused and stared at the two of them, the black man in his white T-shirt and shabby jeans, the little white man with the thick glasses and the ballooning belly. "One of you two is gonna hang for this," said the cop. Then he turned to Brandley. "Since you're the nigger, you're elected." Nick Davies in "White Lies", quoting testimony leading to Clarence Brandley's release.

Capital punishment: Them without the capital get the punishment. John Spenkelink's last words at his electrocution.

There are at least three hundred fifty documented cases that show that innocent people were sent to death row. With the recent applications of DNA tests more and more on death row are shown to be innocent.

Most of the democratic nations including Canada have abolished the death penalty. Even Russia has commuted all of the death sentences of its prisoners and has stopped all executions.

Until Death Do Us Part.

There is a growing awareness that serious, reversible error permeates America's death penalty system, putting innocent lives at risk, heightening the suffering of victims, leaving killers at large, wasting tax dollars, and failing citizens, the courts and the justice system.

68% of all death verdicts imposed and fully reviewed during the 1973-2003 study period were reversed by courts due to serious errors.

Analyses presented reveal that 76% of the reversals at the two appeal stages where data are available for study were because defense lawyers had been egregiously incompetent, police and prosecutors had suppressed exculpatory evidence or committed other professional misconduct, jurors had been misinformed about the law, or judges and jurors had been biased. Half of those reversals tainted the verdict finding the defendant guilty of a capital crime as well as the verdict imposing the death penalty. 82% of the cases sent back for retrial at the second appeal phase ended in sentences less than death, including 9% that ended in not guilty verdicts.

Why does our death penalty system make so many mistakes? How can these mistakes be prevented, if at all?

Heavy and indiscriminate use of the death penalty creates a high risk that mistakes will occur. The more often officials use the death penalty, the wider the range of crimes to which it is applied, and the more it its imposed for offenses that are not highly aggravated, the greater the risk that capital convictions and sentences will be seriously flawed.

Most disturbing of all they permit that he **conditions evidently pressuring counties and states to overuse the death penalty and thus increase the risk of unreliability and error include** race, politics and poorly performing law enforcement systems. Error is linked to overburdened and underfunded state courts.

The higher the rate at which a state or county imposes death verdicts, the greater the probability that <u>each</u> death verdict will have to be reversed because of serious error.

Four disturbing conditions are strongly associated with high rates of serious capital error. Their common capacity to pressure officials to use the death penalty aggressively in response to fears about crime and regardless of how weak any particular case for a death verdict is, may explain their relationship to high capital error rates.

...The warm water feels wonderful, a little more heat would feel good...

Chapter IX
Police Power

"In Germany, the Nazis first came for the communists, and I didn't speak up because I wasn't a communist. Then they came for the Jews, and I didn't speak up because I wasn't a Jew. Then they came for the trade unionists, and I didn't speak up because I wasn't a trade unionist. Then they came for he Catholics, and I didn't speak up because I was a Protestant. Then they came for me, and by that time there was no one left to speak for me."

-Rev. Martin Niemoeller (sent to Dachau, 1938)

We Serve ourselves and don't Protect

Some of you may remember the cop walking the street in your neighborhood. He knew everybody good and bad and he was our friend.

Gone are the days when you could trust most police.

The newspapers and the TV is replete on a daily basis of the corruption in the various police departments. The suburban cop who sits all day in his squad car hiding in a private parking lot to catch people exceeding the arbitrary 30 mile per hour limit.

The cop that plants a joint in your ashtray to arrest you on his lie.

The woman who is pulled over just because she is pretty and the cop makes her perform an indecent act on him under the threat of a phony arrest.

Go to a store and pay with a twenty dollar bill that you received in change at the gas station a few minutes ago. The bill is an apparent forgery, but you get arrested for trying to pass a forged twenty-dollar bill.

Laws are enforced that can incarcerate you for 90 days or pay a $500.00 fine for feebling a parking meter.

Play your radio a little loud and you can get arrested.

Even the Supreme Court stated in an opinion that the police duty is not to protect.

The simple citizens you and I have become to fear the police, while real criminals have come not to and have no reason to . The police have become the antagonists.

They carry guns, use military technology against civilians, are given special privileges, have extraordinary responsibility, and are entrusted with the protection of society as a whole-but do some Cops really break the Law? We know they do-and often. Some of the best criminals work in law enforcement, and you fate lies in their integrity.

Mind you-the broad brush does not apply here. Merely being a cop doesn't mean a person is all bad, however, the "blue wall of silence" tends to show the "good" cops supporting the "bad" cops so as not to betray their brethren.

Business as Usual

A federal jury found three Gresham District police officers guilty of scheming to rob undercover agents posing as drug dealers.

"Corruption will not be tolerated, and we will do everything to root it out," Assistant U.S. Attorney Jerome Krulewitch said.

Tactical unit officers in the South Side district, and one other were convicted of conspiracy to commit extortion in connection with a plot to steal $23,000 from undercover police during corruption stings set up by investigators. They also were convicted of carrying out the robberies, illegal use of a firearm, and violating the civil rights of the robbery victims. Jurors also found two cops guilty of drug possession. And one was convicted of a separate charge of drug distribution.

The convictions come as federal prosecutors ready their case against seven Austin District tactical officers, who are accused of robbery, gun crimes and shaking down an undercover FBI agent posing as a drug dealer.

Cops Other Alleged Victims

The most terrifying ordeal in the life of the Rev. Jorge Morales, he said, came at the hands of a man who had more than bravado. He had a weapon, a badge and the protection of a blue wall.

"These memories are still very vivid," said Morales, pastor of First Congregational Church in Humbolt Park. "I have lived with fear for many years."

Joseph Miedzianowski, A Chicago police officer serving in the Gang Crimes Unit, allegedly brutalized morales in front of his own church. Morales says his life was nearly ruined by a yearlong review process following his complaints against Miedzianowski, a process that Morales says placed him, not the officer, on trial.

On Wednesday, federal authorities charged Miedzianowski, a 22-year veteran of the force, with another serious form of misconduct. They say he sold his badge to drug dealers for $12,000 per month. A year later, authorities charge, Miedzianowski graduated, gaining control of a Chicago drug ring that poured crack cocaine, heroin and guns onto the city streets.

Federal officials said the case involves some of the most serious allegations of police corruption they've ever seen.

Now Morales and others who have dealt with Miedzianowski are wondering how a police officer facing serious charges of misconduct throughout his career could have stayed on the streets for so long.

"Today we see that this system of the police policing themselves does not work," Morales said from his church. Miedzianowski survived the police review process. He got his job back, along with back pay, despite a recommendation from then-Police Supt., Fred Rice that he be fired

Almost seven years ago, ATF agent Diane Klipfel thought she was working with a corrupt Chicago cop, a gang unit officer she believed stole thousands of dollars recovered in a raid. Klipfel, a supervising agent with the Federal Bureau of Alcohol, Tobacco and firearms, blew the whistle on that cop-Joseph Miedzianowski-and her life became a living hell.

"Your husband and you both work in the city. Remember that. Always remember that," Klipfel said an angry Miedzianowski told her, after she confronted him about the alleged theft.

In a federal lawsuit against ATF and the City of Chicago, Klipfel said Miedzianowski became irate that day, kicking the door of her car. "And you better watch you darling kids," he allegedly threatened. "Your house could get lit up."

Miedzianowski was accused of similar conduct, with federal authorities alleging he enforced his reign in a drug ring with threats of serious violence, including murder.

Klipfel claims in the suit that her supervisors didn't believe her charges against Miedzianowski, and that they didn't believe her husband, fellow ATF agen Michael Casali, who also suspected Miedzianowski.

Miedzianowski again survived, with police officials determining there wasn't enough evidence against him. But the Klipfels claim they were demoted, and their badges and guns stripped from them as they faced their own internal charges stemming from Miedzianowski's allegations against them.

Even though they won a case in front of the federal Merit Systems Protecting Board that said they were legitimate whistleblowers and were wronged by the agency.

"We were never vindicated until yesterday because for seven years they were liars," their attorney, Sally Saltzberg, said. "My clients are very happy."

Meanwhile, rumors swirled that several other Chicago police officers are targeted in the probe, but sources familiar with the case say there is only one officer, referred to in the FBI affidavit as "Individual B," currently under scrutiny, as well as a correctional officer with the Cook County Sheriff's Department.

Sources familiar with the case also said some of the Miedzianowski's 11 co-defendants are expected to cooperate with authorities. Those deals could become apparent: detention hearings, originally scheduled for next week, are expected to be moved up.

$100,000 award in shooting by cop.

A federal jury on Friday awarded $100,000 to the family of a Hoffman Estates man who was shot and killed by a police officer.

The award, however, is less thank the $2 million the family was seeking and less than the $545,000 the family received from a different federal jury. The first verdict was overruled because of an error by the trial judge.

The jury ruled that officer Marylu Redmond, who has since retired, violated the constitutional rights of Ricky Allen, 31, when she killed him with a single gunshot to the neck. But in ruling in favor of Redmond and Hoffman Estates on a wrongful death count, the jury determined her actions were not "willful an wanton." The first jury had ruled against the defendants on both counts.

Redmond, responding to a fight at the Canyon Estates apartment complex, shot Allen because he was about to stab another man, she testified. But the lawsuit filed on behalf of Allen's two sons charged that Allen was unarmed and that Hoffman Estates police planted a knife next to the body to cover for Redmond. Lawyers for the family said the verdict indicates the jury believed their version of events. But Gregory Rogus, the lawyer for Redmond and Hoffman Estates, said the jury also would have ruled for the Allen family on the wrongful death count of it had determined the knife was planted.

The decision also means Hoffman Estates must pay the family's legal costs, which their lawyers said would far exceed $300,000.

Cruelty in Control?

Police use of weapons intended to stun or temporarily disable suspects- such as chemical sprays and Electro-shock weapons have also led to serious injuries and deaths.

29-year-old woman, Kimberly Lashon Watkins, died in Pomona, California, after being shot by police with a taser – a hand-held device which shoots two barbed hooks attached to wires into the victim through which a high voltage current is transmitted.

The use of so-called "less than lethal" weapons is increasing- at least 3,000 police departments authorize the use of Oleoresin Capsicum (OC) spray. The use of these technologies, some of which invite abuse, is of particular concern give the absence of adequate monitoring systems and national standards for their use.

It is time that the US government took steps to end abusive practices by police and to make police forces more accountable. As a first step the authorities should establish effective independent bodies to monitor police use of force.

Murder Conviction Thrown Out by Court

A federal appeals court overturned the murder conviction of a Chicago man who has spent the last 20 years in prison, finding that the evidence against him was thin and that his defense attorney erred badly.

Ramiro Hernandez, serving a 50-year sentence for his 1979 conviction in the murder of Jorge Orosco, must be released or granted a new trial within 120 days of the ruling, the U.S. 7th Circuit Court of Appeals in Chicago ruled.

Spokeswoman for Illinois Attorney General and Cook County State's Attorney declined to say whether prosecutors would set a new trial.

The decision, written by the Chief Judge, said, "no reasonable jury could have convicted Hernandez" on the scant evidence presented at trial.

The Chief Judge also suggested that a key witness was the actual killer and got a sweetheart deal in return for implicating Hernandez. He also said the prosecutor's closing argument in the case was "reprehensible," though not a factor in the decision.

Gestapo USA

We have all seen in movies the depiction of German Gestapo and SS people blasting their ways into people's homes, killing or torturing them, and on nothing more than the suspicion they might be or might be hiding

Jews during WWII. We have seen it and thought of how awful it was and that it is just a movie we are watching.

Many of us have read the book and/or seen the movie, 1984, written by George Orwell. Many were frightened by the movie but calmed with the thought it was make believe, that it could never happen in the good old US of A. It was science fiction and always would be.

But, as time went on, we also found that good science fiction was the best predictor of the future. What was considered so far out as to being impossible is now reality. Space vehicles, television, computers, automobiles, individual flight equipment, and so on are common every day actualities to this society. It is a society of youth who have never seen or heard of what was considered modern 40 to 60 years ago, just as society 50 years from now will not be able to imagine sitting at a computer desk using a keyboard.

Just as modern inventions and the like have advanced far beyond the science fiction of my youth, so has society reached, maybe even exceeded, Orwell's Big Brother concept.

Mario Paz thought he was safe after migrating to this country legally. After all, he now lived in the United States of America, the melting pot of the world, the haven of freedom and individual liberty. That is, right up to the moment bullets tore first through the locks on his doors and windows and then through his body leaving him a lifeless lump of human tissue.

Twenty law enforcement officers, members of the El Monte police force, blew the locks off of the Paz residence and kept shooting as they entered while the family slept. Mr. Paz was shot twice in the back and his then widow, taken to the police station wearing only panties and a towel someone threw over her to cover her breasts.

Six others in his family were also incarcerated, none of who at had anything to do with dealing or using drugs. Neither a trace of drugs, nor any other evidence of wrong doings could be found in the home.

It was still up to those who lived to prove their innocence. Mrs. Paz had a receipt from the bank clearly showing Mr. Paz had withdrawn his savings because of the fear of Y2K losses. Had he only been able to foresee it would lead to his violent death by law enforcement organization suspecting he was a drug dealer.

You know what, though, even had he been a drug dealer, there is a proper way to investigate and it is not to force entry while blasting away indiscriminately into a home. There is always the risk of innocents being killed, just as happened. But, that is another story, a story that is being repeated all over this nation. Not only that but the war against drugs will not be won by needless slaughtering of innocent, or guilty people.

We think we have privacy and that our homes are our castles, our place of solitude away from the rest of the world, a place we can relax without any worries of intrusion. Well, it just isn't true. The police can receive an anonymous tip and act on the tip without any investigation whatsoever, just as with Mr. Paz. Even worse, they can just get mad at a person and take actions pretending to be against drugs while actually knowing the person is innocent.

You may be sitting watching TV, having sex eating your dinner, and suddenly, find yourself in a hail of bullets fired by the very people hired to protect you and your rights. But, your rights mean little to these 'law enforcement' agencies.

You may be traveling and find yourself pulled over, your vehicle confiscated, your money taken, your family terrorized, and be subjected to the possibility of some trigger-happy freak wearing a badge killing you or other members of your family. It means little to them to stop and harass innocent people. Their pleasure comes from holding a loaded gun, either literally or figuratively, to other people's heads.

And, what will happen to the 'upstanding' officers who do kill or terrorize or beat the crap out of you and yours? Well, here are the comments of the chief of the El Monte.

El Monte Assistant Police Chief Bill Ankeny said an explosive entry is a standard SWAT procedure and can involve opening a door with a battering ram or a round of gunfire.

"We throw flash-bang grenades. We bust open the doors. You've seen it on TV," Ankeny said. "We do bang on the door and make an announcement- 'it's the police'-but it kind of runs together. If you're sitting on the couch, it would be difficult to get to the door before they knock it down." (No doubt if you did approach the door to answer it or defend your home, you would be blasted into oblivion.)

What we see on TV are actual drug dealers and they have been properly investigated. We do not see innocents shot to death on TV.

First of all, without any evidence whatsoever, they shouldn't even have been at the Paz residence. In reality, those in or near the residence thought a robbery was occurring. As a matter of fact, Myrna Serrano, 44, a friend of the family who lives in a converted garage at he front of the house, said she awoke to gunfire.

"I didn't even hear them say they were police," said Serrano, an employee at an art frame factory. "I thought they were thieves coming to rob us. I never dreamed they would be police busting into the house in camouflage and hoods."

Has the El Monte police force been held accountable? Not no, but hell no. Two officers were suspended but are back at work.

Has there been an apology for the death of Mr. Paz and the terrifying of the other residences? Certainly not.

John Bellizzi, director of the International Narcotics Enforcement Assn. in Albany, N.Y., said surprise is an essential element in getting evidence for SWAT team raids. Because of the danger of fighting drug dealers, officers "have to take serious precautions to safeguard their lives, and sometimes unforeseen things happen. It's unavoidable sometimes. These drug dealers are better equipped sometimes than the police are." As our President says they are just collateral damage.

No apology, no remorse. Just the American Gestapo in action.

Blasting away can always be avoided. No healthy person stays in their home 24 hours a day everyday of their lives, which means an arrest could be affected outside the home.

Second, the people weren't drug dealers. The people on this force think they have the right, though, to shoot away at any person without any proof of guilt. That means you, me and any people you know and don't know.

You don't have to be a criminal. All you have to be is someone picked out for terroristic actions to be taken against.

Then, you, if you survive their invasion, must prove your innocence.

That, ladies and gentlemen, is Gestapo America in action.

In Florida, prisoners call the scam "jumping on the bus," and it is as tantalizing as it is perverse. Inmates in federal prisons barter or buy information that only an insider to a crime could know- often from informants with access to confidential federal crime files.

The prisoners memorize it and get others to do the same. Then, to win sentence reductions, they testify about crimes that might have been committed while they were in prison, by people they've never met, in places they've never been. The scam succeeds only because of the tactic approval of federal law enforcement officers.

Cocaine smuggler Jose Goyriena used "jump on the bus" testimony to help federal prosecutors put three men in prison for life, and he was set to do it again for prosecutors who promised to cut his 27 year sentence by 10 years or more.

Prosecutors knew Goyriena had bragged about his lies to cellmates, but the prosecutors didn't reveal what they'd heard to any of the men Goyriena had helped condemn-violating one of the fundamental tenets of American justice. It was defense attorneys who finally caught Goyriena in the scam.

In this nation's war on crime, something has gone terribly wrong.

A two year investigation by the Post-Gazette found that powerful new federal laws designed to snare terrorists, drug smugglers and pornographers are being aimed at business owners, engineers and petty criminals.

Whether suspects are guilty has come to matter less than making sure they are indicted or convicted or, more likely, coerced into pleading guilty.

Promises of lenient sentences and huge government checks encourage criminals to lie on the witness stand. Prosecutors routinely withhold evidence that might help prove a defendant innocent. Some federal agents work so closely with their undercover informants that they become lawbreakers themselves.

Those who practice this misconduct are almost never penalized or disciplined. "It's a result-oriented process today, fairness be damned," said Robert Merkle, whom President Ronald Reagan appointed US Attorney.

"The philosophy of the past 10 to 15 years [is] that whatever works is what's right."

The Justice Department did not respond to questions the newspaper posed in writing about concerns raised in this series. Nor would it return phone calls requesting comments.

Thieves with Badges

-Under any other name, a thief is still a thief.

Has the American public gone nuts? Are people in government of the people, for the people, and by the people?

The answer to the first is the public must have gone nuts to allow the taking of liberty as is being done by the federal and state governments with the help of their law enforcement agencies.

The answer to the second is NO, at least in the cases for the people and of the people.

The most important statement concerning liberty in my mind comes from the Declaration of Independence, which, without a doubt, the finest piece of writing ever expressing the goal of a nation being born. It states: **"We hold these truths to be self-evident, that all men are created equal, that they are endowed by their Creator with certain unalienable Rights that among these are Life, Liberty and the pursuit of Happiness."**

Everything else in the original draft of the Constitution, the Bill of Rights, is there in support of this statement, a statement of the individual, not the majority.

In the introduction, the Declaration states: "When in the Course of Human events, it becomes necessary for one people to dissolve the political bands which have connected them with another, and to assume among the powers of the earth, the separate and equal station to which the Laws of Nature and of Nature's God entitle them…"

The key statement as to this essay is "…to which the Laws of Nature and of Nature's God entitle them…" The laws of nature are applied to the individual. Granted, the individual is part of society and, as long as all respect and observe the rights of all others, then all are free to pursue happiness by applying those God-given liberties as necessary.

If an individual violates the rights of others, then the laws of Man may be applied.

What this means is government cannot make laws removing rights of the individual under any pretext, such as "for the children" the so-called "drug war", or to control crime.

I would almost wager that as many people innocent people are terrorized, beaten, mugged, or killed by law enforcement people as have been killed by firearms in the hands of civilians in the last ten or so years. I use this comparison since their weapons stop legal resistance in many cases. We won't get the facts because law enforcement protects its own and without videos and the like by civilians, we might not even know of the cover-ups that we do know of. So watch yourself if you are ever stopped on a lonely stretch of road.

…Little bubbles rise in the water, how nice and warm…

Chapter X
Invasion of Privacy

"Necessity is the plea for every infringement of human freedom. It is the argument of tyrants; it is the creed of slaves."

-William Pitt

"A society that will trade a little liberty for a little order will lose both, and deserve neither."

-James Madison

Anyone who cares about the privacy of his personal data is fighting a multifront war against the government, and losing badly. The secretary of state sells driver's license photos to a private security firm. With computers making information easily cross-referenced and immediately accessible, the huge databases of information collected by the federal and state government on each of us have become windows into our lives. The privacy protections once in place are being swept aside in the name of convenience and expedience.

It may be reasonable for the government to gather highly personal financial and health records for the collection of taxes or to administer government health programs. But the danger is that once it's collected, it will be used for an unrelated purpose, a kind of "function creep" that has already begun.

For example, a new state law obligates the Department of Labor to sell the information it collects on the wages of Florida residents. Private credit agencies will be able to buy the information, with the consumer's consent, for income verification purposes. The government defends the new law by saying it's a consumer service. It will cut down on the wait for someone applying for a bank loan, because employment and salary verification would be done almost instantaneously. Nonetheless, employers report quarterly to the DOL about their employees' salaries so the state can assess unemployment taxes, not to assist consumer-reporting companies. Why should we trust that the government would stop there? Next it might decide to sell our salary data to telemarketers or retail firms.

In addition to selling our personal information to private industry, the government is increasingly demanding that private industry turn over what it collects on us.

A three-year-old law to crack down on deadbeat parents forces private businesses to submit reports on every new hire and the names, addresses, salaries and Social Security numbers of all their workers. The database, which has information on virtually every working American, was part of the welfare programs' revamping and is designed to catch parents who are delinquent in their child support. It's an unjustified electronic fishing expedition, because most American workers have no history of skipping out on child support.

Then, under the misnamed Bank Secrecy Act, the government has created a huge database of suspicious financial transactions by requiring banks to spy on their customers and report and dealings out of the ordinary-all without a court order or the knowledge of the customer.

Privacy.

What exactly is the right of privacy? Who has the right to know anything other than what I wish to tell them about myself?

Being a free person, protected by a Constitution providing guidelines thousands have fought for and defended with their lives, my idea of the right of privacy is no one has any right to know anything about me- except what I choose for them to know.

My neighbors haven't any right, my banker hasn't any right, other businesses, including any I might work for, haven't the right to know anything about me except, in the case of the bank, knowing who I am in order to keep track of my money or a place of business I work for knowing who to pay (the person, not the number)

Does that take a social security number?

Does any business have any right to know my social security number?

Does anyone have any right to know any medical facts about me, excepting a health insurer or my doctor/s?

Heck, do I even have to have a social security number? By law, no. By misapplication and perpetuation of a gigantic hoax, yes.

Just having my picture and description on a driver's license should suffice to prove my identity to any bank or any business in which I choose to write a check. Then, my signature will add additional verification. If either doesn't match, then the check shouldn't be cashed or anything about my account given to the person. Excepting, of course, if it is me.

I value my privacy and don't want it invaded by anyone other than those I choose to allow entering of my space. I don't want anyone so to speak, knowing anything about me. I am not a criminal and I do not break laws. I even stop at all stop signs.

If some one in the store asks me for my phone number I then ask if they will call me and then I tell them I don't have a phone. If they want to know my zip code I tell them I live in a P.O. Box.

How did we hand over our rights in the Constitution, the Declaration of Independence and the Bill of Rights to let the government take out rights.

People in government are not all powerful but the people of the nation are. We must control government and limit it as it was meant to be limited.

The movie of Welles' 1984 has kept me scared since I first saw it decades ago. And, now, here it is. And, quite frankly, I don't like it; whether it be a government database or some databases collected by some business who somehow believes it is their business to know my business.

Keeping track of known criminals I can understand. However, I am not a criminal but the government's increasing intrusion into my business, my right of privacy, is.

The money I earn legally is none of the government's business, including any interest earned from banks or income from investments as long as I pay the proper taxes. How I legally spend the money I earn is none of their business. If I sell something (legal, of course), it is none of the government's business.

You may think it doesn't matter if the government knows everything there is to know about you but it does. If liberties are taken, there will become a time when the Declaration of Independence, and the Constitution along with its amendments will be worthless documents gathering dust in forgotten crypts.

We will not be free people living in a Republic formed for the protection of the inalienable rights of the individual. Hearts of people who love the principles this nation was founded on will no longer swell when hearing the National Anthem, or the Pledge of Allegiance.

The flag will be the symbol of oppression; the symbol of greedy, powermad elected or appointed officials along with government's enforcers, such as CIA, FBI, DEA, TSA, AFF, US Post Office, and IRS employees.

These are the people, you know, who will be enforcing whatever the government does even if it is unconstitutional. And, then, as now, they will hold with no boundaries of misbehavior against people they suspect of wrongdoing.

The first, second, fourth, fifth, ninth, and tenth amendments are already being violated by a government that has vowed to protect and preserve the Constitution.

The Post Office only needs to know the address on an envelope matches the address of a specific building or post office box. It is actually none of their business who the mail is going to.

The FBI hasn't any right to know anything about any of your activities as long as it is legal yet the FBI maintains a file of every American that has a passport and the CIA is only supposed to operate outside the nation.

The DEA is supposed to be tracking drug trafficking and making arrests concerning illegal drugs. And, as with the FBI, CIA, and other law enforcement organizations, must make sure they have the right place before they bust in and start shooting or beating the crap out of the residents.

And with all these people armed, when they bust in, they presume guilt, not innocence. Some bit of misinformation in your database could lead to them invading your home and scaring the living hell out of you and your family at the least, or killing any or all of you family.

They enter with safeties off and fingers on triggers. What if they accidentally shoot the wrong people, innocent people? What does it take to cover it up? Nothing more than putting weapons in peoples' hands and going to the trunk of their car, or van, or pocket and 'hiding' some illegal drug in your home or on your person. The cover-up is so simple it is scary. Repeatedly we read that a vehicle is searched and nothing is found and only later a recheck finds drugs in the glove compartment.

Even if they don't shoot you or your family, it is now up to you to prove you innocence. Out system supposedly based of the presumption of innocence has been changed by inaccurate information to presumption of guilt. And sometimes the information comes from some drug-high informant. Or, just a neighbor that is mad at one of his neighbors.

Soon, when stopped on highways or city streets, should you refuse to allow your fingerprints to be taken in order to check databases, you may sit in jail for a couple of years.

Or, if there is any information that is inaccurate or been intentionally entered in your database illegally, you may be in the fight of your life trying to prove your innocence, a task that may have very well become impossible since all law enforcement and courts, regardless of the organization, will assume your guilt because – "how could the database be wrong?"

Maybe everyone should watch the movie, The Net, or any movie that has computer hacking in it, in particular, changing information on people.

Most of these possibilities would never have come about if it weren't for the government starting illegal databases on innocent, law-abiding, peace-loving citizens. Most would not have come about if we hadn't begun to be numbered an act I am now finding most offensive.

Can we fix it? Sure, but not with the hidden agendas and the people we now have in government remaining in control. Every problem is a possibility. In this case, we the people, just need to decide we want it fixed and all databases violating our rights to be totally, absolutely, even if it means melting down government computer hard-drives.

Probably too much to hope for so I guess I will pray for it instead. But you see I value my privacy, I want it, and I do not want a government to take from me what is inalienably mine.

Keep your identity to yourself

Your right to privacy has been stripped away. You cannot walk into your bank, or apply for a job, or access your personal computer, without undergoing the scrutiny of strangers. You cannot use a credit card to buy clothes to cover your body without baring your soul. Big Brother is watching as never before.

Encouraged by an act of Congress, Texas and California now demand thumbprints of applicants for drivers' licenses – treating all drivers as potential criminals.

Using a phony excuse about airplane security, airlines now demand identification like those licenses to make sure passengers don't exchange tickets to beat the company's rate-cutting promotions.

In the much-applauded pursuit of deadbeat dads, the Feds now demand that all employers inform the government of every new hire, thereby building a data base of who is working for whom that would be the envy of the KGB.

Although it makes it easier to zip through tolls at bridges and highways, electric eyes reading licenses plates help snoopers everywhere follow the movements of each driver and passenger.

Hooked on easy borrowing, consumers turn to plastic for their purchases, making records and sending electronic signals to telemarketers who track then down at home.

Stimulated by this demographic zeroing-in, Internet predators monitor your browsing, detect your interests, measure your purchases and even observe your expressed ideas.

Nor are Big Brothers limited to government and commerce. Your friends and neighbors secretly tape regular calls you make to them, and listen in to cellular calls to third parties, enhancing the video surveillance of public streets by government and private driveways by security agencies.

Enough. Fear of crime and terrorism has caused us to let down our guard against excessive intrusion into the lives of the law-abiding. The ease of minor borrowing and the transformation of shopping into recreation has addicted us to credit cards. Taken together, the fear and the ease make a map of our lives available to cops, crazies and con men alike.

Crime is real; some court-ordered taps of Mafiosi and surveillance cameras of high-violence playgrounds are justifiable. So are random drug and alcohol tests of nuclear-response teams. The Securities and Exchange Commission should monitor insider stock trades, and no sensible passenger minds the frisking for bombs at airports.

But doesn't this creeping confluence of government snooping, commercial tracking and cultural tolerance of eavesdropping threaten each individual America's personal freedom? And isn't it time to reverse that terrible trend toward national nakedness before it replaces privacy as an American value?

Here's how to snatch your identity back form the intruders:

•Sign as little as possible.
•Write you local legislator demanding that a Privacy Impact Statement be required before passage of any new law.
•Use snail mail, which is harder to intercept than e-mail. And resist mightily requests for your Social Security number.
•Persuade a foundation to issue a quarterly "Intrusion Index," measuring with scholarly authority the degree to which your privacy is being violated by polls and peepers.

•And, above all, pay cash. It costs less than borrowing and keeps you in control of your own records. Remember: Cash is the enemy of the intruders. Use it to buy back your freedom. Believe me, cash will be outlawed in the future.

There is no privacy

The federal government has a "fine" program in place to locate and seize the assets of divorced parents who skip out on paying child support. Every three months, banks are required to search their databases for names on lists provided by state agencies of deadbeat parents.

Unfortunately that costs money, and when state agencies fall to fund it, banks are often resistant to infringing on their profit margins. So they've found another solution within the law. They are simply handing over their entire financial records to the state so public agencies can do the searching. In California, for example, 197 out of 388 reporting financial institutions have simply turned over their customer databases to the state Franchise Tax Board. And that is without even being asked to do so. Think what cooperation that state could get if they said, "Please" and "Thank you" or "Hand it over now."

In the name of catching a few guilty people, the privacy of millions of innocent people is violated. Perversely, those innocent people may have the most to fear when their state adopts the Financial Institution Data Match program. For example, California government officials have already:

- Seized the bank accounts of innocent people. An investigation last fall discovered the Los Angeles County district attorney's office had seized the bank accounts of dozens of men who were later determined not to be the fathers of the children in question.
- Incredibly, politicians who enacted the Financial Institution Data Match program made it almost impossible to protect yourself from false seizures, because it's illegal for your bank to tell you that it has forwarded your account information to the state. The only thing that's private is the governments' power to snoop on you.
- Tried to sell millions of individual bank account records to private companies.
- Jailed innocent people. Last fall, an innocent California man was imprisoned for 26 hours before it was discovered that he had the same name as a man sought for back child support.

Only the government would claim it is protecting children by destroying their parents' privacy, seizing their bank accounts, and hauling them off to jail. If politicians really care about protecting children, let them prove it by abolishing the Deadbeat Dads Law and getting out of the bank spying business entirely.

An invasion of privacy

There is a proposal by the banking industry and the federal government known as "know your customer." The concept is to allow the banking industry to forward confidential, personal monetary information to the federal government. This would be done to find money-laundering schemes typically used by drug dealers.

This idea is utterly ludicrous! To put this under the guise of a "war on drugs" is basically insulting the intelligence of the public. Please tell me where the upstanding dug dealers are that will put hundreds of thousands of dollars in the bank! Are they doing it for the wonderful gifts? If they are, then the government should search houses to see who has an abundance of toasters, blenders and wall clocks.

Why would any corrupt individual send up a flag to the establishment, "Hey, I've got tons of money! I put it in a safe place, a bank." If the money were in a bank to begin with, then it is reportable income to the IRS. The IRS should be able to track "discrepancies" by auditing tax returns.

Dare to Declare Independence

The Declaration of Independence of the Thirteen Colonies

In Congress, July 4, 1776

The unanimous Declaration of the thirteen United States of America,

When in the course of human events, it becomes necessary for one people to dissolve the political bands which have connected them with another, and to assume among the powers of the earth, the separate and equal station to which the laws of nature and of nature's God entitle them, a decent respect to the opinions of mankind requires that they should declare the causes which impel them to the separation.

We hold these truths to be self-evident, that all men are created equal, that they are endowed by their Creator with certain unalienable Rights, that among these are life, liberty, and the pursuit of happiness. That to secure these rights, governments are instituted among men, deriving their just powers form the consent of the governed. That whenever any form of government becomes destructive of these ends, it is the right of the people to alter or to abolish it, and to institute new government, laying its foundation on such principles and organizing its powers in such form, as to then shall seem most likely to effect their safety and happiness.

Prudence, indeed, will dictate that governments long established should not be changed for light and transient causes; and accordingly all experience hath shown, that mankind are more disposed to suffer, while evils are sufferable, than to right themselves by abolishing the forms to which they are accustomed.

But when a long train of abuses and usurpations, pursuing invariably the same object evinces a design to reduce them under absolute despotism, it is their right, it is their duty, to throw off such government, and to provide new Guards for their future security.

Such has been the patient sufferance of these colonies; and such is now the necessity which constrains them to alter their former systems of government. The history of the present king of Great Britain is a history of repeated injuries and usurpations, all having in direct object the establishment of an absolute tyranny over these states. To prove this, let facts be submitted to a candid world.

He has refused his assent to laws, the most wholesome and necessary for the public good.

He has forbidden his governors to pass laws of immediate and pressing importance unless suspended in their operation till his assent should be obtained, and when so suspended, he has utterly neglected to attend to them.

He has refused to pass other laws for the accommodation of large districts of people, unless those people would relinquish the right of representation in the legislature, a right inestimable to them and formidable to tyrants only.

He has called together legislative bodies at places unusual, uncomfortable, and distant form the depository of their public records, for the sole purpose of fatiguing them into compliance with his measures.

He has dissolved representative houses repeatedly, for opposing with manly firmness his invasions on the rights of the people.

He has refused for a long time, after such a dissolution, to cause others to be elected; whereby the legislative powers, incapable of annihilation, have returned to the people at large for their exercise; the state remaining in the meantime exposed to all the dangers of invasion from without, and convulsions within.

He has endeavored to prevent the population of these states; for that purpose obstructing the laws for naturalization of foreigners; refusing to pass others to encourage their migrations hither, and raising the conditions of new appropriations of lands.

He has obstructed the administration of justice, by refusing his assent to laws for establishing judiciary powers.

He has made judges dependent on his will alone, for the tenure of their offices, and the amount and payment of their salaries.

He has erected a multitude of new offices, and sent hither swarms of officers to harass our people, and eat out their substance.

He has kept among us, in times of peace, standing armies, without the consent of our legislatures.

He has affected to render the military independent of and superior to the civil power.

He has combined with others to subject us to a jurisdiction foreign to out constitution and unacknowledged by out laws; giving his assent to their acts of pretended legislation:

- **For quartering large bodies of armed troops among us**
- **For protecting them by a mock trial form punishment for any murders which they should commit on the inhabitants of these states**

•For cutting off our trade with all parts of the world
•For imposing taxes on us without our consent
•For depriving us in many cases of the benefits of trial by jury
•For transporting us beyond seas to be tried for pretended offenses
•For abolishing the free system of English laws in a neighboring Province, establishing therein an arbitrary government, and enlarging its Boundaries so as to render it at once as example and for instrument for introducing the same absolute rule into these colonies
•For taking away our charters, abolishing our most valuable laws and altering fundamentally the forms of our governments
•For suspending our own legislatures, and declaring themselves invested with power to legislate for us in all cases whatsoever.

He has abdicated government here by declaring us out of his protection and waging war against us.

He has plundered our seas, ravaged our coasts, burnt our towns, and destroyed the lives of our people.

He is at this time transporting large armies of foreign mercenaries to complete the works of death, desolation and tyranny, already begun with circumstances of cruelty and perfidy scarcely paralleled in the most barbarous ages, and totally unworthy the Head of a civilized nation.

He has constrained our fellow citizens taken captive on the high seas to bear arms against their country, to become the executioners of their friends and brethren, or to fall themselves by their hands.

He has excited domestic insurrections amongst us, and has endeavored to bring on the inhabitants of our frontiers, the merciless Indian savages, whose known rule of warfare is an undistinguished destruction of all ages, sexes and conditions.

In every stage of these oppressions we have petitioned for redress in the most humble terms. Our repeated petitions have been answered

only by repeated injury. A prince, who character is thus marked by every act, which may define a tyrant, is unfit to be the ruler of a free people.

Nor have we been wanting in attentions to our British brethren.

> **•We have warned them from time to time of attempts by their legislature to extend an unwarrantable jurisdiction over us.**
> **•We have reminded them of the circumstances of our emigration and settlement here.**
> **•We have appealed to heir native justice and magnanimity, and we have conjured them by the ties of our common kindred to disavow these usurpations, which would inevitably interrupt our connections and correspondence.**

They too have been deaf to the voice of justice and of consanguinity. We must, therefore, acquiesce in the necessity, which denounces our separation, and hold them, as we hold the rest of mankind, enemies in war, in peace friends.

We, therefore, the representatives of the United States of America, in General Congress, assembled, appealing to the Supreme Judge of the world for the rectitude of our intentions, do, in the name, and by the authority of the good people of these colonies, solemnly publish and declare, that these united colonies are, and of right ought to be free and independent states; that they are absolved from all allegiance to the state of Great Britain is and ought to be totally dissolves; and that as free and independent states, they have full power to levy war, conclude peace, contract alliances, establish commerce and to do all other acts and things which independent states may of right do. And for the support of this Declaration, with a firm reliance on the protection of Divine Providence, we mutually pledge to each other our lives, our fortunes, and our sacred honor.

Privacy and Human Rights
An International Survey of Privacy Laws and Practice

Privacy is a fundamental human right recognized in the UN Declaration of Human Rights, the International Covenant on Civil and Political Rights and in many other international and regional treaties. Privacy underpins human dignity and other key values such as freedom of association and freedom of speech. It has become one of the most important human rights issues of the modern age.

Nearly every country in the world recognizes a right of privacy explicitly in their Constitution. At a minimum, these provisions include rights of inviolability of the home and secrecy of communications. Most recently written Constitutions such as South Africa and Hungary's include specific rights to access and control one's personal information.

In many of the countries where privacy is not explicitly recognized in the Constitution, such as the United States, Ireland and India, the courts have found that right in other provisions. In many countries, international agreements that recognize privacy rights such as the International Covenant on Civil and Political Rights or the European Convention on Human Rights have been adopted into law.

In the early 1970's countries began adopting broad laws intended to protect individual privacy. Throughout the world, there is a general movement towards the adoption of comprehensive privacy laws that set a framework for protection. Most of these laws are based on models introduced by the Organization of Economic Cooperation and Development and the Council of Europe.

Threats to Privacy

The increasing sophistication of information technology with its capacity to collect, analyze and disseminate information on individuals has introduced a sense of urgency to the demand of legislation. Furthermore, new developments in medical research and care, telecommunications, advanced transportation systems and financial transfers have dramatically increased the level of information generated by each individual. Computers linked together by high-speed networks with advanced processing systems can create comprehensive dossiers on any person without the need for a single central computer system. New technologies developed by the defense industry are spreading into law enforcement, civilian agencies, and private companies.

Defining Privacy

Of all the human rights in the international catalogue, privacy is perhaps the most difficult to define and circumscribe. Privacy has roots deep in history. The Bible has numerous references to privacy. There was also substantive protection of privacy in early Hebrew culture, Classical Greece and ancient China. These protections mostly focused on the right to solitude. Definitions of privacy very widely according to context and environment. In many countries, the concept has been fused with Data Protection, which interprets privacy in terms of management of personal information. Outside this rather strict context, privacy protection is frequently seen as a way of drawing the line at how far society can intrude into a person's affairs. It can be divided into the following facets:

- Information Privacy, which involves the establishment of rules governing the collection and handling of personal data such as credit information and medical records.
- Bodily privacy, which concerns the protection of people's physical selves against invasive procedures such as drug testing and cavity searches.
- Privacy of communication, which covers the security and privacy of mail, telephones, email and other forms of communication.
- Territorial privacy, which concerns the setting of limits on intrusion into the domestic and other environments such as the workplace or public space.

The Right of Privacy

Privacy can be defined as a fundamental human right. The law of privacy can be traced as far back as 1361, when the Justices of the Peace Act in England provided for the arrest of peeping toms and eavesdroppers. In 1765, British Lord Camden, striking down a warrant to enter a house and seize papers wrote, "We can safely say there is no law in this country to justify the defendants in what they have done; if there is, it would have to destroy all the comforts of society, of papers are often the dearest property any man can have." Parliamentarian William Pitt wrote, "The poorest man may in his cottage bid defiance to all the force of the Crown. It may be frail; its roof may shake; the wind may blow through it; the rain may enter

– but the King of England cannot enter; all his forces dare not cross the threshold of the ruined tenement."

The modern privacy benchmark at an international level can be found in the 1948 Universal Declaration of Human Rights, which specifically protected territorial and communications privacy.

Article 12 states:

No one should be subjected to arbitrary interference with his privacy, family, home or correspondence, nor to attacks on his honor or reputation. Everyone has the right to the protection of the law against such interferences or attacks.

On the regional level, these rights are becoming enforceable. The 1950 Convention for the Protection of Human Rights and Fundamental Freedoms, article 8 states:

> (1)Everyone has the right to respect for his private and family life, his home and his correspondence.
> (2)There shall be no interference by a public authority with the exercise of this right except as in accordance with the law and is necessary in a democratic society in the interests of national security, public safety or the economic well-being of the country, for the prevention of disorder or crime, for the protection of health or morals, or for the protection of the rights and freedoms of others.

Carnivore

"Carnivore" is a new FBI system—software installed on a dedicated PC—that can be set up in an Internet service provider's (ISP) location to scan all incoming and outgoing e-mail wiretap.

According to the ACLU and other privacy groups, Carnivore violates the search and seizure clauses of the Fourth Amendment by capturing the e-mail addresses of both the sender and receiver, as well as the subject of all e-mails serviced by the ISP's e-mail servers.

Opponents of Carnivore argue that the system is more intrusive than a telephone wiretap in that Carnivore is controlled completely by the law enforcement agency. In a telephone wiretap, the tap is maintained and controlled by the telephone company. Privacy groups argue that Carnivore is the equivalent of a super wiretap capable of listening to all calls placed by all customers of the telephone service.

Carnivore is Not Echelon

In terms of privacy concerns as well as raw technological power, Carnivore looks like a toy compared to Echelon. Echelon is almost certainly the world's most sophisticated network monitoring system and, if anyone who feels uncomfortable with the secrecy surrounding Carnivore should feel downright paranoid where Echelon is concerned.

The Echelon system was allegedly developed in secret during the Cold War by the USA and UK, with work beginning perhaps as early as the 1940's Canada, Australia, and New Zealand later "joined" the network. The Echelon network ostensibly monitors worldwide communications including telephone calls, faxes, and e-mail. To do this, it allegedly utilizes satellite-monitoring stations. It has been claimed that Echelon snoops on "billions of messages per hour."

Yes, we have allowed Big Brother to take away our privacy.

...Wow, it's now a steam room atmosphere, hot, but it really gets the pores open...

Chapter XI Dealing with the Internal Revenue Service

"Ninety-eight percent of the adults in this county are decent, hardworking, honest Americans. It's the other lousy two percent that get all the publicity. But then, we elected them."

-Lily Tomlin

"It is error alone which needs the support of government. Truth can stand by itself."

-Thomas Jefferson

IRS-Guilty until you prove your innocence and then it may be too late.

In 23 years of practice before the Internal Revenue Service, I could write volumes of books citing Internal Revenue Service abuse, vendettas and stupidity.

I personally saw as Internal Revenue Service collector padlock a bakery on Friday 8:25 a.m. with the shelves filled with bread, the display case filled with cakes and cookies and the back room filled with products for the weekend.

The owner owed one thousand twelve dollars in back taxes and the Internal Revenue Service collector would not come back or accept a pre-dated check.

She took twelve dollars and change out of the register, red tagged and padlocked the shop, which we could not open until Tuesday by court order. Then, all the products were spoiled and four days of revenue was lost.

I have seen a Revenue Agent's report citing no need to inform a quote "Tax Protester" who was in Federal Prison to inform him that the IRS was selling his house since in the Revenue Agent's mind what could the owner do while in prison.

It is a known fact that red-faced Internal Revenue Service agents and Justice Department lawyers voiced to get even when a Judge held against them. Within 30 days the Judge was being audited.

There is no federal agency more feared by the American people than the Internal Revenue Service. They have the power to destroy a person, his business and family.

Ex-President Clinton has used the Internal Revenue Service as a tool to get even with his enemies. His Gestapo have investigated Billy Dale, the White House Travel Office Director, when he went public after being fired by Hillary. Paula Jones received her secret-police notice a few days after she rejected his offer to settle the sexual harassment case. It even includes his ex-girlfriend, Elizabeth Word Gracer, after she went public with her story of their affair. Any organization that has opposed the president's view also received their notices.

The Internal Revenue Service admitted that it ranked employees on their aggressiveness in collecting delinquent taxes and in conducting seizures of property, a practice that violated laws intended to protect Americans from overzealous tax enforcement.

The use of quotas and statistics to evaluate Internal Revenue Service employees is explicitly banned by federal law, based on concerns that such measures would foster abusive tax collection practiced. But the investigation found that the Internal Revenue Service has used statistics to evaluate the performance of employees and supervisors. It also ranked the tax collections of its district offices.

Allegations that the Internal Revenue Service was violating the law and its own internal policies were first raised at Senate Finance Committed hearings held by Sen. William V. Roth, R-Del.

Anonymous Internal Revenue Service agents, testifying behind a screen, said at the hearing that they were coming under increasing pressure to browbeat and abuse taxpayers to inflate their office's national rankings. Internal Revenue Service officials said they were not preciously aware of such allegations and vowed to investigate the charges.

The Internal Revenue Service report corroborated those allegation, finding that the Internal Revenue Service has erected a system that focused on capturing delinquent tax dollars with scant regard to whether taxpayers are treated fairly or their rights are protected.

"Statistics drive the organization…The tail wags the dog," one Internal Revenue Service inspector testified.

The inspector and the five other secret witnesses, concealed by devices usually reserved for organized crime hearings, also asserted that the agency retaliates against whistleblowers and does too little in investigating internal misconduct. "Retaliation in our office is almost on a daily basis," said another witness, described as a long-term revenue officer.

Still another witness, identified as a criminal investigator, said the agency's "climate and culture" often hinders investigations of employee wrongdoing. IRS managers have weakened administrative sanctions to the point "where they have no effect in controlling employee misconduct," the witness said.

"Numbers are extremely important…They are constantly comparing one group to another group and one employee to another employee," said the witness, identified as a 25-year veteran. "This type of behavior leads to very adverse collection practices."

Avoiding Tax Audits

There are two pieces of advice that you should keep in mind about audits:

- If you've done your homework, kept good records, and your return is truthful, you don't have anything to worry about.
- It's better not to be audited.

First, let's talk about the second point.

The average taxpayer has a very small chance of being audited. But if you are self-employed, your return is definitely not typical of the millions of returns filed by employees. You may be waving some red flags at the IRS and increasing your chances of being audited.

The IRS does not provide details on its audit criteria – in fact, they are a closely guarded secret. However, we offer the following suggestions for minimizing your risk:

•Make sure that the information provided on any W-2 forms you receive from employers, and 1099s or 1098s you receive as an independent contractor or from banks, mutual funds, brokerages, retirement plans, or any other source, are accurately reflected on your return. If there is a mistake, get the issuer of the form to correct it. The IRS computer matches these figures with the figures on your return, and it will question any mismatch. If you have many of these forms, report each one separately somewhere on your tax return, or on a separate schedule that you attach to the return. The computer will not catch it if you lump the numbers together.
•If you are claiming an unusual deduction or there is something confusing on your return, attack a written explanation. Any statements should be as brief and to the point as possible – don't ramble or provide unessential details.
•If you are claiming home office expenses or significant travel or entertainment expenses, make sure you have the records. The IRS scrutinizes these expenses very carefully. The same is true of all business expenses if you haven't yet established a track record, and especially if your business is not profitable.
•Sign your return. Fill out all the information required. For example, it's common to omit the social security number of an ex-spouse from a return, but you are required to supply it if you are paying alimony. Make sure your return is complete.
•Make sure your math is correct. Arithmetic errors are the most common errors turned up by the IRS.
•Make sure that all social security numbers for your dependents are correct.
•Do not round number to $50 or $100 amounts. Show actual dollars.

•If you do estimate amounts, don't use round numbers. For example, $193.50 is a more 'credible' estimate than $200.
•File on time even if you can't pay all of the tax.
•Be kind and respectful to all IRS employees you deal with. IRS agents are people, too. Don't create an adversarial attitude in your relationship! They'll see your point of view better if you can see theirs. They will appreciate it and work with you in a better way.

…It's like and interrogation, pretty hot, but we can still take it…

Chapter XII
The Meaning of the Second Amendment

"A well regulated militia, being necessary to the security of a free State, the right of the people to keep and bear Arms, shall not be infringed."

"Conformity is the jailer of freedom and the enemy of growth."

-John F. Kennedy U.S. Democratic politician and president

There is a great deal of controversy going on about the meaning of the second amendment. The Supreme Court and some government officials insist that the proper interpretation of the above second amendment means that the army may have weapons but not ordinary citizens.

"Since the Second Amendment...applies only to the right of the State to maintain a militia and not to the individual's right to bear arms, there can be no serious claim to any express constitutional right to possess a firearm."

U.S. v. Warin (6th Circuit, 1976)

The case U.S. v. Miller is the only modern case in which the Supreme Court has addressed this issue. A unanimous Court ruled that the Second Amendment must be interpreted as intending to guarantee the states' rights to maintain and train a militia. "In the absence of any evidence tending to show that possession or use of a shotgun having a barrel of less than 18 inches in length at this time has some reasonable relationship to the preservation or efficiency of a well-regulated militia, we cannot say that the Second Amendment guarantees the right to keep and bear such an instrument," the Court said.

The basis for a well-regulated militia being formed is its necessity to the security of a free State. 'State does not mean a geographical or other arbitrary grouping of people but, instead, the state of the individual being free. It has nothing whatsoever to do with governing and is not subject to governing but only the unalienable right of freedom of the individual.

In order to form a meaningful, effective militia, and to protect one's self from tyranny or other threats to God-given unalienable right regardless of any militia or military, the People have the right to keep and bear Arms.

Finally, not one of these rights, the right to form a well-regulated militia, the right to keep firearms, the right to bear firearms, as dictated by the last phrase 'shall never be infringed upon'. These are God-given, not government nor majority granted rights.

In other words, we, the individual citizens who make up the people of this Nation, have for all time the right to keep and bear arms and the right to form militia groups in order to protect our rights, our liberty. If necessary, these rights were to be used against the federal government should it begin infringing or over-stepping its limited power.

That was the intent of our forefathers regardless of any modern, interpretation-of-the-government so-called expert's opinion, regardless of what any Supreme Court decision rules, regardless of any unconstitutional laws passed to the contrary.

Understand this. This Bill of Rights was incorporated into the Constitution as the rights of the individual and is in no way related to government, such as military, other than to prevent government or any other persons, organizations, from intruding on the rights of the individual.

Here are a few quotes from our forefathers followed by brief comments…

"…The said Constitution be never construed…to prevent the people of the United States who are peaceable citizens from keeping their own arms." Samuel Adams, during Massachusetts's Convention to Ratify the Constitution (1788).

"No free man shall ever be debarred the use of arms." Thomas Jefferson, Proposed Virginia Constitution (1776).

“Americans need not fear the federal government because they enjoy the advantage of being armed, which you possess over the people of almost every other nation.” James Madison, The Federalist 46 (1788).

“The strongest reason for the people to retain the right to keep and bear arms is, as a last resort, to protect themselves against tyranny in their government.”—Thomas Jefferson.

“I ask sir, what is the militia? It is the whole people. To disarm the people is the best and most effectual way to enslave them.” George Mason, during Virginia’s Convention to Ratify the Constitution (1788).

“A militia when properly former are in fact the people themselves and include all men capable of bearing arms…To preserve liberty it is essential that the whole body of people always possess arms…” Richard Henry Lee, Addition Letters From The Federal Farmer 53 (1788).

“Laws that forbid the carrying of arms disarm only those who are neither inclined nor determined to commit crimes. Such laws make things worse for the assaulted and better for the assailants; they serve rather to encourage that to prevent homicides, for an unarmed man may be attacked with greater confidence than an armed man.” Thomas Jefferson quoting Cesare Beccaria in On Crimes and punishment (1764)

“Arms discourage and keep the invader and plunder in awe, and preserve order in the world as well as property…Horrid mischief would ensue were the law-abiding deprived of the use of them.” Thomas Paine, Thoughts on Defense War (1775).

“The people never give up their liberties but under some delusion.” Edmund Burke (1784).

“The supreme power in America cannot enforce unjust laws by the sword, because the whole body of the people are armed, and constitute a force superior to any band of regular troops.” Noah Webster, An Examination into the Leading Principles of the Federal Constitution Proposed BV the Late Convention (1787)

“Arms in the hands of individual citizens may be used at individual discretion in private self-defense.” John Adams, A Defense of the

Constitutions of Government of the United States of America (1787-1788).

"Guard with jealous attention the public liberty. Suspect everyone who approaches that jewel. Unfortunately, nothing will preserve it but downright force. Whenever you give up that force, you are ruined." Patrick Henry, during Virginia's Convention to Ratify the Constitution (1788)

"(The Constitution preserves) the advantage of being armed which Americans posses over the people of almost every other nation…(where) the governments are afraid to trust the people with arms."—James Madison, The Federalist Papers.

"Suppose that we let a regular army, fully equal to the resources of the country, be formed; and let it be entirely at the devotion of the federal: still it would not be going to far to say that the State government with the people at their side would be able to repel the danger…half a million citizens with arms in their hands"—James Madison, The Federalist Papers.

"False is the idea of utility that sacrifices a thousand real advantages for one imaginary or trifling inconvenience; that would take fire from men because it burns, and water because one may drown in it; that has no remedy for evils except destruction. The laws that forbid the carrying of arms are laws of such a nature. They disarm only those who are neither inclined nor determined to commit crime." Cesare Ceccaria, quoted by Thomas Jefferson.

So, why is there a question concerning the intent of the Second Amendment, our last defense against a tyrannical government? Our forefathers ratified the second amendment based, in part, on the ideas States by these men. It is quite clear to them as to the meaning of the amendment being ratifies and written into the Constitution.

Based on the intent of our forefathers, the Fear of and the knowledge that men (women, too, so as to avoid being Sexist) in power are corruptible, we should never give up our rights to bear arms.

You see, not even the Supreme Court had the right to remove rights of the individual as stated in the Constitution.

Nor does the majority rule.

Nor does the Congress of the United States.

Gun Control
Vs. Gun Rights

What's the issue?

A recent spate of deadly school shootings—including the April 1999 massacre of 14 students and a teacher at a suburban Colorado high school—have added momentum to gun control measures long pending before Congress. Among other things, proponents of stricter firearm laws are calling for mandatory child safety locks, tougher background checks, and other controls that they believe will curb the rise of gun-related violence. Such proposals come just months after a host of cities—including New Orleans, Miami, and Los Angeles—filed suit against firearm manufacturers, blaming the companies' marketing practiced for violence caused my guns.

That's how our freedoms have been, and continue to be, lost. One at a time, incrementally—in such a way that most people don't really notice—until it's too late.

And, of course, it's not just Americans—and not just the USA. But when the "land of the free" slides down the slippery slope of satism—it makes freedom lovers the world over get very edgy!

United Nations Going For Global Gun Control

A United Nations Committee passed a resolution calling for member nations to adopt measures to limit the private ownership of firearms in an effort to consolidate central-government monopolies of firearm ownership.

New York—In an effort to reduce firearm-related crime and violence worldwide, a U.N. commission is drafting recommendations it hope will curb gun ownership and use.

The draft resolution, passed without objection last month by the 54-member U.N. Economic and Social Committee, encourages member states to consider adopting regulations dealing with illegal or unsafe use of firearms.

Such U.N. promoted regulations would include (a) licensing of all firearms businesses, (b) amnesty programs for the surrender of privately owned illegal firearms, (c) mandatory gun safety training where ownership is legal, (d) standardized penalties for firearms violations, and (e) creating a universal serial-number system to keep track of all privately owned firearms.

Reasons given by U.N. officials as to why such global gun control is necessary:

In North America, for example, firearms might be closely linked with robbery and homicides.

The illicit-drug trade is a primary cause of robbery and homicide, but if we ignore that fact we can promote more prohibitions leading to yet more negative side effects. While illicit drugs enrich the super-mega-wealthy through trafficking and money laundering, gun control would disarm their workers.

In Washington D.C., with one of the highest rates of homicide in the U.S., private gun ownership is 100% illegal, giving armed thugs free rein to exploit an unarmed population. Since firearms are the last defense of private property, armed thugs profit from gun control. Another U.N. reason for global gun control:

In Africa and the Balkins, he said, gun trafficking is tied to civil unrest.

If we could stop the flow of guns to those ethnic subsets targeted for extermination in Africa and the Balkins we could indeed reduce the amount of "civil unrest." For example, consider two Nazi death camps, in Nazi camp 1 all prisoners are unarmed, in 2 all are armed. There will be more "unrest" in Nazi camp 2. To maximize "civil rest" the Nazis enforced 100% gun control to keep prisoners unarmed. It seems that the U.N. has similar plans.

The last example given by a U.N. official for gun control is an example of the need for the traffic in firearms to people in areas where they are being targeted for extermination.

Firearms can defend the weak and can thereby ensure justice. All gun control measures work toward building a monopoly of gun ownership by the central authorities, who are those with the maximum strength. By definition, gun control strengthens the strong and weakens the weak, and in so doing, gun control will tend to maximize injustice,

While the U.N. is very concerned about private citizens with private guns killing other people, perhaps we should consider the fact that central authorities have murdered tens of millions with the aid of gun control. Gun control is a key to tyranny, exploitation, and mass murder.

Gun Control Gone Wrong

Extensive reports have shown that gun ownership by the majority of the population especially when the gun is carried or concealed weapon reduces crime. Yet you have cities like Chicago and many other were the ownership of a handgun is illegal and the city in turn then sues the gun manufacturers for any murders committed by a person with a gun within the city. Let's see owning a gun in the city is illegal, and I think murder is also illegal, therefore we need to sue the gun manufacturers for producing the guns. Maybe citizens who are victims of an assault or the estate of a death person wounded by a gun should sue the city for is it not up to the city to enforce its law and one of the laws is that no guns are allowed to be owned within the city.

Except of course, if you are a politician who exempt themselves and are allowed to carry guns and who have body guards or a judge with sheriff personnel protecting the working environment.

One of the more typical altitudes by the government is the example of a recent incident in Wilmette, a suburb of Chicago that has a "Gun Ban Ordinance."

A homeowner was twice invaded by a robber within a twenty four hour period. The first time the robber stole the homeowners vehicle. The second time the robber broke into the house, the homeowner fired a gun and injured the robber who was later arrested.

And, the homeowner was also arrested for violating the hand gun ordinance, and, the homeowner faces the threat of a lawsuit from the robber for violating the "no gun ordinance" and causing bodily harm.

At a Village Board hearing, the police chief defended the arrest of the homeowner by being smug and arrogant stating that "Wilmette residents are much safer without a handgun in their homes". Implying that the homeowner should have locked himself and his family into a room and call 911.

...Yippee – get me outta here, it's too hot...

Chapter XIII
What is obscenity?

"The function of government is to protect me from others. It's up to me, thank you, to protect me from me."

-Arthur Hoppe

"Those who cast the votes decide nothing. Those who count the votes decide everything."

-Josef Stalin

Americans are obsessed with sex, yet we are the prudist people in the world. There are millions upon millions of web sites on the internet featuring pornographic photos, the sex industry in Hollywood and other California towns are the biggest export that we have, yet a six year old expelled from school for kissing a girl.

A father is arrested for kissing his ten year old daughter at a bus stop and we have lists of sex offenders published on the internet and a requirement that sex offenders register within the neighborhood where then intend to live.

There are laws in the books that confiscate the car from a driver that solicits an undercover police officer posing as a prostitute on a street corner in a suggestive pose.

Judges in Michigan upheld the confiscation of a wife's car who had no knowledge that her husband who was driving her car was going or did solicit an undercover police officer.

Magazines are banned from the local Wal-Mart store that have sexy titles or beautiful models in swim suits on the cover. The showing of a naked breast hidden by a nipple disc at a Super Bowl half time show causes a need for Congressional hearings.

A sex offender having served his or her time may be incarcerated for an unlimited additional time until the government feels that the offender is no longer a danger to society.

Having sex one day before a girls eighteenth birthday is considered a felony, depriving the offender of ever getting a proper job and never being allowed to vote for the rest of his or life. One day later it is legal and acceptable.

Justice Harlan once said, "the subject of obscenity has produced a variety of views among the members of the Court unmatched in any other course of constitutional adjudication." The court has struggled mightily over the years to define "obscenity," Justice Potter Stewart fared no better in defining obscenity, but exclaimed, "I know it when I see it." Another federal judge has said, "Obscenity- like beauty- is often in the eyes of the beholder."

The Court formulated guidelines for determining obscene material in Miller v. California, 413 U.S. 15 (1973). The three basic provisions are:

> •(a) whether the average person, applying contemporary community standards would find that the work taken as a whole, appeals to the prurient interest;
> •(b) whether the work depicts of describes, in a patently offensive way, sexual conduct specifically defined by state law; and
> •(c) Whether the work, taken as a whole, lacks serious literary, artistic, political, or scientific value.

The "local community standards" has troubled many. Some have argued for a national obscenity standard. The problem with different obscenity standards magnifies itself when dealing with allegedly obscene material transmitted over the Internet. What standards will apply?

Justice William Douglas concluded that courts could and should not resolve obscenity questions. Douglas wrote: "We deal with highly emotional, not rational questions. To many the Song of Solomon is obscene. I do not think we, the judges, were ever given the constitutional power to make definitions of obscenity."

Film ruled obscene; Police raid home.

Michael Camfield had not finished watching the movie he had rented. The Tin Drum, when police knocked on his front door and demanded that he give them the Academy Award-winning foreign film.

"I got the strong impression that verbal resistance on my part was futile and they were going to get that tape one way or another and arrest me if they had to" said Camfield.

The officers had used video store records to find Camfield. They also had seized copies of the movie from six video outlets within hours of a judge's ruling that the film was obscene.

Some critics labeled the movie about Nazi Germany, as seen by a little boy, as smut, but civil libertarian Joann Bell likened the police seizures to "book burnings organized by Hitler's Gestapo."

This kind of insensitive disregard of our fundamental rights of expression and free speech is outrageous.

District Judge Richard Freeman said Wednesday that the movie was obscene under Oklahoma law, which says that any depiction of a person under 18 – or anyone portraying someone under 18 – having sex is obscene.

The Tin Drum, which won an Oscar for best foreign film, is German director Vloker Schlondorff's acclaimed adaptation of Gunter Grass' novel. The movie includes a scene where a boy has oral sex with a teenage girl.

Police had watched part of the movie but Camfield said he surrendered the video after a debate with the officers on "constitutional law and artistic merit." And then it became clear they were not going to leave without it.

Obscenity and Prostitution

The Supreme Court recently held that it was proper for the police in Michigan to confiscate the car of a woman whose husband was caught picking up a prostitute with his wife's car. Obviously it was without her knowledge but it does not matter. Her car is gone.

A police officer dressed as a hooker either walks or stands in a suggestive pose on the street and if approached a swat team of officers arrests the individual and they impound the vehicle. There may never have been any solicitation.

In many cities the police will publish the names and pictures of people arrested for soliciting a prostitute in sting operations. They will also impound the car and a heavy fine is imposed for the solicitor.

It seems strange that we are one of the few countries where, except for one county in Nevada, prostitution is illegal. The USA also has one of the highest rates for rape and assault. Most other countries regulate the oldest trade by licensing and regular medical checkups. Guess what, those countries have almost no rapes or assaults. Could it be that there is an outlet for some one whom cannot find a sexual partner and instead of assaulting or raping someone these services can be purchased. Who is hurt? Could all of the police attention not be focused on real crime protections?

The proponents of anti prostitution state that prostitution is not a victimless crime. Women and men are forced into prostitution. Ask the Mayflower Madam or Heidi Fleiss if their girls were forced to make thousands of dollars a week?

In 1996 the city and county of San Francisco created a task force to study the impact of prostitution. Below is an extensive summary of the finding.

In San Francisco, prostitution can be summed up in one word: prosecution. Most health and social services are secondary to, or inter twined with, the enforcement and prosecution of soliciting crimes. Moreover, this approach is directed almost at street prostitution, which is estimated to comprise only 10-20% of prostitution in the city.

The Task Force concluded that the current prosecutorial response does a great deal of harm but little good. It has not solved the quality of life concerns voiced by neighborhood residents; it has cost the city millions of dollars; it deprives residents of positive services, which would ameliorate the problems. Moreover, city residents overwhelmingly oppose enforcement and prosecution of prostitution crimes.

The Task Force therefore recommended that the city departments stop enforcing and prosecuting prostitution crimes. If further recommended that the departments instead focus on the quality of life infractions about which neighborhoods complain and redirect funds from prosecution, public defense, court time, legal system overhead and incarceration towards services and alternatives for needy constituencies.

The Task Force recommended that the city maintain a working group on prostitution to oversee implementation and use the cities dispute resolution resources to engender greater communication among neighborhood and business concerns and prostitute representatives.

Law and Law Enforcement

Most laws against prostitution activities are written by the State Legislature. These are the misdemeanors and felonies most used against alleged prostitutes. The penalties include sentences of up to six months in jail for misdemeanors and state prison terms of 16 months to eight years for felonies. Because these laws were written in Sacramento, San Francisco does not have the power unilaterally to change them. Because of these same laws, the city may not unilaterally legalize or decriminalize prostitution.

The San Francisco Municipal Police Code also contains some ordinances against prostitution. Many of these duplicate state laws. Others are patently vague and archaically written. The City Attorney has concluded that most of the San Francisco ordinances are unconstitutional and should be repealed. Nevertheless, these ordinances occasionally are used to arrest suspected prostitutes, though they are usually discharged before they ever make it to court. The reality is that enforcement and prosecution of these laws merely creates a revolving door in the criminal justice system.

The San Francisco Police Department does not consistently enforce laws against any sex workers except the most visible, those working on the street. Most people arrested spend no more than a weekend in jail before being released. Though enforcement may increase, there is no evidence that it does any more than force street workers to move from one place to the next. The Task Force concluded that prosecution of prostitution has exacerbated problems in the industry including violence and chemical dependency, while enforcement further marginalizes prostitutes.

The Task Force heard evidence that prostitutes are afraid to call the police when they are crime victims, for fear of being arrested themselves. Once a person gets a rap sheet as a known prostitute, she/he may be trapped and stigmatized for life, and may be unable to pursue other jobs.

The Task Force findings indicate that decriminalization of prostitution could eventually reduce street prostitution and would enable the city to address other problems.

Adequate state and local laws already exist to respond when noise, trespassing and littering are problems. These infractions are punishable by fines, not by incarceration. Since they cannot be jailed upon conviction, people charged with these infractions do not have the right to a jury trial or an attorney. Since they are handled in traffic court, prosecution, defense and Sheriff's resources are not needed. Failure to pay fines is a criminal offense, however; those who refuse to pay their fines may be prosecuted. Infractions are therefore a more cost-effective enforcement option than misdemeanors and felonies.

Under no circumstance, however, should these infractions be used to harass suspected prostitutes. Harassment and abuse of suspected prostitutes is a serous problem in the San Francisco Police Department, which is only recently coming to light. The very methods of enforcement encourage abuse: police officers pose as prospective clients and try to get suspects to say the words that will get them arrested. The police are most successful who most convincingly behave like clients. Many women complain of vice officers fondling them or exposing themselves before arresting them. These women refuse to report abusive officers because they fear retaliation or that they will not be believed.

Despite the difficulty of uncovering and uprooting abuse, a police officer was arrested for forcing a massage parlor worker to orally copulate him; and the City paid $85,000 in damages to a registered nurse who was falsely arrested and held when the officers suspected her of being a prostitute. In the course of that litigation, The Federal District Court Judge recommended that US Attorney's Office investigate the arresting officers for perjury during their testimony.

Law enforcement policy also affects public health policy. This issue is discussed in the Health, Safety and Services section but one particular law should be highlighted here. State law requires that anyone convicted of soliciting prostitution be tested for HIV infection. The results are kept on file in Sacramento; if a person is re-arrested for soliciting, any District Attorney may learn their results. If the person was HIV positive at the time of the previous conviction, the new charge is elevated to a felony. The person charged faces state prison for offering or agreeing to perform a sex act for money. The law does not distinguish between offers of safe sex and offers of unsafe sex. Civil libertarians and AIDS activists point out that this law stigmatizes a group of people for their immunodeficiency status, without any evidence that they are actually causing harm.

Moreover, the forced testing law assumes that prostitutes represent a threat to public health. There is no evidence that sex workers as a group have greater incidence of HIV infection then the general population or that they spread HIV disease. In fact, evidence shows that San Francisco sex workers are highly educated about safe sex.

Completely contrary to the policy of improving public health, the San Francisco Police Department had a policy of confiscating condoms from people arrested for prostitution related offenses. Many of the condoms taken had been given to street workers by the City Department of Health. Further, if a person charged with soliciting prostitution had condoms when arrested, the District Attorney's office used the condoms as evidence against them in court. The Task Force unanimously added a resolution condemning the Police and the District Attorney's actions. Under pressure, the District Attorney promised to stop using condoms as evidence. Nevertheless, some police officers are still acting in contradiction to the policy.

The Task Force Recommended as Follows:

Immediately stop enforcing and prosecuting misdemeanor and felony laws. Dismiss all current prosecutions in order to begin immediately reallocating resources.

Respond directly to complaints of excessive noise, loitering and trespassing by enforcing ordinances specific to those complaints. The police should not use any laws to harass suspected prostitutes.

Vigorously enforce laws against coercion, blackmail, kidnapping, retraining individual's freedom of movement, fraud, rape and violence regardless of the victim's status as a sex worker.

Redirect resources currently allocated to police investigation, incarceration, prosecution and defense of sex workers to augment resources for housing, outreach and other service for these populations.

Curtail expenditures for Police investigation of prostitution venues where there are no accompanying complaints, including hotel, cafes and bars.

Remove authority for the licensing of massage parlors, masseuses and masseurs and escort services form the Vice Crime Division's jurisdiction and place it with agencies already qualified to grant other standard business licenses.

Provide training and circulate directives to Police Department and Sheriff's Department personnel to eliminate harassment and abuse of prostitutes by law enforcement personnel.

Provide training to improve the ability of the District Attorney's office to successfully prosecute cases of rape and other assault in which prostitutes and other sex workers are the victims.

Authorize city lobbyists to identify legislators who will commit to carrying legislation towards the following goals:

- •Repeal state laws that criminalize engaging in, agreeing to or soliciting prostitution or laws and policies, which can be interpreted to deny freedom of travel and the right to privacy to prostitutes.
- •Repeal state laws which can be interpreted to deny freedom of association, or which criminalize prostitutes who work together for safety.
- •Repeal mandatory HIV testing and felony enhancements of HIV+ prostitutes.

•Repeal minimum mandatory sentencing laws for second and subsequent convictions.

Currently, and as long as there are people accused and convicted of prostitution-related offenses in our jails, the Task Force recommends the following:

Conduct a study of the accessibility and relevance of services in the city and county jails, and the juvenile detention center, to individuals involved in the sex industry.

Develop peer based pre-release planning programs relevant to prostitutes to connect them to social service programs that respond to their specific needs, including sex worker's rights organizations, as well as other programs that help them obtain housing, jobs, clothes, child custody and child care, health care and other post-release need they have.

Formulate a proactive policy within the Sheriff's Department, that charges related to prostitution should not be excluded from release programs.

For prostitutes, being labeled as a criminal can mean that a woman may lose custody of her children, especially since there is a mandatory jail sentence on second conviction. Very often, prostitutes "lead double lives" forced underground for fear of being evicted from their homes, losing their jobs, and the break-up of family and other relationships. Immigrants who work as prostitutes, particularly people of color, have fewer economic alternatives due to institutional racism and can face deportation if convicted of prostitution. Therefore they are unlikely to report violence against them.

Labor Policy Issues

Strip clubs and erotic performance theaters, erotic film and video production, porn magazine publishing and phone sex switchboards, commercial parties and sex clubs-are all part of the legal sex industry in San Francisco.

Youth Issues and Policy

Youth are involved in prostitution for a wide variety of reasons, similar to adults. These reasons are compounded because of legal restrictions based on age, especially in employment and housing. Because of labor laws, establish to "protect" those under the age of eighteen, most youth are not legally able to work more than part time. For young people who are living on their own and can legally work only part time at a job that pays minimum wage and offers little in terms of skill development and advancement, there are few opportunities for survival other than working in the underground economy, which includes sex work.

Many young people are forced to survive on their own to escape violent and abusive family situation. The dangers they face on the streets may be less than the dangers they face at home. While on their own, there is a total lack of affordable housing options for those under the age of eighteen, unless they are emancipated. In order to become emancipated, however, it is necessary to prove a legal means of supporting oneself.

Recommendations below emphasize strategies to reduce the harm done by legal restrictions and an arcane system of "child care."

While we realize that our society has a long way to go to adequately address civil and human rights for young people, and young women in particular because of the disparity in social service for youth, and that limited financial resources compete for the most effective interventions, the Task Force submits the following recommendations:

The Task Force recommends that the City focus on independent housing, job development and specific shelter alternatives for incarcerated young women. Provision of services, no detention, should be the first priority for youth. Therefore the Task Force recommends that the City:

Ensure that service available for adults are also available for youth. These should include housing, health care including prenatal care and abortions, rape and abuse counseling, drug treatment and detox programs, methadone programs, needle exchange, and self-defense training. Accessibility of services should not be dependent on parental consent.

Increase the number of Public Defenders available to people under the age of eighteen.

Increase services available to young women in order to end the gender disparity in social services for youth.

Increase the number of shelter beds for young women in the juvenile court system who cannot be released to parents or guardians.

Increase funding for peer-run support groups for youth in the sex industry, including transitional services and programs to provide alternatives.

Youth with experience in prostitution or survival sex should be employed as peer educators, consultants and speakers.

The Task Force recommends the following:

Change current policy and modify current contracts to provide access to a full range of health services indicated for all residents, including drug treatment programs, without discrimination regarding sex work history or continuation in prostitution.

Provide adequate resources for services to battered women, the homeless, youth, immigrants and refugees, and those needing rape crisis services regardless of whether they have a history of, or are currently working in prostitution.

With the revenues made available by eliminating budgets to enforce prostitution laws, support current and develop new peer-guided programs and services. These should include outreach, including mobile outreach, drop-in centers and low threshold emergency and transitional housing. Programs should include occupational and educational programs, health and other programs for those who continue working as prostitutes, as well as those who wish to transition into other occupations including financial assistance to escape abusive and violent situations.

Provide in-service training to health and social service workers who work with prostitutes to increase sensitivity and accessibility of services.

Legalize Prostitution

In many communities throughout the U.S., the police periodically focus their attention on arresting persons involved in prostitution. A careful examination of this practice shows that it reduces the quality of life in society.

By forcing prostitution out of places where it would more naturally be found, such as in brothels or near motels, the police drive that activity into the streets of neighborhoods where it otherwise would not exist. The result is that residents of the neighborhoods are exposed to the activity against their will.

Also because of prostitution being forced into the streets, the dangers to many prostitutes greatly increase. Prostitutes whose jobs involve working at night and getting into cars with complete strangers can be, and often have been, easy pickings for serial killers and other sociopaths. James Alan Fox, a criminal justice professor at Northeastern University, reports that prostitutes are the most frequent targets for serial killers.

A sensible solution to these problems would be to follow the example of some European cities, where prostitution and soliciting are allowed in certain designated areas. People who are interested in those activities go to the places where it is permitted, and they leave alone the neighborhoods that don't wish to be associated with it. And the prostitutes can work in environments where they are much safer.

Another problem with prostitution arrests is that they cause long-term increases in crime and drug abuse in society. Margo St. James, a former social worker and a leading advocate of legalizing prostitution, writes: "When a woman is charged for a sex crime, it's a stigma that lasts her lifetime, and it makes her unemployable."

St. James identifies that stigma as a major reason that a large percentage of women who are in jail were first arrested for prostitution. The arrest record forecloses normal employment possibilities, keeps the women working as prostitutes longer than they otherwise would, and sets them up for a lifetime of involvement with drugs and serious crime.

Keeping prostitution illegal also contributes to crime because many criminals view prostitutes and their customers as attractive targets for robbery, fraud, rape or other criminal acts. The criminals know that such people are unlikely to report the crimes to police, because the victims would have to admit they were involved in the illegal activity of prostitution when the attacks took place.

If prostitution were legal, these victims would be less reluctant to report to police any criminal acts that occurred while they were involved in it.

This would significantly improve the probability of catching the criminals and preventing them from victimizing others. In many cases, it could deter them from committing the crimes in the first place.

Additionally, laws against prostitution violate Americans' fundamental rights of individual liberty and personal privacy. Thomas Jefferson and other founders of the U.S. envisioned a society where people can live without interference from government, provided they don't harm others.

As Jefferson said in his First Inaugural Address: "A wise and frugal government, which shall restrain men from injuring one another, shall leave them otherwise free to regulate their own pursuits of industry and improvement."

Similar to issues such as birth control, this issue involves people's fundamental rights to control their own bodies and decide the best way to conduct their lives. Alan Soble noted, "The freedom to choose one's reasons for engaging in sex is an important part of sexual freedom."

In a free society, it makes no sense for the government to be telling persons-particularly the poor-that they cannot charge a fee for harmless services they otherwise are at liberty to give away. Many people work in the sex industry because they see it as their only means of alleviating serious financial problems. Other sex workers aren't poor but simply enjoy that type of work and receive both income and personal satisfaction from it.

Likewise for the customers, there is no reason their freedom should not include the right to purchase the companionship and affection they may want but, for whatever reason, do not find in other aspects of their lives.

For example, one disabled man told researchers he was lonely and visited prostitutes because "I'm ugly, no women will go out with me... It's because of my disability. So prostitutes are a sexual outlet for me." Another man reported that he did the same for a number of years due to being "anorexic and very reclusive. There was no chance of forming a relationship." A physically unattractive man added, "I pay for sex because that is the only way I can get sex."

Another person related that his experiences with prostitutes and other sex workers helped him overcome an extreme aversion to physical intimacy, which had resulted from years of physical and emotional abuse while growing up. He said: "I very likely would have died a virgin if I hadn't somehow gotten comfortable with physical intimacy, and sex workers enabled me to do that. At least for me, it's been a healing experience."

Sr. John Money, a leading sexologist and a professor at the Johns Hopkins University, similarly notes that sex workers, with proper training, can assist clients in overcoming "erotic phobia" and various other sexual dysfunctions. He says that for the clients, "the relationship with a paid professional may be the equivalent of therapy."

Can anyone, other than the ignorant or cruel, argue that sex workers should not be permitted to help such persons?

Further, numerous legal commentators point out the using law enforcement resources against prostitution reduces substantially the resources available to fight serious crimes committed against persons or property. This nation desperately needs more efforts applied to solving these crimes, because arrests are being made in connection with less than 20% of them.

And according to the Multinational Monitor, massive amounts of white-collar crime are not being prosecuted. The magazine also reports that the damage inflicted on society by corporate crime and violence far exceeds the harm caused by all the street crime combined. The victims of the Enron and WorldCom scandals-many of whom lost their life savings-could probably support that claim.

As Ralph Nader stated "Law enforcement, which is supposed to protect the incomes of consumers from corporate crime, fraud and abuse is a farce, devoid of resources and the will to apply necessary law and order. Hundreds of billions of dollars are being looted from consumers yearly."

Some researchers assert that a reason for the inordinate amount of police attention to prostitution is that certain officers prefer duties enabling them to be with attractive women in hotel rooms or massage parlors. The duties are more pleasant, far less dangerous, and less complex than assignments requiring them to be among violent criminals who may be carrying weapons.

For instance, at least one of the vice-squad officers in Columbus, Ohio, was regularly having sexual intercourse with prostitutes before arresting them. After receiving negative publicity about that practice, the police division issued new guidelines that limited officers to getting completely naked with prostitutes, being masturbated briefly, and "momentarily" having sex "in spite of all reasonable efforts of the officer to stop." (In practice, though, the officers apparently find it necessary to use those tactics only in arresting female -not male-prostitutes.

Despite the revised guidelines, the Columbus Dispatch quoted one court clerk as describing the officers' arrest reports as sometimes being so steamy that she "should have a cigarette after reading it." The head of the vice squad acknowledged to the newspaper that "It appears officers are engaging in sexual contact."

His officers give new meaning to being "in hot pursuit." Unfortunately for the public, this nonsense goes on at the same time that Columbus has over 350 unsolved murders since 1990, including several prostitutes brutally murdered by a possible serial killer.

In regard to white-collar crime, the police undoubtedly know that their jobs and careers are safer by making prostitution arrests than by investigating criminals who cause serious harm, but either wield political power or have strong connections to those who do. And when the corruption involves others in the police force, the notorious "Blue Wall of Silence" leads all too many officers to ignore and protect the wrongdoing of badge-wearing criminals, too.

Our society would be better served if the police directed their efforts away from the activities of consenting adults and toward preventing and solving real crimes involving clear victims and injustices.

Benefits of Legalization

Currently, most everywhere in the United States, our legal system penalizes prostitutes and their customers for what they do as consenting adults. Money is still spent on law enforcement efforts to catch prostitutes and their customers. Once caught, justice departments have to process these people through very expensive systems.

What are the end results? Police personnel and courtrooms are overburdened with these cases, having little or no impact on prostitution. The prostitutes and their customers pay their fines and are back to the streets in no time in a revolving door process. Catch and release may work for recreational fishing, but it has no deterring affect on prostitution.

Making prostitution legal will allow the act to be managed instead of ignored. Pimps and organized crime figures, who regularly treat their workers on subhuman levels, would no longer control women. In some countries, prostitution rings buy and sell women on the black market, force their women to comply through violence and create unhealthy working conditions. When prostitutes operate independently and in secret, many times they become abused by their own customers.

Legalizing prostitution would prevent underground prostitution that occurs today. When men want to pay for sex, they find prostitutes. These people work in massage parlors, escort services, strip bars and modeling agencies or still work corners as traditional streetwalkers. There are legitimate parlors, dating services, bars and agencies but of the hundreds that exist within newspaper classified advertisements and telephone directories, there are a large number that provide sexual services.

A very important problem in our society is teen prostitution. If we allow prostitution to remain hidden from view and basically invisible to the law as it is today, we allow a number of teens to be swept up into prostitution every year. When adult women decide to exchange money for sex, it is a personal choice open to them under the philosophy of a free, democratic society. When troubled minors who do not yet have the social survival skills decide to prostitute, they are often manipulated by opportunists who exploit these teens, typically leading to horrific ends. Legalizing prostitution will help prevent these instances through regulation.

Legalized, regulated prostitution has many benefits. Encounters can happen within controlled environments that bring about safety for both the customers and the prostitutes. Prostitutes would no longer be strong-armed by pimps or organized crime rings. Underage prostitution would be curtailed. There would also be health-safety improvements.

The Role of Government

Whether one is a liberal or conservative, republican or democrat, the role of government is to carry out necessary duties its citizens cannot perform. Politicians are elected to government positions to solve the problems countries face. Some Democratic politicians insist government should be designed to act as a safety net for people who need help, by providing citizens with various social programs including public safety and healthcare entitlements. Other Republican representatives believe in freedom of choice through responsible action and rather institute high standards in education and healthcare to enable citizens with opportunities. Libertarians feel compelled to ensure civil rights and allow citizens to be self-governing members of society.

In these cases, the issue of morality aside, it can be plainly seen how each political view contains strong elements supporting legalization. Maintaining the status quo has the U.S. healthcare system is currently reactionary at best; it passively handles STDs after they occur instead of instituting mechanisms to prevent them from happening in the first place. Political philosophy has not changed from immaturity and clings to a prohibitory model form the 1920's even though it was proven to be devastating to its citizens.

The best way to understand the current state of affairs concerning prostitution is to entertain an analogy. Pretend government is a business. Politicians would be the managers and prostitution would be a certain procedure the company had to manage. Would a successful business ignore a procedure when it performed poorly? Would it allow a poor procedure to continue or would a successful business instead rethink its position and improve it? All successful companies must evolve over time if they are to stay in business and excel. Fortunately, the U.S. constitution allows its citizens to view government like a dynamic business because it is a work in progress. Laws can change and adapt to meet the demands of a modern civilization. It is a far better strategy than hoping it will go away and clean up itself.

Where are the limits for two consenting adults in privacy? How government is shaped to handle that question will decide how women's rights, social programs, public healthcare, the safety of youth and possibly the general safety of citizens are valued. If moral obstacles prevent citizens from obtaining a government that helps its people while preserving freedoms, then a paradigm shift must be considered. A movement away from values that are harmful is difficult only if one decides to cling to outdated, self-destructive traditions.

Think it through. A couple meet at a bar, they have a few drinks, drives and then have sex in one of their homes. No law was broken. The next day, he sends her some flowers and a Neiman Marcus gift certificate to have a beauty treatment for $200.00.

Where do we draw the line? In Europe, in most major cities, there are red light districts that have the girls sitting in a showroom window.

No police, no crime and no victims. Most European cities have almost no sex crimes for there is an outlet for any person who does not have a wife, girlfriend or significant other.

How many marriages are based on rewards for sexual favors yet there are no arrests? What's wrong with two consenting adults to make a deal over sex?

Politicians should be careful how they address the philosophical limits of adult privacy. Government should have no right deciding how adults conduct their sexual lives, even when an exchange of money is involved.

Comparing Prostitution Rights to Abortion Rights

Abortion was decided to be legal by The Supreme Court in 1973 in a landmark case: Roe vs. Wade. Intellectuals have weighed the issue and decided in favor for women's rights in part due to public safety.

Considering the safety gains, the decision was proper, despite perpetual moral objections from religious groups ignoring longstanding facts to this day. Pre-1973, 17% of all deaths due to pregnancy and childbirth were the result of illegal abortions. Pre-1973, 17% of all deaths due to pregnancy and childbirth were the result of illegal abortions. Pre-1973, 1.2 million women resorted to illegal abortions yearly and botched illegal abortions caused as many as 5,000 deaths a year. Untrained physician in unsanitary conditions using primitive methods often performed illegal abortions.

As with the treatment of alcohol in the '20s, prohibiting abortions did not stop them. In fact, illegal abortions were commonplace and hazardous to the health of women. Again, we see the outcome of a prohibitory philosophy. The facts indicate we must abandon abolitionist thinking and insist society rest on what is best for it.

If society must accurately decide whether regulated prostitution is better than illegal prostitution, then scientists must analyze the wealth of information that exists. Social scientists and common voting citizens must look at data from countries having legal prostitution and compare them to the United States. Canada, Mexico and most of Europe have legal forms of prostitution as does Israel, Greece, Denmark, Singapore and the United Kingdom. Saudi Arabia allows polygyny and Iran offers "temporary wives". Examining these countries in the broad areas of crime, healthcare, and social conditions will help determine if prostitution should be legalized.

The United States has problems with violent crime despite great efforts to prosecute criminals and imprison them. The U.S. prosecutes almost five times the number of people as Canada and over eight times the number that Mexico reports. The U.S. is also unrivaled in terms of imprisonment. France comes the closest to the U.S.'s number of inmates, confining one-sixth the number as the U.S.

It is unknown if there is a correation between laws that prohibit sex and higher crime rates, but the reverse appears to be more enlightening. The countries where prostitution is legal do not suffer from a high number of violent crimes. It appears legalized prostitution does not make societies more of a crime hazard. Contrary to the prohibitionist's philosophy, this data may give reason to implement and regulate prostitution to reduce crime because crime in countries where prostitution is legal is lower than the U.S.'s rates.

A measure of the overall citizen happiness may be obtained by looking at suicide rates for each country. The U.S. is third highest on the list and has over 50% more suicides per capita than Denmark. Only Greece and Mexico have higher rates, which may be a result caused by the low socio-economic conditions permeating those countries. Also, we see a trend occurring for countries that have legal prostitution; they have lower suicide rates, suggesting yet another benefit of industry regulation.

If we compare divorce rates between countries, we will understand the success of institutional monogamy under different social conditions. The United States is second highest, with eight times the divorces as Mexico, twice as many as Canada and 55% more than Denmark. It is clear that the U.S. has a high turnover rate. Meanwhile, most countries with legal prostitution have less of a problem with institutional monogamy.

Upon a close examination of the Netherlands reveals interesting findings. Amsterdam is the capitol of the Netherlands and is internationally known for its redlight district. Critics to prostitution might be stunned to learn that the Netherlands has the least number of murders and rapes. It prosecutes a considerable amount of criminals but has a low number of prisoners. It does not suffer from an HIV/AIDS epidemic, like the U.S. and the U.K., and has the second lowest suicide rate listed. This news will literally stop critics (who are open to reason) in their tracks when they are confronted with such information.

When critics mention neighborhood safety, they do not offer meaningful alternatives. Their plan is to heighten police patrols, encourage undercover sting operations, and stiffen penalties. We have seen the results of prohibition in the 1920s. It drives the industry further underground, making it harder to stop the spread of HIV/AIDS and various other sexually transmitted diseases in a community.

If critics of prostitution wanted to truly help prostitutes and the neighborhoods where prostitution occurs, they would reconsider their position. Prohibitionists retain their view as a result of moral codes, not because of unbiased scientific study. Research shows the many benefits of legalization. Allowing prohibitionist propaganda to drive laws and the way civil liberties are viewed will guarantee: drug dependency will not be abated, physical abuse will continue, and STDs will spread. Most important, the women who need help will continue their lives on the same harmful paths.

Prostitution as a Career

Prostitution has been in existence for millennia, going back to the Byzantine, Roman, Greek, and Egyptian Empires. Ironically, the ancient religions of those eras dealt with the needs of the group and consequently developed protocols for dealing with sexual relations that have propagated throughout time to the modern era. As a result, prostitution is not about to disappear anytime soon, despite relatively recent local laws.

There are three strata of prostitutes. Within the top layer rests discrete call-girls for the affluent, much like the services Heidi Fleiss offered. The middle layer holds bordello-dwelling prostitutes or others in less subtle environments such as strip clubs and massage parlors that offer backroom services. Streetwalkers occupy the lowest layer. Some people entertain a controversial notion that the role of wife is akin to being a prostitute; their placement within the strata may depend on what socio-economic class they reside once married.

The lowest layer prostitutes are plagued with the most problems. It is the group that usually remains perpetually vulnerable. They work in conditions that make them prove to violence due to lack of supervision. And, there are healthcare risks due to unsafe sexual contact with unscreened clients.

These lower strata prostitutes are the women who require help. The others benefit from physically safe environments, decent to lucrative wages, and operate among clients that are more likely to be healthy. Lower strata prostitutes cannot afford decent medical services and are frequently physically assaulted by pimps or clients. These women are either lured into the industry by drugs or they turn to drugs as a means to cope with their careers. They contribute large portions of their revenue to pimps or drugs, making their condition inescapable.

Bottom strata prostitutes remain trapped, but the upper two-thirds are far less constrained. For the upper two strata of prostitutes, free will is present. They are able to carefully parlay their gains into real estate or financial investments even within localities having laws against prostitution. They can choose to leave prostitution for other careers or simply retire. Since it is impossible to stop prostitutes, the upper two-thirds will continue to make a fiscally respectful living from it and the lowest third will suffer.

If modern society rests itself on principles claiming to assist those who cannot help themselves and create structures where opportunities, not dead ends, are the norm, then these lower strata prostitutes do not deserve the abandonment from which they are suffering. Instead, politicians and community activists have become influenced by religious dogma. The entities that long ago managed prostitution, hypocritically exile prostitutes to lives they may identify as depraved; yet, they use their services, engage in adulterous relations and cover up widespread pedophilia. Prostitutes continue to suffer due to these long-standing traditions maintained in part by such religionists. No longer do these traditions serve humanity.

Sexual relations are handled differently in countries around the world. Most countries encourage varied forms of monogamy, others polygyny. Even in the case of monogamy, there are numerous countries that impose no restrictions on prostitution, unlike a majority of the communities within the United States.

In order to discover if legalization is proper, one has to first familiarize oneself with the U.S. prohibition of alcohol in the 1920's and the legalization of abortion in the 1970's. The implementation of prohibition was a result of an abolitionist philosophy and caused great harm to the country through lost taxes, increased crime rates and higher suicide rates. Similarly, when the U.S. abandoned its abolitionist stand on abortion, the country benefited from fewer deaths from botched back alley abortions. This proved prohibitionist thinking to be baseless and actually detrimental to communities.

There are many benefits to legalized prostitution. The benefits include (1) allowing law enforcement agencies to respond to more important crimes, (2) freeing justice systems from nuisance cases, (3) helping women who are trapped by prostitution, and (4) preventing teens from being ensnared into prostitution.

When data from countries that ban prostitution is compared with data from countries that do not, many startling discoveries can be observed. Countries without anti-prostitution laws have less murders, less rapes, and prosecute/imprison less people. HIV/AIDS is less of a problem; suicide rates are lower as are divorce rates, too.

Critics of the legalization of prostitution offer no alternative to a troublesome problem. These people would rather adopt the status quo model, which virtually abandons lower strata, low socio-economic prostitutes. Instead of managing the problem, these critics view the continued downward spiral of this subgroup as acceptable.

The critics of legalized prostitution rest comfortably within relatively new moral codes. The religions that now reject prostitution once used to manage it. However, even though religionists publicly denounce prostitution, too many hypocritically entertain like services and commit adultery. The Catholic Church has covered up institutional pedophilia at the expense of demeaning religious values and the lives of those who aspire to follow them.

...No more, let's turn the control down, I have had enough...

Chapter XIV
Privacy in the Workplace.

"Watching the world-wide growth of compulsory health insurance, I noticed something that seemed to be overlooked: that all modern dictators – Communists, fascist, or disguised – have at least one thing in common. They all believe in social security, especially in coercing people into governmentalized medicine."

-Melchior Palyi (1892-1970)

Let's Outsource our President

Employers may as a condition for employment check your credit, do a background check, submit you to mandatory drug testing, random drug testing.

Depending on your professional and personal habits, a company can require you to alcohol tests, join fitness programs or perform your job under electronic surveillance.

Theoretically, you have a right of privacy in your workplace but the employer may ask as a condition of employment, to have you waive these rights.

Employers even have the right to establish non-smoking policies even when in your personal vehicle on the company parking lot.

More and more controls have been put into place to assure the surveillance of your person in the workplace.

The company may require that you carry a picture identifications at all times in order to gain entry into the workplace.

There may be codes or swipe cards that allow you to enter certain floors or rooms within a building. Your computer may gave a password that requires you to log-in and the computer software will track all of the sites that you visit but it also may limit you to only certain programs that you are authorized to enter.

The employer can bar-code each tool that to access in order to determine who used what tool and to reach in the shop which machine you signed in on to establish which parts were produced by you and to determine your productivity and quality.

If you use a copier, phone, fax or e-mail, your employer may monitor each of these and verify that they were used for proper business only.

If you are salesman, your car may be equipped with GPS (geographical Positioning System) that trends where the vehicle is driven at any time. If you are a truck driver, your employer may track the time and place of your stop and may ask for an explanation of your stop. The employer and the government may check that you complied with the appropriate authorized and allowed rest stop and your employer may check your print-out to check your compliance to speed regulations.

If you are a service person your employer may require you to have a GPS on your vehicle and on your person to determine at all times your whereabouts and may even bill customers directly by GPS for the time spent at each location. Parts may even have an embedded chip to track the use of parts for theft and billing purposes.

About the only place an employer may as of yet not keep you under video surveillance is in the companies rest rooms, but may monitor the time you spend on a cigarette break, coffee break or the time and times you visit the restroom.

Firms liable for home offices

Americans who work at home should expect to be covered by the same safety standards that apply in their company's offices, says a federal advisory that outlines how traditional workplace protections affect the growing number of people who telecommute.

"Ensuring safe and healthful working conditions for the employees should be a precondition for any home-based work assignments," said the Labor Department's Occupational Safety and Health Administration.

OSHA's advisory said companies must provide necessary protective equipment and guidance against hazards that will ensure home offices are set up safely. An example of such a hazard, it said, is a computer that could overload electrical circuits in a residence and create a fire hazard. According to the advisory, employers can be held liable if they know or should reasonably have known about home workplace hazards.

Workplace Surveillance

Employees in nearly every country are vulnerable to comprehensive surveillance by managers. Legal protections are generally more lax in such circumstances because surveillance is frequently imposed as a condition of employment. In many countries employers can tap phones, read email and monitor computer screens. They can bug conversations, analyze computer and keyboard work, peer through CCTV cameras, use tracking technology to monitor personal movements, analyze urine to detect drug use, and demand the disclosure of intimate personal data.

The technology being used to monitor workers is extremely powerful. It can analyze "keystrokes" on a terminal to determine whether employees are making efficient use of their time between telephone conversations. Software companies call this process "performance monitoring." Even in workplaces staffed by highly skilled information technology specialists, bosses demand the right to spy on every detail of a workers performance. Modern networked systems can interrogate computers to determine which software in being run, how often, and in what manner. A comprehensive audit trail gives managers a profile of each user, and a panorama of how the workers are interacting with their machines. The software also gives managers totally central control over the software on each individual PC.

A manager can now remotely modify or suspend programs on any machine.

The technology being used extends to every aspect of a worker's life. Miniature cameras monitor behavior. "Smart" ID badges track an employee's movement around a building. Telephone Management Systems analyze the pattern of telephone use and the destination of calls.

Psychological tests, general intelligence tests, aptitude tests, performance tests, vocational interest tests, personality tests and honesty tests are all electronically assessed. Surveillance and monitoring have become design components of modern information systems.

While companies assert that all surveillance is justified, it is clear that not all uses of monitoring are legitimate. Following some organizing activity by a local union, one U.S. employer installed video cameras to monitor each individual workstation and worker. Although management claimed that the technology was being established solely for safety monitoring, two employees were suspended for leaving their workstations to visit the toilet without permission. According to a report of the International Labor Office, the activities of union representatives on the floor was also inhibited by a "chilling effect" on workers who knew their conversations were being monitored.

A spate of well-publicized cases of similar abuses of visual surveillance has prompted concern in the workplace. A survey of employees throughout the U.S. revealed that 62 percent disagreed with the use of video surveillance. Nevertheless, a recent report by the American Management Association revealed that two thirds of American bosses spy on their workers, often through email and phone interception.

The report also says that "as the use of computers spreads throughout the world, workers in many countries are being subjected to new pressures, including electronic eavesdropping by superiors…" A survey of telecommunications workers sponsored in part by the Communications Workers of America revealed that 84 percent of monitored employees complained about high tension as opposed to 67 percent of unmonitored workers. A later study by the U.S. Office of Technology Assessment also found that workplace monitoring "contributes to stress and stress-related illness."

In Britain and the United States, there are few legal constraints on video surveillance, unlike the laws of Austria, Germany, Norway and Sweden, under which employers are obliged to seek agreement with workers on such matters.

This situation has been challenged in the European Court of Human Rights, Former British Assistant Chief Constable Allison Halford had complained that following her sex discrimination complaint against the police, her office phone had been bugged. While the British government asserted that this was an entirely lawful and proper activity, Halford maintained that it breached the right to privacy contained in the European Convention on Human Rights. The court agreed, and ruled that the police had acted improperly in bugging Ms. Halford's phone.

The practice is likely to breach laws which form in the wake of the European Telecommunications Directive. Currently, however, the court's decision appears to do little more that oblige bosses to notify workers that they should have no expectation of privacy on the phone. And accordingly, most businesses are moving to routine monitoring of phone calls.

Respecting Privacy Rights of Employees

The FOURTH amendment of the U.S. Constitution provides that "the right of the people to be secure in their persons, houses, papers, and effects, against unreasonable searches and seizures, shall not be violated."

We should know that this guarantee generally only applies to state action, and by statute to situations in which rights are violated under color of state law. Nonetheless, the rapid modern growth of statutory and common law privacy torts and statutory recognition of privacy rights in electronic and mail communications have given Americans privacy protection in contexts in which state action is usually absent.

The government should be cognizant of the privacy rights of employees, particularly in situations in which employees or prospective employees become targets of corporate investigations. We should not suppose that employees who are suspected of fraud or theft relinquish all privacy rights in the workplace. In particular, counsel should advise management and investigative personnel not to assume that a laudable end necessarily justifies the means of an expansive search into the employee's personal affairs and effects.

This article will briefly review the principal employee privacy concerns of which a corporation should be aware when involved in an internal investigation of an employee or prospective employee.

Common Law Rights

The common law right of privacy encompasses four distinct causes of action, only three of which are generally relevant as workplace torts. The four are: misappropriation of the plaintiff's name or likeness without his consent; intrusion by the defendant into an area in which the plaintiff's reasonable expectations of privacy are violated; public disclosure of private facts about the plaintiff; and portrayal of the plaintiff in a false light in the public eye.

Intrusion rights must be considered whenever employee's desks or work areas are searched, or personal records such as credit card accounts or bank records obtained, in an Amendment claim, an employee will claim that the employer violated his legitimate expectation of privacy. The question of whether such an expectation should exist is generally an issue of fact.

Whether a reasonable expectation of privacy will be deemed to exist will often hinge on the circumstances of each case. In K-Mart v. Trotti, a reasonable expectation of privacy was found in an employee locker which the employee had locked at her own expense and with the employer's consent. The court reasoned that the employer might have legitimately searched the locker had the lock been that of the employer, but held that "(w)here…the employee purchases and uses its own lock on the lockers, with the employer's knowledge, the fact finder is justified in concluding that the employee manifested, and the employer recognized, an expectation that the locker and its contents would be free from intrusion and interference."

Other privacy torts that might be implicated in an investigation are those of public disclosure of private facts and false light invasion of privacy. A claim for public disclosure of private facts is stated when an employer makes a public statement about an employee which, although concededly true, is nor a matter of public concern, the test is whether the disclosure would be highly offensive to a reasonable person.

A false light case, like a defamation claim, is premised upon false statements about the plaintiff. Although the connection need not be a defamatory one, a statement must be objectionable to a reasonable person in order to be actionable. Of course, even in states, like New York, that lack a common law privacy right, false and defamatory statements are still actionable. Thus, investigative personnel should be extremely circumspect about publishing any statements based upon findings or tentative conclusions of an internal investigation.

Polygraph Testing

Another area of concern is that of employer administration of polygraphs, or similar testing against an employee. Employers will often want to administer such tests because of legitimate concerns about possible employee theft or fraud, as well as about workplace safety and absenteeism. Employers should bear in mind that in New York; employer administration of polygraph testing to employees is unlawful.

Outside New York, employer polygraph testing is generally governed by the Employee Polygraph Protection Act of 1988, which broadly prohibits the use of polygraphs by employers. Generally, the Act makes it unlawful for any employer to require, request, suggest or cause any employee to take or submit to any lie detector test, or to use or rely upon the results of any polygraph test for the purpose of discharging or disciplining any employee. Employees have a private cause of action under the terms of the Act, and may not waive their rights under the Act. The Act imposes restrictions on the nature of the testing, the persons to whom the test results may be disclosed, and the uses to which the information derived from the test may be put.

A limited exception to the prohibitions of the Act exists in cases of ongoing investigations. An employer may administer a polygraph test to an employee if the test is administered in connection with an ongoing investigation involving economics loss or injury to the employer's business, such as theft, embezzlement, misappropriation, or an act of unlawful industrial espionage or sabotage, if (a) employee had access to the property that is the subject of the investigation; (b) the employer has a reasonable suspicion that the employee was involved in the incident to activity under investigation; and (c) the employer executes a statement, provided to the examinee before the test, that meets statutory requirements.

The test must set forth with particularity the specific incident or active being investigated, and the basis for testing particular employees must be signed by a person authorized to legally bind the employer, be retained by the employer for at least three years, and contain an identification of the specific economic loss or injury to the business of the employer, a statement indicating that the employee has access to the property that is the subject of the investigation, and a statement describing the basis of the employer's reasonable suspicion that the employee was involved in the incident or activity under the investigation.

An employer must be scrupulous about observing each of the requirements of the statute. In **Blackwell v. 53rd Ellis Currency Exchange**, an employer conducting an investigation into the loss of notary seals and cash shortages subjected all employees to a polygraph examination. The plaintiff was required to sign a statement acknowledging that she and other employees were required to the test. Shortly after the plaintiff was informed that she has passed the test, she was fired for a variety of reasons apparently having nothing to do with the matter under investigation.

The court held that the polygraph examinations violated the Act. Since the employer required all employees to take the polygraph examination, the court held that there was no "reasonable suspicion" of plaintiff personally. The court rejected the employer's preferred reasoning that plaintiff had access to the missing property. Also the statement signed by the plaintiff did not, as required, set forth with particularity the specific incident being investigated and the basis for testing particular employees.

Monitoring

The Electronic Communications Privacy Act of 1986 generally prohibits the interception of any wire, oral or electronic communication. This statute generally prohibits the monitoring of employee telephone conversations or external email (courts have not generally addressed the situation with respect to internal email).

An employer may, however, intercept the electronic communications of employees if the interception is made in the ordinary course of business, However, an employer must be able to state a legitimate business purpose, and there must be minimal intrusions into employee privacy. Employer monitoring of all conversations on employee phone lines will not pass muster under the ordinary course of business exception, and employers must not monitor calls that are evidently personal in nature.

An employer may be exempt from liability under the Act if it obtains the permission of the employer or other party to the conversation. Consent will not generally be implied.

Finally, an employer should be careful not to conduct searches of an employee's mail before it has been delivered. Federal law prohibits any person from taking a letter, postcard or package from the mail before it had been delivered, with design to obstruct the correspondence.

Conclusion

It is important for employers to be able to conduct investigations of employees when circumstances give rise to a suspicion of theft or fraud. In considering the means to conduct an investigation, an employer should ensure that employee privacy rights are safeguarded at all times, when appropriate, the employer should consider obtaining the written permission of the employee. Nonetheless, no workplace investigation, however carefully conducted, can possibly be immune to claims that employee privacy rights were violated. However, considering privacy issues beforehand, will minimize the chance that an employer investigation will result in a costly lawsuit.

Surveillance

One of the most controversial and significant workplace issues in the 90s and beyond is that of workplace and employee surveillance. Employees' concerns over the extent to which their activities are conduct are monitored by employers by the use of the telephone, computer, electronic mail or video cameras have resulted in an increasing number of lawsuits-a trend which will certainly continue.

Balanced against these concerns are the valid business interests of employers such as the need to assure that work is performed and efficiently, that customer calls are being properly handled, and that company assets, including valuable and confidential information, are not misused or misappropriated by employees. The challenge is to pursue these valid business interests in a way that does not infringe upon employee's valid personal and private communications.

The most significant federal law in this area is Title III of the Omnibus Crime Control and Safe Streets Act of 1968 and its amendments contained in the Electronic Communications Privacy Act of 1986, collectively known as the Federal Wiretap Statue. While this statue was intended primarily to regulate government use of wiretaps and other surveillance media, it also applies to private individuals and business. These various forms of surveillance are also subject to scrutiny under the principles of invasion of privacy, so it is no surprise that the cases decided under the Federal Wiretap Statue borrow concepts form this body of law.

The statutes prohibit, among other things, the actual or attempted willful interception of any wire, oral or electronic communication. The definition of "electronic communication' brings email within the coverage of the statutes. The statutes provide for criminal penalties, as well as civil damages, including punitive damages and attorney's fees in appropriate cases.

There are exceptions to the statues that give employers significant leeway to protect their legitimate business interests. For example, it is not a violation of the statues if an employer has obtained the consent of one party to a communication to intercept or listen in on the communication. In addition, employers with private phone and computer networks are permitted to intercept communication made by employees under a business use" exception to the statues, as long as the interception is done for the purpose of rendering services or to protect rights or property.

Company policy should make it clear that computers and communication systems and other assets can only be used for business purposes. The employer should provide notice that the contents of communications over these systems are business property, subject to access and monitoring by the employer, To minimize the impact on morale, an employer should establish and stick to clear guidelines.

As in the area of privacy, employers have been found in violation of the Federal Wiretap Statute when monitoring has gone beyond business interests and invades the employees' legitimate rights to privacy. The recording of person-to-person communications in the workplace may also violate the statue if the employee has a reasonable expectation of privacy in the conversation being recorded.

Video (only) surveillance is not addressed by the wiretap statutes but would be subject to the same general privacy guidelines as other types of surveillance. As long as the camera does not invade a place where the employee has a reasonable expectation of privacy, then the surveillance should not rise to a claim of invasion of privacy.

Employer efforts to provide a safe and secure work environment involves a balancing of employer business interest and employee rights. By implementing security measures in a well-planned and controlled manner and keeping employees informed of the reason and deeds for them, employer should be able to establish an effective security program with a minimum of disruption or legal risk.

...No More Heat. Too much of a good thing is not good...

Chapter XV
News Media

"Now it's no good to have such rights if they're not used- a right of free speech when no one contradicts the government, freedom of the press when no one is willing to ask the tough questions, a right of assembly when there are no protests, universal suffrage when less than half the electorate votes, separation of church and state when the wall of separation is not regularly repaired. Through disuse they can become no more that votive objects, patriotic lip-service. Rights and freedoms: Use 'em or lose 'em.

-James Madison

Media Bias

1) Most Americans think that the media are biased. Almost half (49%) think that the media usually don't "get the facts straight."

2) Some two-thirds believe the media don't "deal fairly with all sides" in social and political reporting.

3) Almost three-fourths of Americans see a "fair amount" or "great deal" of political bias in the news. And by more than a 2-to-1 ratio, poll respondents said that bias is liberal rather than conservative (43%-19%).

4) More than 60% of Americans surveyed prefer the media to "simply report the facts" and not "weigh the facts and offer suggestions about how to solve problems." This is a sharp break from ABC News' motto "News With Solutions."

5) Some 65% do not believe that "journalists should point out what they believe are inaccuracies and distortions in the statements of public figures."

6) Nearly 60% believe the news media have "too much influence."

7) Some 47% think journalists have values different from their own.

Misleading headlines are an especially devious form of media bias. Anyone who scans newspaper headlines to get an idea of what the news is can get a totally skewed perception of the information contained within the article.

Rewriting History

George Orwell penned the following about the tyrannical and totalitarian State described so vividly in his chilling novel, 1984:

The past is whatever the records and the memories agree upon. And since the party is in full control of all records, and in equally full control of the minds of its members, it follows that the past is whatever the party chooses to make it.

The White House misled the public into war in Iraq. Now the Administration argues it didn't happen that way.

There was a pretty damning article in The Washington Post about the way President George W. Bush and his administration sold the claim that Iraq was developing nuclear weapons. The article makes clear the extent to which the White House lent credence to worst case scenarios and assumptions about Saddam Hussein's intentions at the expense of plausability. The White House also misled the American public and its allies in the United Nations by selectively releasing intelligence.

After September 11, the CIA and other intelligence sources were condemned for their conservatism in analyzing intelligence. Unless something was verified, they dismissed it, and thus were unable to "Connect the dots" leading to Al Qaeda's terrorist attack.

To those who didn't know any better-that is, almost everyone except the Iraqi and U.S. intelligence agencies – the case against Iraq seemed overwhelming.

Consider this quote from Cheney, cited in The Washington Post: "We now know that Saddam has resumed his efforts to acquire nuclear weapons. Among other sources, we've gotten this from firsthand testimony from defectors, including Saddam's own son-in-law." This sounds definitive.

Unfortunately, The Washington Post reports, the Vice President was lying:

That was a reference to Hussein Kamel, who had managed Iraq's special weapons programs before defecting in 1995 to Jordan. But Saddam Hussein lured Kamel back to Iraq, and he was killed in February 1996, so Kamel could not have sourced what U.S. officials "now know."

And Kamel's testimony, after defecting, was the reverse of Cheney's description. In one of many debriefings by U.S., Jordanian and U.N. officials, Kamel said on Aug. 22, 1995, that Iraq's uranium enrichment programs had not resumed after halting at the start of the Gulf War in 1991. According to notes typed for the record by U.N. arms inspector Nikita Smidovich, Kamel acknowledged efforts to design three different warheads, "but not now, before the Gulf War."

Using the newer aggressive mode of interpreting intelligence, Bush placed Saddam in a no-win situation. Based on prior experience, the Bush administration decided Saddam was an untrustworthy villain who wanted to take over the world and destroy the United States. Given this assumption, the White House further assumed Saddam was hiding weapons and commanded him to prove he did not. If you believed Saddam was hiding his weapons this made some sense. But if you allowed the remote possibility that these weapons did not exist, then a catch-22 was revealed, because Saddam could never prove the negative, that he wasn't hiding the weapons in a country the White House never failed to remind us is "the size of California."

Although there was scant evidence for man of their allegations, the White House – and British Prime Minister Tony Blair –made specific and bold claims about Saddam's "weapons of mass destruction" programs. Bush's claim, made in the State of the Union and other speeches, that Iraq had sought to purchase uranium sounded unequivocal. The claim was based, however, on the scantest of intelligence and it was not true.

The claim that Iraq attempted to buy uranium from Niger has now become famous as the 16 words, but a claim that stood out in the speech for its specificity and the confidence with which it was made, and part of a pattern of deception.

Citing a newly released unpublished draft white paper on Iraq, The Washington Post finds several misleading arguments the White House codified in unpublished form but repeated in speech after speech:

Much as Blair did at Camp David, the paper attributed to U.N. arms inspectors a statement that satellite photographs show "many signs of the reconstruction and acceleration of the Iraqi nuclear program." Inspectors did not say that. The paper also quoted the first half of a sentence from a Time magazine interview with U.N. chief weapons inspector Hans Blix: "You can see hundreds of new roofs in these photos." The second half of the sentence, not quoted, was: "but you don't know what's under them."

As Bush did, the white paper cited the IAEA's description of Iraq's defunct nuclear program in language that appeared to be current. The draft said, for example, that "since the beginning of the nineties, Saddam has launched a crash program to divert nuclear reactor fuel for…nuclear weapons." The crash program began in late 1990 and ended with the war in January 1991. The reactor fuel, save for waste products, is gone.

Given that no weapons of mass destruction or any nuclear program has been uncovered in Iraq since the United States took control, two interpretations are possible. Using the intelligence community's previous, conservative mode of analysis, one would conclude the weapons never existed. White House has dismissed this mode of analysis, however, as insufficiently imaginative, so one must consider other possible cases. If one wishes to continue to give the President the benefit of the doubt, the most likely scenario is that Saddam's active weapons programs and chemical and biological stockpiles are hiding in the same cave as Osama bin Laden. And if that is the case, we are very much worse off than before the war.

If you don't take this possibility seriously-and the White House doesn't seem to, since they haven't mentioned it-then you have to acknowledge a hole in the Administration's case for war large enough to drive two mobile hydrogen-producing trailers through.

Weapons of mass destruction

President Bush for whom I really voted for broke all of his campaign promises when he invaded Iraq.

First, he stated that Saddam had supported the 9/11 attack. So much propaganda was spewed that over 50% of the Americans were made to believe that Saddam himself was behind the attack.

Then Bush claimed Saddam had biological and nuclear weapons that were ready to be used against the United States. When none were found, rocket parts buried behind a rose bush were shown to be buried nuclear weapons.

President Bush than stated that the USA must enforce the UN resolution that Saddam did not comply with. Nothing was said on the twice as many resolutions that Israel did not comply with.

Finally, history was rewritten by the Bush administrations that we went there to free the Iraqis from an oppressive dictator. Where was the U.S. in Rowanda when over a million people were slaughtered. Or where in the U.S. to enforce human rights violations in china.

Did you notice how President Bush triumphantly entered Bagdad last Thanksgiving with his plastic turkey. Yes, he flew in under cover of night to spend a few minutes with his troops. If the USA really freed and liberated the Iraqis, why does the President have to sneak in at night? Now history is re-written again with the question, "Aren't the Iraqi better off than before and we have given them democracy and a free world.

The whole election and the News Media lives on political spin.

Political aphorisms don't get any more cogent: "Who controls the past controls the future; who controls the present controls the past."

George Orwell's famous observation goes a long way toward explaining why -—a full year after the invasion of Iraq – the media battles over prewar lies are so ferocious in the United States. Top administration officials are going all out to airbrush yesterday's deceptions on behalf of today's. and tomorrow's.

The future they want most to control starts on Election Day. And with scarcely seven months to go in the presidential campaign, the past that Bush officials are most eager to obscure is their own record. In late 2002 and early last year, whenever the drive to war hit a bump, they maneuvered carefully to keep the war caravan moving steadily forward.

There was no doubt, they were a hard-driving bunch. The most powerful squad of the Bush foreign-policy team ran on the fuel of certitude at such a prodigious rate that even their momentum had momentum – maybe, in part, because their lives' trajectories seemed to demand it. War had been declared first within themselves.

Perhaps such steeliness has been almost boilerplate in history; excuses for aggressive war have never been hard to come by. In this case, no amount of geopolitical analysis –from media pundits, academics and other commentators –could really do more to shed light than the light bulb comprehension that these people in charge had from the outset made the determination that war it would be.

So, every attempt at civic engagement and demonstrations against the war scenario was, in effect, trying to impede "leaders" who had already gone around the bend. A very big bend. One of the American mass media taboos was to seriously suggest the possibility that the lot of them –Bush, Cheney, Rumsfield, Rice and, yes, Powell –were, in their pursuit of war on Iraq, significantly deranged.

Working back from their conclusion of war's necessity, top Bush administration officials –with assistance from many reporters and pundits –were reading the calendar backwards, hell-bent on getting the invasion underway well before the extreme heat of summer.

There was also political weather to be navigated. Though much more susceptible to manipulation than the four seasons, the electoral storms would be starting for the 2004 presidential contest, and a secured victory over Iraq well in advance seemed advisable.

The peace-seeking pretense was dripping with charade in the months before the invasion. Journalists kept writing and talking about the chances of war as though President Bush hadn't already made up his mind to order it. Yet what Bush said in public was exactly opposite to reality – a "one-eighty." When he talked about preferring to find an acceptable alternative to war, he was determined to bypass and destroy every alternative to war.

Rational arguments would not work to forestall the presidential order to unleash the Pentagon. Despite the obstacles, which included vital activism and protests for peace, the chief executive easily got to have his war – the best kind, to be fought and endured only by others.

Key questions of the past are also crucial for the future. For instance, can the United States credibly wage a "war on terrorism" by engaging in warfare that terrorizes civilians?

Close to 10,000 Iraqi civilians have died because of the war during the past year.

Does the mix of mendacity and deadly violence from the Oval Office really strike against terrorism, or does it fuel terrorist cycles?

And, in the realm of news media, how many journalists are willing and able to go beyond reliance on official sources enough to bring us truth about lies that result in death?

As with all wars in the past the victor rewrites the history, putting himself as the righteous person and soon the world believes the new history.

The best proof of how the news media distorts the news (truth) is to listen to a speech and the minute it is over, we are told what was said and what was meant by the speech and it may be totally different as to what was meant by the speaker, than what you heard. You look puzzled, but you know what you heard and it was different.

... Steam rises from the kettle and we can barely stand the heat, enough is enough...

Chapter XVI
Property Rights

"The only thing that saves us from bureaucracy is inefficiency An efficient bureaucracy is the greatest threat to liberty."

-Eugene McCarthy

"Government employees (Bureaucrats) like to solve problems. If there are no problems handily available, they will create their own problems."

-George Van Valkenburg

For nearly 227 years America has prospered because this nation has operated under a rule of law that was designed to protect the individual's right to pursue his own life in the way he chooses. To work, to play, to invest, to own property and to use it in the way that best suits his or her needs. Yet, today, we are witnessing courts that toss aside election laws, that take over whole school systems and then demand taxes be imposed to implement their rulings, a function of legislatures and local communities.

The Founding Fathers, particularly James Madison, took those ideas of limited government to heart and put them in the Fifth Amendment of the Constitution. It limits government taking of private property, saying no American shall "be deprived of life, liberty or property without due process; now shall private property be taken for public use without just compensation." This is a guarantee to Americans that they are safe and free to pursue their own lives without interference from government. It says it is the government's job to protect those liberties. Without that guarantee there can be no society. Chaos and tyranny would replace order and prosperity.

Guaranteed by those protections, Americans began to work their land. With their free minds they invented new approaches, and created new jobs, and found new ways to prosper. As a result, our standard of living improved. Science improved health care. Life expectancy increased. And wealth followed. Americans have created an incredible society out of a barren wilderness.

Liberty became our birthright and visions of freedom became our legacy to much of the world's people still yearning to be free. Today, as we are under attack by terrorists, the nation rallies around our belief in freedom. Flags fly from our homes and car antennas. Bumper stickers declare "God Bless America." Banners shout "Let Freedom Ring."

The question must be asked; do we still have those freedoms or is our pride in America now based mostly on propaganda and memories from another era? The answer is that today, an army of bureaucrats care nothing about those rights and the politicians, the ones who seek our votes every few years, don't care either. They keep passing laws to give the bureaucrats the power to run roughshod over our rights.

Their only true concern is that you are verbally appease until Election Day while they wink at the radical environmentalists who slip money in their pockets. Step by step, American liberty is disappearing. Americans are being ruled, regulated restricted, licensed, registered, directed, checked, inspected, measured, numbered, counted, rated, stamped, censured, authorized, admonished, refused, prevented, drilled, indoctrinated, monopolized, extorted, robbed, hoaxed, fined, harassed, disarmed, dishonored, fleeced, exploited, assessed, and taxed to the point of suffocation and desperation.

We lost the wisdom of the need for individuals to have the right to own and control private property. The fact is no other rights can exist without property rights. How can you have free speech if you aren't allowed to control your own property? Step by step, property rights are being eliminated in America and that means we are eliminating freedom.

Too many people in America have accepted the idea that they have the right to tell other people what to do with their private lives and their private property. And they believe there is nothing wrong with using the power of government to enforce those ideas. They have become the Sustainable Development lynch mob.

Ask yourself these questions. Do you support zoning laws? Do you support land-development plans and restrictions? Do you support restrictions on where businesses can be placed? Do you support how waterways are used? Do you support historic preservation? Do you support restrictions on building designs to create uniformity? Do you support community growth management? Are you an active member of a homeowners association?

In every case, you are licensing the government to infringe on someone else's property rights. And what happens if a bigger mob doesn't like what you are doing with your land? Once the precedent has been established the monster is out of the bag. There is no turning back.

If and when Sustainable Development is implemented and imposed, every one of these things are to be controlled by decisions made for you by government bureaucrats, members of private, non-government organizations in partnership with private businesses and elected representatives, working together in specially organized councils with names like sustainability councils, stakeholder councils.

John Adams said, "The moment the idea is admitted into society that property is not as sacred as the laws of God and there is not a force of law and public justice to protect it, anarchy and tyranny commence."

We keep electing politicians who offer the best argument on how to use government power. We select our leaders today based on which ones have the best plan for collecting taxes; the best plan for restricting land use; the best plan for providing government-restricted medical care and drug prescription and soon, if some get their way, the best plan to even control what we eat.

We seem to have one property right left. The right to keep paying taxes and the mortgage payments as we live by the permission of the government. We have been losing our freedoms because we have lost the knowledge of why this nation was founded.

The government now can tell you what kind of fence you must build on your property if you can build one at all.

A few years ago, I had an eight flat building built. The Village approved the construction and provided a building permit and an occupancy permit for the construction. Then for years, the village collected an annual tax for eight units and inspected each unit.

Then a few years later, the building was put on the market for sale and all of a sudden the Village stated that the building is only a six flat instead of an eight flat for two apartments on the lower floor had only one exit instead of two and obviously the buyer refused to pay as much as contracted for the property. Do you think the Village reimbursed me for the loss of value?

Europeans are stunned to hear that my annual real estate tax is higher than six hundred dollars a month.

They don't understand that ever though you pay for the lot, and build a house, the government can sell your house for non payment of taxes. It is as if we don't own our houses, just lease them from the government and if we fail to pay the real estate tax on our home, we loose it. A similar tax on a home in Europe is less than $20 a year.

The Government can stop you from cutting trees you have in your yard even though you planted them and they can stop you from planting trees without their permission.

In villages where there is no more land to develop, the building department creates obstacles to perpetuate its existence.

If you want to replace a small roof over the front entrance you need an architectural reading and a material list certified by an architect and pay a hefty permit fee to just change the appearance of the roof.

A church wishing to develop part of it's land for single family housing had to go through five years of zoning law meetings, civil engineering drawings, agree to keep one lot for water detention and pay for the village to bring all utilities to the premises including paying for a sewer lift station that the village had wanted already for a long time.

Not, that the city was happy that twelve houses would bring in about sixty thousand a year in Real Estate Taxes since the church was exempt from those taxes the village wanted more.

To develop a parcel of land, flood plan maps, wetland, environmental inspections, water retention, detention and flow, soil baring, civil engineering, historical society cleaning, wild life and plant growth and approval from many other numerous governmental agencies.

...Wow is it hot, my skin is burning, no more heat...

Chapter XVII
Children's Rights

"Man creates problems. Government and bureaucrats magnify them 100 times."

-George Van Valkenburg

"Politicians are like diapers. They should both be changed frequently and for the same reason."

-Anonymous

If you listen to former President Clinton and former first lady, Hillary, it seems that everything they did was for the children.

Children's rights have expanded world wide through the efforts of the United Nations that the government has become the protector of children giving parents less and less rights in deciding what's the best for the children. It's almost as if the US Government is following the formula spelled out in George Orwell's book 1984.

Children have been given the right to sue their parents for a divorce, not providing a good education or a myriad of things that parent's previously held sacred as their right as a parent.

In the U.S., the government has a right to give to children a drug called Ritalin without notifying the parents. Children are given drugs to calm them down. They get exposed to drugs and as they get older and when we have high school students that are drugged, we should not be surprised.

It is a horribly sobering realization that Columbine, Colorado, while devastating in its consequences, is only the latest in a tragic trail of incomprehensible acts of mayhem and murder. One need only read a newspaper or watch a television news broadcast to know that schools are not the only place these assaults have taken place. A review of media reports from the last fifteen years reveals that these incidents are also occurring on our highways, in restaurants, post offices and homes and factories from coast to coast. While the number of these incidents continues to escalate, a more disturbing fact is the increasingly bizarre nature of these pointless murders and suicides.

Acts of criminal violence have been with us since time immemorial but what we have been witnessing over the last couple of decades staggers the mind and assaults the senses. These grotesque acts, devoid of any possible sense of moral decency strike us as completely incomprehensible-mothers blowing the brains out of their small children, fathers slashing their young children to pieces, employees "calmly" walking through their offices or factories murdering their fellow co-workers as they go and young children going on maniacal shooting sprees in school yards.

As each new incident is reported, we sit in stunned horror in front of our television sets and wonder what is happening to our way of life. How can we be in the twenty-first century with technology snowballing us into a space age future and yet continue to find ourselves without a solution to the escalating number of acts of random, senseless violence? The reason is that we have been fed all manner of wrong reasons for why these tragedies have taken place and so they continue.

It is not guns that are common denominator to these horrific events some occur with knives, axes and even automobiles. Nor is it clothing, age, gender, or political orientation. The fact missed by most is that psychiatric, mind-altering drugs have been found to be the common factor in an overwhelming number of these acts of random senseless violence. These drugs, on an ever-increasing rise in society and amongst school children, particularly over the last two decades, are actually creating acts of violence. In short, the rise in senseless violence in America is date-coincident with the increased use of psychiatric mind-altering drugs.

In the U.S., there are now approximately four million children on the psychiatric drug, Ritalin, a drug which the Drug Enforcement Agency (DEA) places in the same category as opium, morphine and cocaine.

Psychotic episodes and violent behavior are associated with chronic Ritalin abuse. Ritalin is the amphetamine like drug widely prescribed to children for the contrived mental disease, "Attention Deficit Hyperactivity Disorder" (ADHD).

Even Ritalin's manufacturer warns that "frank psychotic episodes can occur" with abusive use. While the American Psychiatric Association's Diagnostic and Statistical Manual of Mental Disorders states that the major complication of Ritalin withdrawal is suicide.

If this were not bad enough, over 909,000 children and adolescents between the ages of six and eighteen are on psychiatric antidepressant drugs.

And in this regard, it is important to note that there were reports of over 90 children and adolescents who had suffered suicidal or violent self-destructive behavior while on the newer antidepressant Prozac.

Now imaging that a school nurse or administrator can give your child Ritalin without asking you. What happens as children get older or become adults when they are raised on drugs?

The scientific research documents the connection between violence and suicide and psychiatric drugs is overwhelming.

Brief excerpts from some studies documenting the violence/suicide connection follow:

Testing revealed that Eric Harris, one of the dead suspects in the Colorado incident, had therapeutic levels of Luvox in his blood.

"Luvox is the trade name for fluid which research shows can induce mania...One symptom of mania can begin behavior."

The New York Post reported that they had obtained documents (through Freedom of Informant Law) that the New York Psychiatric Institute was testing Prozac on six-year-olds. The documents obtained by the Post showed that under these drug trials the psychiatric researchers own documents noted that "Some patients have been reported to have an increase in thoughts and/or violent behavior." Another side effect with manic episodes was in the researchers' records.

A study of children taking Ritalin found that some grew hysterical or hostile. One of the kids began "exhibiting excessive irritability and anger, pacing excessively and declaring that he was not afraid anymore, that he was 'not chicken anymore'."

A study found that patients taking the drug Elavil, an anti-depressant, appeared progressively more hostile, irritable, and behaviorally impulsive increase in demanding behavior and assaultive act was statistically significant.

Another little known fact is that from psychiatric drugs can turn people horrifically violent. The fact that these create this effect can be obscured because frequently after a violent crime has been committed, psychiatrists blame person's violent behavior on his failure to continue his medication, but the truth is that extreme violence is a documented side-effect of withdrawal from psychiatric drugs.

Viewed against this and the dramatic increase in the use of mind-altering drugs by children and adults alike the cause for the rise of senseless violence becomes all too clear.

● ● ● ●

The government has become so involved in deciding who has what rights over children that we hear new reports that leave us wondering if parents have anything to say at all over their children.

Russian immigrant Tatiana Glotova appeared in court on charges she left her seven-year-old son, Dennis, alone in a New York City park for two hours while she worked.

Glotova, twenty-five, of Paterson, NJ, denied she left the boy unsupervised. According to a statement read in court, Glotova said she could see the boy from where she worked.

" I could see the boy from my building. I didn't know I couldn't leave him outside," she said.

Glotova was released without bond on charges of endangering the welfare of a child. Her son was placed in foster care while the case was investigated.

● ● ● ●

Danish officials charged city authorities with overreacting after they arrested Annette Sorensen, a Danish actress, for leaving her fourteen month old daughter In a baby stroller on the sidewalk while she and the infant's father had drinks in a restaurant.

Sorensen said that leaving babies in carriages outside shops and restaurants was common in Denmark. The case against Sorenson and the child's father was dropped. Both of them were jailed and charged with child neglect when the incident occurred.

● ● ● ●

A six-year-old boy was charged with a crime for kissing a schoolmate.

● ● ● ●

A nine-year-old was arrested and strip searched and taken out of school for putting his handprint on fresh cement on school grounds.

● ● ● ●

A mother was arrested for leaving two small children in her fenced back yard alone while she was in the house.

● ● ● ●

The government has sided with the UN definition of a child and what rights a child has.

A child is recognized as a person under eighteen, unless national laws recognize the age of majority earlier.

All actions concerning the child shall take full account of his or her best interests. The State shall provide the child with adequate care when parents, or others charged with that responsibility, fail to do so.

The child has a right to a name at birth. The child also has the right to acquire a nationality and, as far as possible, to know his or her parents and be cared for by them.

The child has a right to live with his or her parents unless this is deemed to be incompatible with the child's best interests. The child also has the right to maintain contact with both parents if separated from one or both.

The State has an obligation to prevent and remedy the kidnapping or retention of children abroad by a parent or third party.

The child has the right to express his or her opinion freely and to have that opinion taken into account in any matter or procedure affecting the child.

The child has the right to express his or her views, obtain information, and make ideas or information know, regardless of frontiers.

Parents have joint primary responsibility for raising the child, and the State shall support them in this. The State shall provide appropriate assistance to parents in child raising.

The State shall protect the child from all forms of maltreatment by parents or others responsible for the care of the child and establish appropriate social programs for the prevention of abuse and the treatment of victims.

The child has a right to the highest standard of health and medical care attainable. States shall place special emphasis on the provision of primary and preventive health care, public health education and the reduction of infant mortality. They shall encourage international cooperating in this regard and strive to see that no child is deprived of access to effective health services.

A child who is placed by the State for reasons of care, protection or treatment is entitled to have that placement evaluated regularly.

Every child has the right to a standard of living adequate for his or her physical, mental, spiritual, moral and social development. Parents have the primary responsibility to ensure that the child has an adequate standard of living. The State's duty is to insure that this responsibility can be fulfilled, and is. State responsibility can include material assistance to parents and their children.

The child has a right to education, and the State's duty is to ensure that primary education is free and compulsory, to encourage different forms of secondary education accessible to every child and to make higher education available to all on the basis of capacity. School discipline shall be consistent with the child's rights and dignity. The State shall engage in international co-operation to implement this right.

Children of minority communities and indigenous populations have the right to enjoy their own culture and to practice their own religion and language.

The child has the right to be protected from work that threatens his or her health, education or development. The State shall set minimum ages for employment and regulate working conditions.

Children have the right to protection from the use of narcotic and psychotropic drugs, and from being involved in their production or distribution.

The State shall protect children from sexual exploitation and abuse, including prostitution and involvement in pornography.

No child shall be subjected to torture, cruel treatment of punishment, unlawful arrest or deprivation of liberty. Both capital punishment and life imprisonment without the possibility of release are prohibited for offenses committed by persons below eighteen years. Any child deprived of liberty shall be separated from adults unless it is considered in the child's best interests not to do so. A child who is detained shall have legal and other assistance as well as contact with the family

Yet, the USA is only one of six nations that authorizes the execution of persons for crimes committed below the age of eighteen.

Too young to love

How far does the state go? Enclosed are excerpts from an article in an issue of St. Petersburg Tribune with the headline "Teenage love may be a crime to court."

Because he loves her, Tim Smith went to the Pasco County Courthouse in Dade City with every intention of marrying his girlfriend, Jessica Berggren, the mother of his unborn child.

The wedding didn't come off for the young couple because sixteen-year-old Jessica forgot to bring identification.

Smith, nineteen, will return to the courthouse, but this time it will be to face Circuit Judge Maynard Swanson. He is scheduled to face charges that he committed a criminal sex act against Jessica.

What Timothy and Jessica call love, the state attorney calls a lewd and lascivious act on a child under the age of eighteen.

Like many teen-age lovers, Tim and Jessica expressed their love on the physical level. They made love. And from that love making, there will come a child. And in that child the state has the evidence that it needs, along with Tim's confession, to charge the young man with a felony that could send him to prison for a maximum of fifteen years.

Many sexually active teens and their parents are not aware to the legal consequences of mixed aged romance. But defense attorneys are all too familiar with the growing number of cases like Tim and Jessica's.

"We got these things trough here all the time, consensual sex," said the Assistant Public Defender. "And it's dishearting how many of them go to prison. All I can say is, it's a good thing that Christ wasn't born in Florida, because Joseph would be doing a quick four to five years in prison."

Smith's attorney, Assistant Defender Alan Howell, said that even with Tim's clean record, he would probably face a prison sentence of six to ten years if convicted.

"I think (the law) was meant more for people who are twenty-one or twenty-two." Howell said. "A twenty-four-year-old can't sleep with a sixteen-year-old. And I would be opposed to a twenty-one-year-old and a fifteen-year-old. Still, it's a second-degree felony and he actually faces a maximum of fifteen years in prison. That to me is harsh."

Jessica, seven months pregnant, was several months shy of her sixteenth birthday when she and Tim conceived a fetus. Tim was eighteen years old-an adult-at the time. The disparity in their ages and their ill-advised timing made their actions a violation of state law. It made their love, and how they chose to express it, a crime.

"We just want to be left alone," Jessica said. "I just want to be able to be with him, and not have any problems. He's a good person. He cares about me and loves me, same as I care about and love him. He's not going to get you pregnant and leave you. I just love him for who he is."

"I still love her," Tim said. "I care for her very much. If anything, I think this has brought us closer together."

Tim and Jessica have been "together" for almost a year, except for three months after his arrest when a restraining order prevented him from even talking to Jessica.

Tim graduated from River Ridge High School. He had steady work with his father, who worked at a company installing lawn sprinklers. And he was ready for some independence. Jessica's stepfather, Larry Jones, said Tim was looking for a room to rent. Because the family had an extra room in their home in Cypress Bayou, and because the family needed some extra income, Tim was invited to move in.

Despite the occasional tension in the home, both sets of parents support Tim and Jessica and both speak highly of them.

"He's a clean-cut boy," said Jessica's mother, Sonya Jones. "Nice, short haircut, clean shaved, good manner. He's not one of these hoodlums out here on the street. I mean she could've picked a whole lot worse. He's been brought up strict just like she has."

"He did what a man should do," Larry Jones said. "He didn't pack his bags and say, "I'm gone." He stayed right here and said, "I'll face this with you."

Jessica thought she was pregnant, but it was a false alarm. After her sixteenth birthday on the twenty-seventh of the month, Jessica went to a health department clinic for a pregnancy test, which came back positive.

"I was happy," Jessica said. "We want it. I was scared but not scared scared."

The school resource officer heard about it, Tim said, and soon the Department of Children and Families was on the case and so was the Pasco County Sheriff's Officer.

Things had happened quickly. Jessica turned sixteen on a Wednesday and went to the health department on Thursday. Tim was asked to leave the home he shared with Jessica on Friday, although he said it wasn't because of the positive pregnancy test.

By Monday, Pasco Sheriff's Detective Brett Landsberg spoke with Tim and asked him to come to the sheriff's substation in Land O'Lakes on Tuesday.

Tim told the detectives that Jessica's baby was his. He was charged with one count of lewd and lascivious act on a child under the age sixteen and spent Tuesday night in the Pasco County jail before being released on his own recognizance Wednesday afternoon.

In the span of a week, Tim had become a father, an outcast and an accused criminal facing the same kind of jail time and conditions faced by child molesters, rapists and sexual predators.

Jessica came to court wearing a flowered dress and a pained look on her face. At four-and-a-half months pregnant, she rubbed her hand over her stomach and her face, battling the cramps that had plagued her off and on since Tim's arrest.

Because of the restraining order, Tim was forbidden from seeing or talking to Jessica. He and his attorney went before Judge Swanson seeking to have the order lifted.

Jessica had leaned her head on the bench seat in front of her while her mother massaged Jessica's lower back. At the podium, Tim's attorney was introducing a piece of evidence to support his request.

Jessica's obstetrician, Dr. Reginald L. Simmons, had written a letter asking the judge to allow the young lovers to be together again.

"I do believe that she is under a lot of stress, which could be the cause of the cramping she's having, and that some of the stress is related to the situation with her boyfriend," Dr. Simmons wrote. "I feel that if you allow them to see each other, this might relieve some of the problem."

Swanson granted the request and lifted the restraining order over the objectives of Assistant State Attorney Phil Van Allen.

Outside the courtroom, Tim was all smiles as he held and kissed Jessica.

"You're allowed to hold hands now," Sonja Jones said. "Does she look like a victim? Maybe a victim of love."

Some young girls are victimized by older men and by their misguided concept of love.

Marilyn Anderson, director of education for Planned Parenthood of Southwest and Central Florida, sees them all the time.

Anderson has spent much of the year focusing on a new sex education program called "Unequal Partners," which addressed the growing problem of adult-teen relationships.

"Is teens dating adults an issue? Statistics and research say it's a problem," Anderson said. "The trick is to get young people to acknowledge dangerous relationships, especially young girls who are looking for romance, who are looking for someone to love them forever."

Anderson said the trend in Florida and nationally is prosecution only after a birth. But she questioned the wisdom of jailing a parent who wants to participate in his child's life.

Anderson said a better solution would be to make the "punishment" fit the crime. She suggests "sentencing" people such as Tim to attend parenting to obtain a high school diploma, to get and keep a good job to support his family.

"If we want him to be a productive part of society and we want him to be actively involved in the life of his child, let's set him up to win instead of set him up to fail."

Ritalin Prescription a No-Brainer

"bureaucracy is nothing more than the hardening of an organizations' arteries." -William P. Anthony

Too many Children are diagnosed and treated for attention deficit/ hyperactivity disorder even though they're guilty of nothing more than acting their age.

I don't believe anyone has any idea what Ritalin does to our children. Will they move on to Prozac and live like zombies when they grow up. We should let children be children.

We have let our schools be the guardians of our children. No longer do parents control their children, they have handed over this obligation to the governmental agents, the school masters and the drugs.

We wonder why children grow up and become violent, they never had an outlet to be children and we won't let them. It has been shown that school violence is usually committed by students taking psychotropic drugs.

U.S. Children take over 90% of all Ritalin in the world

Some experts who certify new disorders "receive extravagant annual retainers from pharmaceutical companies that profit from the promotion of disorders treatable by the companies' medications."

One alternative to Ritalin might be school choice – parents finding schools suited to their children's temperaments. When it is difficult to change the institutional environment, "we don't think twice about changing the brain of the person who has to live in it." Psychiatrists believe the rambunctiousness of boys is treated as a mental disorder by people eager to interpret sex differences as personal deficiencies.

...The Frog feels faint as the water around him begins to move, it is almost too late...

Chapter XVIII
Education

"Politics is supposed to be the second-oldest profession. I have come to realize that it bears a very close resemblance to the first."

-Ronald Reagan

> " We ask that the government to provide for all citizens an adequate opportunity for employment and earning a living."
>
> "The activities of the individual must not be allowed to clash with the interests of the community, but must take place within its confines and be for the good of all. Therefore, we demand: an end to the power of the financial interests."
>
> "We demand profit sharing in big business."
>
> "We demand a broad extension of care for the aged."
>
> "We demand the greatest possible consideration of small business in the purchases of the national, state and municipal government."
>
> "In order to make possible every capable and industrious [citizen] the attainment of higher education and thus the achievement of a post of leadership, the government must provide and all-around enlargement of our entire system of public education...We demand the education at government expense of gifted children of poor parents..."
>
> "The government must undertake the improvement of public health by protecting mother and child, by prohibiting child labor

> by the greatest possible support for all clubs concerned with the physical education of youth."
>
> "We combat the materialistic spirit within and without us, and are convinced that a permanent recovery of our people can only proceed from within on the foundation of The Common Good Before The Individual Good."

Now let me surprise you. The above statements are the exact Nazi Party of Germany statements adopted in Munich.

We think that "Public schooling is a distinctively American institution as American as apple pie and free enterprise."

The truth? As Sheldon Richman documents so well in his book, "Separating School and State", twentieth-century American adopted the idea of a state schooling system in the latter part of the nineteenth century from -you guessed it – Prussia! And as Mr. Richman points out, public schooling has proven as successful in the United States as it is in Germany. Why? Because it has succeeded in its goal of producing a nation of "good little citizens' –people who pay their taxes on time, follow the rules, obey orders, condemn and turn in the rule breakers, and see themselves as essential cogs in the national wheel.

In the hands of the state, compulsory public education becomes a tool for political control and manipulation a prime instrument for the thought police of society. And precisely because every child passes through the same indoctrination process learning the same lessons of obedience and the same "civic virtues", the same lessons of obedience and loyalty to the state it becomes extremely difficult for the independent soul to free himself from the straight jacket of the ideology and values the political authorities wish to imprint upon the population under its jurisdiction. For the communists, it was the class struggle and obedience to the Party and Comrade Stalin; for the fascists, it was worship of the nation state and obedience to the Duce; for the Nazis, it was race purity and obedience to the Future. The content has varied, but the form has remained the same. Through the institution of compulsory state education, the child is to be molded like wax into the shape desired by the state and its education elite.

We should not believe that because ours is a freer, more democratic society, the same imprinting procedure has not occurred even here, in America. Every generation of school-age children has imprinted upon it a politically correct ideology concerning America's past and the sanctity of the role of the state in society. Practically every child in the public school system learns that the "robber barons" of the 19th century exploited the common working man; that unregulated capitalism needed to be harnessed by enlightened government regulation beginning in the progressive era at the turn of the century; that wild Wall Street speculation was a primary cause of the Great Depression; that only Franklin Roosevelt's New Deal saved America from catastrophe; and that American intervention in foreign wars has been necessary and inevitable, with the United States government required to be a global leader and an occasional world policeman".

This brings us to the heart of the problem the core of the Nazi mind-set that the interests of the individual must be subordinated to the interests of the nation. This is the principle that controls the minds of the American people, just as it controlled the minds of the German people sixty years ago.

Each person is viewed as a bee in a hive; his primary role in life is to serve the give and the ruler of the hive, and to be sacrificed when the hive and its rulers consider it necessary. This is why Americans of our time, unlike their ancestors, favor such things as income taxation, Social Security, socialized medicine and drug laws; they believe, as did Germans in the 1930's that their bodies, lives, income and property, in the final analysis, are subordinate to the interests of the nation.

As you read the following words of Adolf Hitler, ask yourself which American politician, which American bureaucrat, which American schoolteacher, which American citizen would disagree with the principles to which Hitler subscribed:

> "It is thus necessary that the individual shall finally come to realize that his own ego is of no importance in comparison with the existence of this nation; that the position of the individual ego is conditioned solely by the interests of the nations as a whole; that pride and conceitedness, the feeling that the individual is superior, so far from being merely laughable, involve great dangers for the existence of the community that is a nation: that above all the

> unity of a nation's spirit and will of an individual; and that the higher interests involved in the life of the whole must here set the limits and lay down the duties of the interests of the individual."

Even though the average American enthusiastically supports the Nazi economic philosophy, he recoils at having his beliefs labeled as "Nazi". Why? Because, he argues, the Nazi government, unlike the U.S. government, killed six million people in concentration camps, and this mass murder of millions of people, rather that economic philosophy, captures the true essence of the Nazi label.

What Americans fail (or refuse) to recognize is that the concentration camps wee simply the logical extension of the nazi mindset! It does not matter whether there were six million killed-or six hundred-or six-or even one. The evil – the terrible, black evil is the belief that a government should have the power to sacrifice even one individual for the good of the nation. Once this basic philosophical premise and political power are conceded, innocent people, beginning with a few and inevitably ending in multitudes, will be killed, because "the good of the nation" always ends up requiring it.

Political killings of innocent people could never happen in America, our fellow citizens tell us. America is a democracy. But so was Nazi Germany. Hitler was popularly elected, and his economic policies wee widely favored and acclaimed (by Germans and Americans).

But there is another basic problem with that assertion: it is happening here in America. And like the German people 1930's, Americans either refuse to see it happening, or they rationalize what is happening so that they do not have to deal with it. Now, it is true that the killings do not number in the millions but they certainly do number, so far, in the thousands.

Let's take some examples. The Branch Davidians at Waco, Texas: U.S. Army tanks and gas were used against peaceful, religious, well-armed people. More than eighty Americans, including children were gassed and burned. And is there any remorse-any regret-any independent governmental investigation into this massacre? Not on your life. The government officials, just like their Nazi counterparts, think they did "the right thing" in killing our fellow citizens. And for those of you who look to the judiciary for protection, you had better look elsewhere; the federal judge who presided over the trial of the Waco survivors declared that he would not permit the government to be "put on trial", and then slapped forty-years sentences on the Branch Davidian survivors.

Or take Randy Weaver, his wife, and son, of Idaho. First, they were set up on a gun charge. (Weaver sold a shotgun that was a quarter of an inch too short, at the request of a U.S. Government Agent). Then, they sent Weaver a notice of a wrong trial date. When he failed to appear, they surrounded his house and attacked. A government sniper shot his unarmed wife in the head with a bullet as she was holding her baby. And they shot Weaver's son in the back. Then, at Weaver's trial, they fabricated evidence and committed perjury. Fortunately, Weaver was acquitted. But have any criminal charges been brought against the government agents for the murder of Weaver's wife and son? Did the federal judge in the case even cite the agents for contempt for their reprehensible conduct? Well, did the Nazi government ever bring charges against the SS? Did Nazi judges ever punish Nazi officials for killing Jews?

Government officials killed Donald Scott, a millionaire rancher in California. They claimed that they needed to barge into his house in the middle of the night to look for marijuana. And when Scott obeyed their order to lay down the gun he had picked up in his fear of the intruders, they shot him dead. And it later turned out that they hoped to find marijuana so that they could confiscate his land and convert it to a national park.

But Americans either look the other way, the way the Germans did, or they rationalize what is happening by saying, "The war on drugs has gotta be won."

And it is not just killings. Just as the Nazis did, they are confiscating people's money, land, boats, and cars-anything they can get their hands on. No longer do they need to depend only on taxes for their revenues-they just go grab the money and property directly and keep it, regardless of the guilt or innocence of the victims. And, of course, it's all rationalized because "the war on drugs has gotta be won."

And it's not just confiscation. It is also terror-the terror of the Internal Revenue Service agents barging into people's homes, "visiting' them at work, and levying liens on bank accounts and real estate without notice, hearing, or other semblance of due process.

Yes, it's true-we are not dealing with the killings and mass confiscations and infliction of terror on millions of people. It is happening only to several thousands. But that's today. What happens in a crisis? Suppose an American ruler decided he is not going to get "pushed around" by the ruler of North Korea, Haiti, Panama, Iraq, or Japan? What happens if a war is not over in a few weeks, but instead drags out into months, even years, with higher taxes, more controls, and ...conscription? What happens if Americans, who are already being taxed 50 percent of their incomes, now find taxes at 70 or 80 percent? What happens if there is a massive tax strike in which millions refuse to pay their taxes? What happens if hundreds of thousands of American students refuse to be drafted by a president who refused to be drafted?

Will the government meekly surrender? Will it simply agree to lose "international face"? Not on your life. The Internal Revenue Service, the Department of Justice, the FBI, and the army will simply turn their massive powers against the leaders of the revolt and as many of its followers as possible. And they will do whatever is necessary to teach those "cowards" a lesson. The American people will learn what the German people learned: that the omnipotent state that loves the poor and the needy will remove its velvet glove and use its iron fist to smash those who interfere with the "good of the nation."

Let's look at some more examples of the Nazi mind-set in America-this time in the Department of the Army. The army conducted nuclear radiation experiments on American soldiers. Why? Because the good of the nation required it. The army conducted drug experiments on American citizens. Why? Because the good of the nation required it. The army conducted disease experiments on the American people. Why? Because the good of the nation required it. The army herded innocent Americans of Japanese descent into American concentration camps. Why? Because the good of the nation required it.

In other words, in the past, U.S. government officials have engaged in evil, Nazi-like conduct for the "good of the nation." Would they do so again? You can bet your life they could, if the "good of the nation required it", and even if it entailed the violation of every single restriction on government power set forth in the U.S. Constitution. There is nothing inevitable in all this. Through the power of ideas, we can reverse the trend. If ideas did not matter, governments would not try to suppress ideas. Ideas do matter; they do have consequences; they do influence people into acting, into changing, into reversing course.

But the rights guaranteed by the First Amendment-the right to speak, to write, to disseminate ideas – are not sufficient. The ultimate safeguard against the ultimate tyranny lies instead with the right to bear arms guaranteed by the Second Amendment. If this Amendment is destroyed or severely constricted, the rest of the Constitution becomes worthless, because in a crisis in which their power base is threatened, and in which there are no means of forcible resistance, government officials will squash the things they view as "technicalities" –free speech, habeas corpus, trial by jury, and the other rights guaranteed in the Constitution.

Combine a crisis with a disarmed, discontented citizenry, and the concentration camp for hundreds of thousands becomes a real possibility. But when the citizenry, together with various patriotic sheriffs, police, and members of the armed forces, have the means to inflict severe casualties on their potential oppressors, tyrants think twice before they try to oppress their own citizens too heavily.

Contrary to everything our rulers tell us, and everything that our schoolteachers are teaching the children of this nation, the biggest threat to the lives and well being of the American people lies not with some foreign government. The biggest threat to the American people lies with the United States government.

In his book "The Road to Serfdom," Friedrich Hayek warned Americans in 1944 that despite their military war against the Nazis, they were traveling the philosophical and economic road that the Nazis and the communists were traveling. Our grandparents and parents ignored Hayek's warning. Now, we are left with the consequences; a government of omnipotent size and power using its power to kill innocent peaceful citizens and confiscate millions of dollars of property to feed its insatiable hunger for more power. Today, the number of victims is in the thousands. But at the end of this road lie the concentration camps for the multitudes.

Can the tide be reversed? Can the omnipotent state be dismantled, rather than simply reformed?

Yes, it will take a return to first principles – the principles on which this nation, not Germany, was founded: principles that hold that it is the individual, not the collective, that is supreme; that each individual has been endowed by his creator with inalienable rights; that among these rights are life, liberty, and the pursuit of happiness; that to secure these rights, government are instituted among men, deriving their just powers from the consent of the governed; that whenever any government, including the American government, becomes destructive of these ends, it is the right of the people to alter or abolish it and to institute a new government; and that no individual – his life, liberty, or property – shall ever be sacrificed for the good of the nation. As Ayn Rand put it in her essay, "The Fascist New Frontier".

"If you wish to oppose [statism], you must challenge its basic premises. You must begin by realizing that there is no such thing as "the public interest" except as the sum of the interests of individual men. And the basic, common interest of all men – all rational men – is freedom. Freedom is the first requirement of "the public interest" – not what men do when they are free, but that they are free. All their achievements rest on that foundation- and cannot exist without it.

"A politician will do anything to keep his job even become a patriot."

-William Randolph Hearst (1863-1951) US newspaper publisher, Recalled on his death 14 August 1951

...How did the frog get into this predicament, what first seemed safe and secure now feels hot and uncontrollable...

Chapter XIX
Electronic Eavesdropping

When asked to name the chief qualification a politician should have. "It's the ability to foretell what will happen tomorrow, next month, and next year —-and to explain afterward why it didn't happen."

-Sir Winston Churchill

Big Brother is Listening

National and international surveillance networks are becoming more and more sophisticated and intrusive throughout the world. It is now a widely known fact that if you carry a mobile phone, all your movements are being tracked and recorded-and are readily available to government agencies upon request. In some countries, these records are even routinely analyzed to spy on phone holders who make "suspicious movements"!

While this is shocking enough, it doesn't stop there. Believe it or not, almost all phone calls in the world are routinely scanned for "suspicious words" by various agencies' computer systems. You have certainly heard of ECHELON, the international surveillance system-but that's not all!

There are many others! The European Union is planning its own EU Phone, Fax & Internet Surveillance System. In Germany, all international calls are already automatically scanned by the BND Even in Austria, the country that has become famous for being the last bastion of fully anonymous banking; a secret surveillance system is currently being installed to monitor all national and international calls.

There goes your privacy

I won't go into too great detail about the implications of this technology-here's just one example. If you call your friend and tell him about he latest movie where a Colombian Drug Dealer plans to Bomb the Government, this will almost certainly trigger one of these scanners, and a human being will retrieve the whole call and listen to it.

You say you have nothing to hide?

Think again! While some of these systems seem to be justified buy the goal to catch criminals, the really bad guys know about this technology, too-and thus will only use innocent code words when communicating over the phone.

"The bomb is ready, I'll pick up the drugs at 5 p.m."

may translate to… *"The cake is ready, I'll pick up the flowers at 5p.m."*

…which is a perfectly unsuspicious statement.

What is their real goal?

So, What is the real purpose of these surveillance networks? What do they really want? Scan the phone networks for "unfriendly" remarks about the government? Eavesdrop on individuals who discuss the distribution of powerful encryption software? Find those who discuss tax havens and offshore strategies, and provide their details to tax or financial crime agencies for further investigation?

All of the above is already happening-today.

"Is the real purpose of this system to protect the citizens from crime-or is it to protect the government from its citizens?"

So What's the Conclusion?

When ever you talk on the phone, SOMEONE is listening-be it your country's national surveillance system, or an international system like ECHELON. Thus, never use the phone for confidential discussions unless you have prearranged some "code words" with your communication partners that will leave Big Brother in the dark.

Will We Be Under Total Surveillance?

Imagine a world in which every aspect of your life, past and present, is encrypted on a personal ID card and stored on a nationwide database. Where virtually all communications media-soon to be 100% digital-are automatically monitored by computerized phone taps and satellites from control centers thousands of miles away. Where self-training neural net and artificial intelligence data search systems scan for undesirable lifestyles and target you for automatic monitoring.

Personal privacy was once considered the most sacred of your constitutional rights; agencies were severely limited by law. All that's about to change drastically thanks to a deadly combination of extremely sophisticated surveillance technology, ubiquitous digital information collection, and centralized interagency data exchange.

Until recently the "supersecret" National Reconnaissance Organization did not exist-even though it has the largest budget of any intelligence agency. They are responsible for the design, development and procurement of all US reconnaissance satellites and their continued management once in orbit.

The NRO is eagerly implementing such technologies as ultra-high storage capacity holographic films (allowing huge amounts of personal information to be present on you ID card) and self-training artificial intelligence software that tracks your personal data without human intervention. A new era of ubiquitous surveillance is dawning.

A struggling military-industrial complex searching for new markets for their technologies has merged forces with a government obsessed with ever tighter control over the activities of the general public. Congresswoman, Barbara Jordan, has proposed a "National Employment Verification Card" that will be required for all employment in the U.S. The card will, of course, have a magnetic data strip, and altering of counterfeiting the card will be a federal felony offense.

There is a dedicated and aggressive effort underway to chart various genetic features as part of one's personal information set. The feds goal is to have the ability to screen individuals for everything from behavioral characteristics to sexual orientation, based on genetic information embedded in you personal (and required) national ID card.

Biometric signature technologies have been developed. There is even a technique available to translate human DNA into bar codes for efficient digital transmission between agencies.

Are these science fiction story lines or the ravings of a paranoid lunatic? I wish they were. This technology is on the street today or about to leave the labs. It goes way beyond Orwell's worst nightmares.

A fundamental shift in the legal definition of personal privacy is occurring right now. A court-issued warrant used to be a universal requirement for personal surveillance, such as phone tapping, observing physical papers, and probing financial or medical records. Now, in this new age of monitoring and data tracking systems, there are no pesky people in the loop. A computer doesn't need to seed a court warrant to monitor every aspect of your private life. A self-training automated surveillance system doesn't need permission to observe you movements or communications.

Total data tracking is already commonplace for financial institutions and private security operations. Tomorrow, it will be commonplace for all of us. The technical elements of a massive surveillance engine are in place. It's just a matter of turning the key to fire it up. Let's examine these elements and why you should be concerned.

Universal Encryption Chip

It sounds logical. The feds want to preserve privacy, so their story goes, so they've announced that an encryption chip will go into all phones and computers that they buy. But what do they really want in the long run?

How about a government-issued encryption chip in all personal computers and communication devices? That way, the feds can deal with drug smugglers, terrorists, kiddie porn merchants, and anyone else who uses messages.

Of course, they'd have to prevent tampering with the chip. In fact, the technology to do just that has already been developed at Sandia National Laboratory. Scientists there have developed an optical sensor that uses a powdered silicon optical absorption layer in an optical waveguide embedded in a chip. A micro photodetector detects even the slightest intrusion into the chip package by measuring a slight change in the photonic.

It's Almost Too Late

In an unexpected and near-complete victory for law enforcement, the Foreign Intelligence Surveillance Court of Review overturned a lower court's decision and said that Attorney General John Ashcroft's request for new powers was reasonable.

The 56-page ruling removes procedural barriers for federal agents conducting surveillance under the Foreign Intelligence Surveillance Act (FISA). The law permits sweeping electronic surveillance, telephone eavesdropping and surreptitious searches of residences and offices.

At a press conference, Ashcroft applauded the ruling, characterizing it as a "victory for liberty, safety and the security of the American people."

Ashcroft said the ruling marks a new era of collaboration between police and intelligence agencies such as the CIA and the National Security Agency.

"This decision allows law enforcement officials to learn from intelligence officials, and vice versa, as a means of sort of allowing the information to flow from one community to another," Ashcroft said. "This will greatly enhance our ability to put pieces together that different agencies have. I believe this is a giant step forward."

The lower court, called the Foreign Intelligence Surveillance Court, had said there must be a well-defined wall separating domestic police agencies from spy agencies. It accused the FBI of submitting incorrect information under oath in more than 75 cases, including one signed by then-FBI Director.

The lower court's decision, went so far as to say that changes to the Justice Department's procedures were necessary "to protect the privacy of Americans in these highly intrusive surveillances and searches."

Justice Department lawyers argued that the USA Patriot Act, signed by President George W. Bush, made any such wall obsolete and unnecessary. The Patriot Act also changed the requirements for FISA surveillance, saying that espionage or terrorist acts did not have to be the primary purpose of the investigation but only a "significant purpose."

The review court agreed with Ashcroft, even suggesting that greater use of FISA surveillance conceivably could have thwarted the Sept. 11 terrorist attacks. It ruled that Ashcroft's proposed procedures, "if requirements, certainly come close."

Civil libertarians said they were alarmed by the ruling, the public version of which was censored for security reasons. The American Civil Liberties Union and the National Association of Criminal Defense Lawyers had filed friend-of-the-court briefs urging the appeals court to uphold the lower court's decision.

The Cato Institute, said, "Because the FISA now applies to ordinary criminal matters if they are dressed up as national security inquiries, the new rules could open the door to circumvention of the Fourth Amendment's warrant requirements. The result: rubber-stamp judicial consent to phone and Internet surveillance, even in regular criminal cases, and FBI access to medical, educational and other business records that conceivably relate to foreign intelligence probes."

FISA authorizes judges on the secret court, which always meets behind closed doors, to authorize electronic surveillance for foreign intelligence purposes if "there is probable cause to believe" that a terrorist, spy, or foreign political organization is involved. Police are not required to meet the same legal standards that are required under the Fourth Amendment, which prohibits unreasonable searches and eavesdropping, when conducting surveillance in normal investigations.

The Justice Department began interpreting the law as limiting FISA orders to cases in which no criminal prosecution was planned. Former Attorney General Janet Reno ordered a wall created between FBI intelligence agents—who have security clearances—and Justice Department prosecutors in FISA investigations.

The initial FISA court rejected Ashcroft's procedures as not authorized by the Patriot Act, the review court rejected that analysis saying that congress "clearly did not preclude or limit the government's use or proposed use of foreign intelligence information, which included evidence of certain kinds of criminal activity, in a criminal prosecution.

We are tracked by on-star, our cell phones and even our grocery card. Every purchase on a credit card, every bank deposit, trip on an airplane or a hotel stay traces our whereabouts. It's almost impossible not to be tracked on a daily basis.

...The frog dreams of the nice life he had envisioned letting his fate dictate by the warm water, which has now, began to boil around him...

Chapter XX
Legalize Freedom

"Give a man a fish and you feed him for a day: teach him how to fish and you feed him for a lifetime."

-Lao Tzu

Don't look for the mark of the beast as prophesized in the bible. The mark is your social security number. Without this number, US citizens can't get a job, can't get a driver's license, or open a bank account or get a loan. Certainly can't vote, and can't file a tax return!

With digital technology, gene mapping and other wondrous high tech ideas just around the corner, the grip is getting tighter.

Soon, at birth, each American baby will carry a permanent identification. First, for the convenience and soon thereafter, by government orders.

Sometimes, I really wonder why the Americans bothered having a Boston Tea Party. Just think about it-there they were, being asked to pay a paltry tax on tea. And some of these upstarts just refused-and dumped the tea in the harbor. They even had a war with England over it-then had the nerve to declare independence!

And all for what? So they could slide into the very statist control their forefathers fought so bitterly to escape from.

What would these early Americans think of today's breed? Not a lot I fear. I'm sure they would consider them thoroughly brainwashed.

But let's be charitable. Perhaps it really is like that fable of the frog being boiled to death. You know the story; to kill a frog in a pot of boiling water, all you need to do is turn up the hear very, very slowly-so the frog does not notice the incremental hear increases. And by the time the hapless frog does notice, it is too late.

That's how our freedoms have been, and continue to be, lost. One at a time, incrementally-in such a way that most people don't really notice-until it's too late.

In a matter of a few years, we have lost most of our freedom. Our children will never know what it was like to be able to play cowboy and Indians, our children will never know what "recess" meant in the school playground and they will never know what it meant to be free.

It looks as if the government has found the source of stopping any discontent and all oppositions by college students, who in the past were the source of demonstration and requesting political change, by keeping the children from the time they enter school and are so controlled that the rebel spirit has been eliminated from their life.

In addition, the Patriot Act makes any sort of demonstration against he government a federal offense.

Long gone are the sit-ins and marches on the streets by college students. Like sheep, our college students are led to the slaughter.

You have No right to die

Supreme Court Justice Scalia says there is no constitutional "right t die". It is "absolutely plain that there is no right to die," Scalia said at Catholic University's School of Philosophy. "there were laws against suicide" when the Constitution was drafted. Most states forbid doctor-assisted suicide, but lower courts have struck down bans imposed by New York and Washington state.

You may be familiar with the case of Dr. Kavorkian who is serving a prison sentence in Michigan for his efforts in assistant suicide.

He helped numerous persons who wanted to die to commit assistant suicide. Most of the people he helped were terminally ill and in pain and be videotaped the suicide openly.

Some European countries have enacted laws that allow that a doctor can prescribe life-ending drugs to terminally ill patients who no longer want to live.

Luckily, no law can stop you from swallowing a bottle of Aspirin, but your family may not be able to collect the life insurance policy.

Dare to Declare Independence

The Declaration of Independence of the Thirteen Colonies

In CONGRESS, July 4, 1776

The unanimous Declaration of the thirteen United States of America,

When in the course of human events, it becomes necessary for one people to dissolve the political bands which have connected them with another, and to assume among the powers of the earth, the separate and equal station to which the laws of nature and of nature's God entitle them, a decent respect to the opinions of mankind requires that they should declare the causes which impel them to the separation.

We hold these truths to be self-evident, that all men are created equal, that they are endowed by their Creator with certain unalienable rights, that among these are life, liberty, and the pursuit of happiness. That to secure these rights, governments are instituted among men, deriving their just powers from the consent of the governed. That whenever any form of government becomes destructive of these ends, it is the right of the people to alter or to abolish it, and to institute new government, laying its foundation on such principles and organizing its powers in such form, as to them shall seem most likely to effect their safety and happiness.

Prudence, indeed, will dictate that governments long established should not be changed for light and transient causes; and accordingly all experience hath shewn, that mankind are more disposed to suffer, while evils are sufferable, than to right themselves by abolishing the forms to which they are accustomed.

But when a long train of abuses and usurpations, pursuing invariably the same object evinces a design to reduce them under absolute despotism, it is their right, it is their duty, to throw off such government, and to provide new Guards for their future security.

Such has been the patient sufferance of these colonies; and such is now the necessity which constrains them to alter their former systems of government. The history of the present king of Great Britain is a history of repeated injuries and usurpations, all having in direct object the establishment of an absolute tyranny over these states. To prove this, let facts be submitted to a candid world.

He has refused his assent to laws, the most wholesome and necessary for the public good.

He has forbidden his governors to pass laws of immediate and pressing importance unless suspended in their operation till his assent should be obtained, and when so suspended, he has utterly neglected to attend to them.

He has refused to pass other laws for the accommodation of large districts of people, unless those people would relinquish the right of representation in the legislature, a right inestimable to them and formidable to tyrants only.

He has called together legislative bodies at places unusual, uncomfortable, and distant form the depository of their public records, for the sole purpose of fatiguing them into compliance with his measures.

He has dissolved representative houses repeatedly, for opposing with manly firmness his invasions on the rights of the people.

He has refused for a long time, after such a dissolutions, to cause others to be elected; whereby the legislative powers, incapable of annihilation, have returned to the people at large for their exercise; the state remaining in the meantime exposed to all the dangers of invasion from without, and convulsions within.

He has endeavored to prevent the population of these states; for that purpose obstructing the laws for naturalization of foreigners; refusing to pass others to encourage their migrations hither, and raising the conditions of new appropriations of lands.

He has obstructed the administration of justice, by refusing his assent to laws for establishing judiciary powers.

He has made judges dependent on his will alone, for the tenure of their offices, and the amount and payment of their salaries

He has erected a multitude of new offices, and sent hither swarms of officers to harass our people, and eat out their substance.

He has kept among us, in times of peace, standing armies, without the consent of our legislatures.

He has affected to render the military independent of and superior to the civil power.

He has combined with others to subject us to a jurisdiction foreign to out constitution and unacknowledged by out laws; giving his assent to their acts of pretended legislation:

- For quartering large bodies of armed troops among us
- For protecting them by a mock trial form punishment for any murders which they should commit on the inhabitants of these states
- For cutting off our trade with all parts of the world
- For imposing taxes on us without our consent
- For depriving us in many cases of the benefits of trial by jury
- For transporting us beyond seas to be tried for pretended offenses
- For abolishing the free system of English laws in a neighboring Province, establishing therein an arbitrary government, and enlarging its Boundaries so as to render it at once an example and fir instrument for introducing the same absolute rule into these colonies
- For taking away our charters, abolishing our most valuable laws and altering fundamentally the forms of our governments
- For suspending our own legislatures, and declaring themselves invested with power to legislate for us in all cases whatsoever

He has abdicated government here by declaring us out of his protection and waging war against us.

He has plundered our seas, ravaged our coasts, burnt our towns, and destroyed the lives of our people.

He is at this time transporting large armies of foreign mercenaries to complete the works of death, desolation and tyranny, already begun with circumstances of cruelty and perfidy scarcely paralleled in the most barbarous ages, and totally unworthy the Head of a civilized nation.

He has constrained our fellow citizens taken captive on the high seas to bear arms against their country, to become the executioners of their friends and brethren, or to fall themselves by their hands.

He has excited domestic insurrections amongst us, and has endeavored to bring on the inhabitants of our frontiers, the merciless Indian savages, whose known rule of warfare is an undistinguished destruction of all ages, sexes and conditions.

In every stage of these oppressions we have petitioned for redress in the most humble terms. Our repeated petitions have been answered only by repeated injury. A prince, who character is thus marked by every act, which may define a tyrant, is unfit to be the ruler of a free people.

Nor have we been wanting in attentions to our British brethren.

- We have warned them from time to time of attempts by their legislature to extend an unwarrantable jurisdiction over us.
- We have reminded them of the circumstances of our emigration and settlement here.
- We have appealed to their native justice and magnanimity, and we have conjured them by the ties of our common kindred to disavow these usurpations, which would inevitably interrupt our connections and correspondence.

They too have been deaf to the voice of justice and of consanguinity. We must, therefore, acquiesce in the necessity, which denounces our separation, and hold them, as we hold the rest of mankind, enemies in war, in peace friends.

We, therefore, the representatives of the United States of America, in General Congress, assembled, appealing to the Supreme Judge of the world for the rectitude of our intentions, do, in the name, and by the authority of the good people of these colonies, solemnly publish and declare, that these united colonies are, and of right ought to be free and independent states; that they are absolved from all allegiance to the British Crown, and that all political connection between them and the state of Great Britain is and ought to be totally dissolved; and that as free and independent states, they have full power to levy war, conclude peace, contract alliances, establish commerce, and to do all other acts and things which independent states may of right do. And for the support of this Declaration, with a firm reliance on the protection of Divine Providence, we mutually pledge to each other our lives, our fortunes, and our sacred honor.

The Signers of the Declaration of Independence

New Hampshire: Josiah Bartlett, William Whipple, Matthew Thornton

Massachusetts: John Hancock, Samual Adams, John Adams, Robert Treat Pained, Elbridge Gerry

Rhode Island: Stephen Hopkins, William Ellery

Connecticut: Roger Sherman, Samuel Huntington, William Williams, Oliver Wolcott

New York: William Floyd, Philip Livingston, Francis Lewis, Lewis Morris

New Jersey: Richard Stockton, John Witherspoon, Francis Hopkinson, John Hart, Abraham Clark

Pennsylvania: Robert Morris, Benjamin Rush, Benjamin Franklin, John Morton, George Clymer, James Smith, George Taylor, James Wildon, George Ross

Delaware: Caesar Rodney, George Read, Thomas McKean

Maryland: Samuel chase, William Paca, Thomas Stone, Charles Carroll of Carrollton

Virginia: George Wythe, Richard Henry Lee, Thomas Jefferson, Benjamin Harrison, Thomas Nelson, Jr., Francis Lightfoot Lee, Carter Braxton

North Carolina: William Hooper, Joseph Hewes, John Penn

South Carolina: Wdward Rutledge, Thomas Heyward, Jr., Thomas Lynch, Jr., Arthur Middleton

Georgia: Button Gwinnett, Lyman Hall, George Walton

...And The Price They Paid

five signers of the Declaration of Independence were captured by the British and brutally tortured as traitors. Nine fought in the War for Independence and died from wounds or from hardships they suffered. Two lost their songs in the Continental Army. Another two had sons captured. At least a dozen of the fifty-six had their homes pillaged and burned.

What kind of men were they? Twenty-five were lawyers of jurists. Eleven were merchants. Nine were farmers or large plantation owners. One was a teacher, one a musician, and one a printer. These were men of means and education who launched the Ship of State which you and I have inherited. Yet they signed the Declaration of Independence, knowing full well that the penalty could be death if they were captured.

When these courageous men signed, they pledged their lives, their fortunes, and their sacred honor to the cause of freedom and independence.

In the face of the advancing British Army, the Continental Congress fled from Philadelphia to Baltimore on December 12, 1776. It was an especially anxious time for John Hancock, the President, as his wife had just given birth to a baby girl. Due to the complications stemming from the trip to Baltimore, the child lived only a few months.

William Ellery's signing at the risk of his fortune proved only too realistic. In December 1776, during three days of British occupation of Newport, Rhode Island, Ellery's house was burned and all his property was destroyed.

Richard Stockton, a New Jersey State Supreme court Justice, had rushed back to his estate near Princeton after signing the Declaration only to find that his wife and children were living like refugees with friends. They had been betrayed by a Troy sympathizer who also revealed Stockton's own whereabouts. British troops pulled him from his bed one night, beat him and threw him in jail where he almost starved to death. When he was finally released, he went home to find his estate had been looted, his possessions burned, and his horses stolen. Judge Stockton had been so badly treated in prison that his health was ruined and he died before the war's end. His surviving family had to live the remainder of their lives off charity.

Carter Braxton was a wealthy planter and trader. One by one, his ships were captured by the British navy. He loaned a large sum of money to the American cause; it was never paid back. He was forced to sell his plantations and mortgage his other properties to pay his debts.

Thomas McKean was so hounded by the British that he had to move his family almost constantly. He served in the Continental Congress without pay, and kept his family in hiding.

Vandals or soldiers or both looted the properties of Clymer, Hall, Harrison, Hopkinson, and Livingston. Seventeen lost everything they owned.

Thomas Heyward, Jr., Edward Rutledge and Arthur Middleton, all of South Carolina, were captured by the British during the Charleston Campaign in 1780. They were kept in dungeons at the St. Augustine Prison until exchanged a year later.

At the Battle of Yorktown, Thomas Nelson, Jr., noted that the British General Cornwallis had taken over the family home for his headquarters. Nelson urged General George Washington to open fire upon his own home. This was done, and the home was destroyed. Nelson later died bankrupt.

Francis Lewis also had his home and properties destroyed. The enemy jailed his wife for two months, and that and other hardships from the war so affected her health that she died only two years later.

"Honest John" Hart, a New Jersey farmer, was driven from his wife's bedside when she was near death. Their thirteen children fled for their lives. Hart's fields and his gristmill were laid waste. For over a year, he eluded capture by hiding in nearby forests. He never knew where his bed would be the next night and often slept in caves. When he finally returned home, he found that his wife had died, his children disappeared, and his farm and stock were completely destroyed. Hart himself dies in 1779 without ever seeing any of his family again.

Such were their stories and sacrifices typical of those who risked everything to sign the Declaration of Independence. These men were not wild-eye, rabble-rousing ruffians. They were soft-spoken men of means and education. They had security, but they valued their liberty even more. Standing tall, straight, and unwavering, they pledged.

"For the support of this declaration, with a firm reliance on the protection of the Divine Providence, we mutually pledge to each other, our lives, our fortunes, and our sacred honor."

They gave us an independent America. Do we have the devotion and dedication to keep it?

Drafting the Documents

Thomas Jefferson drafted the Declaration of Independence in Philadelphia behind a veil of Congressionally imposed secrecy in June 1776 for a country wracked by military and political uncertainties.

In anticipation of a vote for independence, the Continental Congress on June 11 appointed Thomas Jefferson, John Adams, Benjamin Franklin, Roger Sherman, and Robert R. Livingston as a committee to draft a declaration of independence. The committee then delegated Thomas Jefferson to undertake the task. Jefferson then made a clean or "fair" copy of the composition declaration, which became the foundation of the document, labeled by Jefferson as the "original rough draft."

Revised first by Adams, then by Franklin, and then by the full committee, a total for forty-seven alterations including the insertion of three complete paragraphs was made on the text before it was presented to Congress on June 28. After voting for independence on July 2, the Congress then continued to refine the document, making thirty-nine additional revisions to the committee draft before its final adoption on the morning of July 4.

The "original Rough draught" embodies the multiplicity of corrections, additions and deletions that were made at each step. Although most of the alterations are in Jefferson's handwriting (Jefferson later indicated the changes he believed to have been made by Adams and Franklin), quite naturally he opposed many of the changes made to his document. Congress then ordered the Declaration of Independence printed and late July 4, John Dunlap, a Philadelphia printer, produced the first printed text of the Declaration of Independence, now known as the "Dunlap Broadside."

The next day John Hancock, the president of the Continental Congress, began dispatching copies of the Declaration to America's political and military leaders. On July 9, George Washington ordered that his personal copy of the "Dunlap Broadside," sent to him by John Hancock on July 6, be read to the assembled American army at New York. In 1783 at the war's end, General Washington brought his copy of the broadside home to Mount Vernon, one of only twenty-four known to exist. On July 19, congress ordered the production of an engrossed (officially inscribed) copy of the Declaration of Independence, which attending members of the Continental Congress, including some who had not voted for its adoption, began to sign on august 2, 1776.

"It is error alone which needs the support of government. Truth can stand by itself."

-Jefferson

Your Freedom is At Risk!

223 years ago, during July and august of 1776, the American Founding Fathers signed the Declaration of Independence, every one of them staking his own life upon the decision to write his name. By that decision came into existence a nation destined to bring to mankind the freedom of making decisions.

The founding Fathers were men of means and education, Yet they signed the Declaration of Independence, knowing full well that the penalty would be death if they were captured.

The result was a free America

But Wait! Something Went Wrong!!

The Founding Fathers, if alive today, would be dismantling the Government, as this is what they fought against originally: A country of increasing oppressed individuals terrorized by a ruling elite. Why does someone spend over one hundred million dollars to run for a senate seat that pays $180,000 a year? It must be obvious that a person running for a political office is not doing it for the money. It is the power and control they can exercise over us.

Imagine

Just close your eyes for a minute and try to look into the future...at the America of the 2010's. Imagine what the world would or could look like by then if the terrocrats have their way. Don't be afraid to imagine the worst—-just for a second.

Worldwide taxation? Never-ending wars? Implanted microchips? A Government camera in every room of every house? Mind control? Slaves to the state? 20% of the population in federal reeducation camps? Constitution officially abolished? Death of slavery? Burning of subversive books? Bombing of offensive internet servers? Slaughter of freedom activists?

Can you feel the fear? The pain? The suppressed, but still ardently burning desire to...break free?

Now, leave these visions behind and instead connect to the Spirit of freedom, which this country was founded upon. Can you feel it – that glorious fire...that pulsating desire...that burning, radiating passion...that uncompromising persistence?

Life, Liberty and the Pursuit of Happiness! Freedom of speech! Laissez-fair capitalism! Private money! Private education! Freedom of choice! Real values! Voluntary association! A new government whose sole purpose is to protect these rights! A society that emphasizes individual responsibility!

What do you prefer? Sooner or later you'll have to decide for yourself.

Choose wisely, and be aware that today's actions create tomorrow's reality.

...It's too late, the heat of the boiling water has overcome the life of the frog and slowly he drifts away into oblivion...

Wake up, don't follow the frog!

www.ingramcontent.com/pod-product-compliance
Lightning Source LLC
Chambersburg PA
CBHW030251290526
45785CB00001B/47
* 9 7 8 1 4 2 0 8 2 0 2 4 9 *